Puritanism and Natural Theology

Puritanism and Natural Theology

Wallace W. Marshall

☙PICKWICK *Publications* • Eugene, Oregon

PURITANISM AND NATURAL THEOLOGY

Copyright © 2016 Wallace W. Marshall. All rights reserved. Except for brief quotations in critical publications or reviews, no part of this book may be reproduced in any manner without prior written permission from the publisher. Write: Permissions, Wipf and Stock Publishers, 199 W. 8th Ave., Suite 3, Eugene, OR 97401.

Pickwick Publications
An Imprint of Wipf and Stock Publishers
199 W. 8th Ave., Suite 3
Eugene, OR 97401

www.wipfandstock.com

PAPERBACK ISBN: 978-1-5326-0274-0
HARDCOVER ISBN: 978-1-5326-0276-4
EBOOK ISBN: 978-1-5326-0275-7

Cataloguing-in-Publication data:

Names: Marshall, Wallace W.

Title: Puritanism and natural theology / Wallace W. Marshall.

Description: Eugene, OR: Pickwick Publications, 2016 | Includes bibliographical references and index.

Identifiers: ISBN 978-1-5326-0274-0 (paperback) | ISBN 978-1-5326-0276-4 (hardcover) | ISBN 978-1-5326-0275-7 (ebook)

Subjects: LSCH: Puritans—England—History | Puritans—United States—History | Natural theology

Classification: BX9322 M178 2016 (print) | BX9322 (ebook)

Manufactured in the U.S.A.   11/03/16

To my father, who introduced me to
the Puritans and so much more.

Contents

Acknowledgments | ix
Abbreviations | x

Introduction | 1

1. Rational Theism and Practical Atheism | 17
2. The Role of Natural Theology | 32
3. Reason, Learning, and the Mystery of God | 59
4. The Limits of Natural Theology | 80
5. Arguments for the Existence of God | 93
6. Providence, Evil, and Immortality | 120

Appendix 1: The Role of John Locke in the History of Natural Theology and Evidentialism | 135
Appendix 2: Table of Puritans Represented in this Study | 141

Bibliography | 145

Index of Persons | 165
Subject Index | 169
Scripture Index | 171

Acknowledgments

I WISH TO THANK Jon Roberts, who read and critiqued each chapter and was an invaluable guide along the path of my doctoral studies, especially on matters pertaining to the historical interaction between science and religion in the West; Michael Himes, a fountain of perspective on Western intellectual history and the most engaging lecturer I have ever heard; Michael J. Buckley, whose writings on the historical origins of atheism in the modern West stimulated my own thoughts on that tremendous subject; and to Gerry Williams and Jim O'Brien, who read the manuscript with eagle eyes and made many helpful comments and suggestions.

Abbreviations

DNB   H. C. G. Matthew and Brian Harrison, eds. *Oxford Dictionary of National Biography.* 60 vols. Oxford: Oxford University Press, 2004.

Introduction

NATURAL THEOLOGY IS SOMETIMES misunderstood as referring only to religious knowledge that can be derived from the study of nature. However, in both historical and contemporary Christian thought, it has the broader meaning of all religious knowledge that is accessible through the use of reason, independently of supernatural revelation. The term was used in this sense by Catholic theologians at least as far back as Raymond of Sebunde's *Theologia naturalis* (c. 1434), and by the seventeenth century it was current among continental Reformed writers. The German encylopedist Johann Heinrich Alsted's *Theologia naturalis* (book III of his *Methodus sacrosanctae theologiae*, 1614) seems to have been the first Protestant treatise published under that title. The first English book so titled was the Puritan Matthew Barker's *Natural Theology* (1675). Until the early nineteenth century, however, Anglo-American Protestants more commonly designated natural theology as "natural religion," "natural revelation," "light of nature," and "reason," terms that were usually contrasted with "revealed religion," "supernatural revelation," or "Scripture."

Puritans and other seventeenth-century divines used these terms for discourse about four main categories of natural theology: the existence and attributes of God, divine providence, immortality, and natural law (in its ethical rather than physical sense). Ethical natural law is so large a field that I have given scant attention to it except insofar as it had a bearing on the duty of worship considered as a dictate of the light of nature, and on the argument for God's existence *ex consensu gentium* (from the universal consent of nations). For several reasons, I have devoted some space to the related discipline of evidentialism, the attempt to prove the divine origin of the Bible through rational arguments. Puritans often presented such arguments right alongside the evidences of natural theology, so that the two sets of proofs taken together were intended to establish a rational grounding for the religion they wished to inculcate in their parishioners. The Puritans' use of evidentialism not only illuminates the wider context in which they used natural theology but is critical for our understanding of the function of reason within their religious thought. Historians of religion have varied widely in their assessment of this issue, and it would have been difficult to adequately address myself to that problem without giving some attention to Puritan evidentialism.

Defining Puritanism is a much more complicated affair than defining natural theology. Christopher Hill once referred to this problem as "that dragon in the path of every student of this period." By now it is clear that the popularly-held image of Puritans as gloomy, obscurantist foes of science, merriment, progress, and learning lacks merit. The Puritanism that has emerged from modern scholarship is in many respects rather un-puritanical, and a far-cry from the American journalist H. L. Mencken's oft-quoted 1925 caricature of Puritanism as "the haunting fear that someone, somewhere, may be happy."[1]

Saying what Puritanism was not, however, is easier than saying what it was. The problem is not so much identifying the characteristics of a typical Puritan clergyman, or at least a clergyman whom most historians would recognize as a Puritan. His views on grace would have been Calvinistic; he would advocate the education of ministers in philosophy, theology, Latin, Greek, and Hebrew; he would have a distaste for liturgical ritualism and champion the centrality of the preached word; he would be wary of sectarian "enthusiasm" yet zealous for ecclesiastical reform; he would believe that work and recreation were unlawful on Sundays; he would strongly encourage his parishioners to engage in family worship and private devotions; his preaching would exhort them to examine themselves carefully to see if they were truly regenerate and would remind them that multitudes were deceived about this matter; and finally, for good measure, if he lived in Restoration England he would have refused the terms of the 1662 Act of Uniformity and accordingly have been ejected from his pulpit.

The problem rather lies in coming up with a set of criteria that can encompass all or at least most of the figures whom historians have called

---

1. Mencken, *A Mencken Chrestomathy*, 624. Hill, *Economic Problems of the Church*, xii. The best general corrective to Mencken's caricature has been provided by Ryken, *Wordly Saints*; also useful is Daly, *God's Altar*.

Introduction

Puritans without being so broad that it becomes useless as a defining concept. That task is challenging enough even if we limit our analysis to the ministerial class, and one notable conclusion of modern scholarship on that matter is that a rigid "Puritan vs. Anglican" paradigm will not work. Figures such as William Gurnall, Edward Reynolds, John Trapp, and Ezekiel Hopkins, for instance, whom almost everyone would recognize as Puritans, subscribed to the Act of Uniformity; and other indisputable Puritans, such as Philip Henry (father of the well-known Puritan biblical commentator Matthew Henry), had to think long and hard about its terms before finally refusing to subscribe.

But as Patrick Collinson and a number of scholars following him have shown, Puritanism was both a lay and a clerical movement, indeed an impulse that became part of England's national fabric and was likewise a communal element of New England society. Is it possible to capture this transatlantic impulse with a useful definition, and if so, where should one set the chronological terminus of the movement? Recent treatments of these questions have emphasized that ambiguities will be inherent in any solution to the problem but have nevertheless maintained that the concept of "Puritanism" is a highly useful if not indispensable tool of historical analysis. Michael Winship aptly concludes that it is "inescapably an approximate identifier, however it is defined, and the point at which it becomes, through change and adaptation, something new and different is inevitably a judgment call."[2]

Happily, it is possible to write about aspects of Puritanism without arriving at a definitive solution to the problem of its definition, especially if, as is the case with this book, it is the thought of Puritan theologians rather than Puritanism as a societal phenomenon that is in view. As Peter Lake remarks, "The definition of Puritanism is an issue which has been both addressed and avoided to great profit by many great scholars."[3] This study adheres to the traditional chronological terminus of the early eighteenth century. An appendix lists the dates and provenance of the sixty-eight theologians represented in this study, and I think I can safely affirm that only

---

2. Winship, "Were There Any Puritans in New England?" 136. Lake, "Defining Puritanism—again?" For a somewhat dated but still excellent overview of scholarship on American Puritanism, see Hall, "On Common Ground." A more recent treatment is Cohen, "The Post-Puritan Paradigm." On the Puritan vs. Anglican paradigm, see Lake, *Anglicans and Puritans?*

3. Lake, "Defining Puritanism—again?" 3.

two of them, John Wilkins and the lay theologian-scientist Robert Boyle, are of debatable Puritan status.

Despite an immense body of scholarship on Puritanism, very little has been written on its relationship to natural theology. Only a few passing references to the subject appear in the place where one would most expect to find it, Perry Miller's classic two volumes on *The New England Mind* (1939, 1953). One significant contribution of the first of those volumes was its demonstration of the Puritan enthusiasm for logic as a divine gift that, while damaged by the fall and distorted by the influence of sin, was nevertheless vital to the Christian's journey back to God and was above all an indispensable tool for the theologian. Miller's primary emphasis, however, was on the Puritan use of reason as an "instrument" for interpreting Scripture and discerning the divine logic mirrored in the theatre of nature. What Puritans believed reason might be able to accomplish on its own in the way of theology was largely neglected. The same omission occurs in all the ink that has been spilled on the question of Puritanism's relationship to science. A number of scholars, including Miller, have argued that Puritans exhibited an unusual degree of interest in natural science, and Donald Fleming has related the swift reception of Copernicanism by New England Puritans to Miller's work on the Puritan embrace of Ramist logic. But no one has connected the Puritans' appreciation of science to the broader question of their natural theology.[4]

This neglect is reflected in the general assumption among historians that Puritans spurned both natural theology and the related discipline of evidentialism. Insofar as the history of Protestantism in the English-speaking world is concerned, natural theology and evidentialism are almost always represented as having arisen during the late seventeenth and early eighteenth centuries, being triggered by the rise of modern science and especially the Enlightenment's emphasis on reason. Thus, under the entry "Natural Religion" in the recently published *Encyclopedia of the Enlightenment*, readers are informed that Samuel Clarke's (1675–1729) attempt in his Boyle Lectures of 1704–5 to prove the immateriality and immortality of the soul and the moral certainty of the Christian revelation was a "breathtaking" project because it "attempted to establish so much by natural reason." "Having conceded so much to natural reason," the article

---

4. Miller, *The New England Mind: The Seventeenth Century* (see esp. 111–235); Miller, *The New England Mind: From Colony to Province*; Fleming, "The Judgment Upon Copernicus in Puritan New England."

predictably continues, "he left relatively little to faith and revelation." Owen Aldridge traces the roots of American natural theology to "the reasoning of Anglican divines who argued, on the basis of the life sciences as well as on Isaac Newton's astronomical discoveries, that nature offers unimpeachable proofs of the existence of God." A leading scholar of American deism juxtaposes deism with, on the one hand, "liberal" theologians like John Locke and Samuel Clarke who in response to Enlightenment science crafted an "uneasy . . . marriage between natural and supernatural revelation," and on the other hand, the claim of Christian orthodoxy that faith was "a nonrational, grace-inspired assent to supernatural tenets." But as a result of the deist controversy, he argues, eighteenth-century orthodox theologians eventually abandoned this claim and came over to the side of Locke and Clarke. Hence one of the legacies of American deism was that it "helped to awaken Christianity from its dogmatic slumber." D. H. Meyer arrives at the same appraisal of the American evidential tradition, except that he places the supposed capitulation in the early nineteenth century: "Instead of trying to suppress the Enlightenment, the Americans assimilated it."[5]

In this "assimilation" narrative, instances of which could be multiplied almost endlessly, Puritanism often functions as the contrasting background against which the rise of natural theology and evidentialism are related. Conrad Wright, for example, in his valuable essay on reason and religion in eighteenth-century America, has drawn a sharp distinction between eighteenth-century evidentialism and "the witness of the Spirit" that "had once assured the Puritan that the Bible was truly the Word of God." The same perspective permeates Winton Solberg's analysis of the significance of Cotton Mather's use of natural theology in his *Christian Philosopher* (1721), which according to Solberg reversed the traditional Puritan approach to the relationship between scripture and nature. Lee Gibbs and Norman Fiering have interpreted the early English Puritan William Ames (1576–1633), whose strong influence on New England Puritanism is well known, as adopting a decidedly anti-natural theology outlook. Ernest Lowrie has written that the question of how to prove God's existence was "seldom faced directly" by Puritans. Mark Noll's magisterial work on American religious history prior to the Civil War has asserted that "Puritans expected divine revelation to provide the starting place for all forms of thought,"

---

5. Dybikowski, "Natural Religion," 3:147; Aldridge, "Natural Religion and Deism in America before Ethan Allen and Thomas Paine," 836; Walters, *American Deists*, 11, 31, 44; Meyer, "The Uniqueness of the American Enlightenment," 181.

which if true would turn the idea of Puritan natural theology (as defined above, at least) into an oxymoron. Indeed, for Noll, the abandonment of this epistemology marks a fundamental point of departure between the religion of Puritans and that of later American theologians, including their conservative Calvinist descendants. James Turner similarly reads the late seventeenth- and eighteenth-century idea of American theologians that "belief in God was entirely reasonable and plausible" as well as the penchant of apologists of this period "not just to glorify God in nature but to *see* him there" as representative of a new emphasis on the capabilities of reason that was radically different from the outlook of pre-Enlightenment Christianity.[6]

When I began my research for this book, I had read enough Puritan literature to suspect that the viewpoint of these scholars might not be the whole story. What I discovered, after an exhaustive study of the primary sources, was that it is *entirely mistaken*. The overwhelming majority of Puritan theologians were firm believers in the legitimacy of natural theology and evidentialism. Even the small minority of dissenters did not categorically reject natural theology but merely expressed reservations about its usefulness. Puritans were persuaded that the existence and attributes of God, the creation of the world, the immortality of the soul, as well as the divine origin of the Scriptures, could be proved by rational arguments made without any *a priori* appeal to special revelation. For all their disagreements with one another on ecclesiology and the fine points of conversion, grace, and law, Puritans forged a firm consensus on the subjects of natural theology and evidentialism. On these two issues, the "intellectual field" of English and American Puritanism was nearly homogenous.[7]

Puritans did not simply embrace these rational arguments on a theoretical level but employed them in a surprising variety of pastoral, evangelical, and polemical contexts. The pastoral element deserves first mention, not only because it is surprising but also because it reveals how significant natural theology and evidentialism were to the Puritan enterprise.

---

6. Wright, "Rational Religion in Eighteenth-Century America," 16. Wright, *Beginnings of Unitarianism in America*, 135–38, 152. Solberg, "Introduction" to Cotton Mather, *The Christian Philosopher*, cxii–cxvii; Kearney, "Puritanism, Capitalism and the Scientific Revolution," 95; Ames, *Technometry*, 180–81; Fiering, *Moral Philosophy at Seventeenth-Century Harvard*, 49n83; Lowrie, *Shape of the Puritan Mind*, 48; Noll, *America's God*, 96; Turner, *Without God, Without Creed*, 29, 259. Also see Noll, "The rise and long life of the Protestant Enlightenment in America," 95–97.

7. On this concept, see Ringer, "The Intellectual Field."

Introduction

Arguments for the existence of God and the inspiration of Scripture were twin features of Puritan catechisms from the late sixteenth century to the early eighteenth century. The polemics of the Reformation were certainly one reason behind the inclusion of proofs for the divinity of Scripture. Since Protestants denied the Roman Catholic view that the Bible was to be received as the word of God on the authority of the church, it was incumbent on them to answer how they presumed to instill this certainty in their parishioners.

The testimony of the Holy Spirit in using the word as a converting instrument was one solution to this challenge. For John Calvin it was the primary and ultimate answer. He availed himself of several of the standard evidential proofs, which he deemed "neither few nor weak," but he insisted that "of themselves these are not strong enough to provide a firm faith, until our Heavenly Father, revealing his majesty there, lifts reverence for Scripture beyond the realm of controversy." Puritans incorporated this testimony of the Spirit into their catechisms and indeed viewed it as the capstone of all such arguments, but they placed greater weight than did Calvin on the so-called "external evidences" from miracles and fulfilled prophecy and on the "internal" evidences such as the majesty and sublimity of Scripture and its suitability to the human condition.[8]

One striking feature of Puritan literature was its frank and forthright approach to the existence of religious doubt among believers: doubt as to the truth of Christianity, and doubt about the existence of God, which as they often repeated was the foundation of all religion. Some of the most prominent Puritans—Richard Baxter, Thomas Shepard, Jonathan Mitchell, Increase and Cotton Mather—experienced severe shakings of their faith that read like those revealed in Mother Teresa's posthumously published letters.[9] Baxter related that he had counseled dozens of similarly shaken individuals over the course of his ministerial career. Consider, for example, the English minister-physician Richard Capel's (1596–1656) remarks when reflecting on the unfortunate fact that the original (autograph) manuscripts of the Bible were no longer extant and that the laity's access to the Scriptures was mediated through fallible human translations. Capel thought he had good answers to this problem and he offered them to his readers, but not without adding that he could not "but confess that it sometimes makes my heart ache," and, "These and such things as these, I

---

8. Calvin, *Institutes*, 1.9.13.
9. Van Biema, "Mother Teresa's Crisis of Faith."

doubt not do stagger the thoughts of weak, & of strong Christians too, and drive many towards Atheism."[10]

Temptation to atheism was a standard theme in Puritan sermons stretching at least as far back as William Perkins in the 1590s. So was "practical atheism," a term used by Puritans to refer not only to nominal Christians who lived like the devil but to sincere believers who fell far short of the ideal of a life lived in continual awareness of an omnipresent Deity. Wrestling with unbelief was a natural corollary to the introspection and desire for intense religious experience that were hallmarks of Puritan piety. For many Puritans, devotional exercises such as prayer and the reading of Scripture were only one half of the solution to this practical atheism. The other half was rational argumentation for the truths in question. Piety, they believed, rose and fell together with the strength of one's belief in the existence of God. "All our baseness, stupidity, wanderings, vanity," preached the English Puritan Stephen Charnock in a series of discourses on the theistic proofs, "spring from a wavering and unsettledness in this principle." By strengthening this foundational conviction, natural theology could prove a tremendous aid to holiness. This was why, as the influential English Puritan John Preston put it in the 1620s, the existence of God was a truth that could "never sufficiently enough be rammed down, as being that that must bear all the weight of the building."[11]

Given this frankness about practical atheism and their strong emphasis on religious experience through the written and preached word, it might be expected that Puritan theologians would have been at least a little ambivalent on the question of how cogent the proofs for God's existence really were; that they would have adopted something like the indecisiveness depicted by Pascal:

> Nature has nothing to offer me that does not give rise to doubt and anxiety. If I saw no sign of a Divinity I should decide on a negative solution: if I saw signs of a Creator everywhere I should peacefully settle down in the faith. But, seeing too much to deny and not enough to affirm, I am in a pitiful state, where I have wished a hundred times over that, if there is a God supporting nature, she should unequivocally proclaim him, and that, if the signs in nature are deceptive, they should be completely erased; that nature

---

10. Capel, *Remains*, 38, 92.
11. Charnock, *Existence and Attributes of God*, 1:85; Preston, *Sermons*, 66.

should say all or nothing so that I could see what course I ought to follow.[12]

But of the nearly seventy Puritans represented in this study (considerably more if one counts all the Westminster Assembly divines), only one, the aforementioned Richard Capel, expressed anything like this sentiment. Instead they simultaneously asserted both the incontrovertibility of the evidences and the reality of the doubt of those evidences they perceived among the godly as well as the godless. Puritans never directly addressed this incongruity. Were they simply being disingenuous, or perhaps subconsciously whistling in the dark, when they avowed such confidence in the logical integrity of their arguments for the existence of God?

My own impression of the sources is that this is unlikely, and that a more plausible explanation for the doubts experienced by some Puritans can be found in the one area of natural theology about which they expressed some ambivalence, namely the ability of reason to fully demonstrate the doctrine of divine providence. While Puritans did strenuously argue for this tenet on purely rational grounds, they usually conceded in the same breath that the course of human affairs sometimes pointed to the opposite conclusion. "Not only wise but good men have sometimes been put to a non-plus here," remarked Increase Mather.[13] Puritan literature abounds with similar sentiments. Calvin and Luther had also stressed this ambiguity, and it was what tempted Cotton Mather at one point in his life to believe that Christianity might after all be a grand illusion. Such reflections were licensed and prompted by the Puritans' interaction with identical quandaries found in the biblical text—in Job, the prophets, and above all the Psalms, which occupied such a prominent place in their hymnody. All of this belies, incidentally, the opinion of some scholars that Calvinists regarded outward prosperity as an informal sign of their election.[14]

Abstractly considered, a denial of providence did not entail a rejection of God's existence. But it is not difficult to see how in the Puritan mind the two beliefs would have been linked together so strongly that they could not imagine one without the other. Their God was the intervening, covenanting, chastening, and judging God, sovereign over every detail of existence. An absentee Deity stripped of these characteristics would have hardly seemed to them like a God at all. Yet they acknowledged that the evidences of an

---

12. Pascal, *Pensées*, no. 429, pp. 162–63. Also see nos. 418, 449, 463, 471, 781.

13. Increase Mather, *Doctrine of Divine Providence*, 43.

14. See, e.g., Howe, "The Impact of Puritanism on American Culture," 2:1067–68.

active divine government over the world sometimes appeared non-existent. And thus, as the English Puritan Matthew Barker described it, there was a kind of natural atheism to which the human mind was drawn: "when men for a long time together have observed that *Nature* keeps its course, and things come to pass by the use of means, they grow into an Opinion that all things are by nature, and that there is no *Providence*, and so no God."[15]

The Puritans' foundationalist conception of natural theology was further manifested in their missionary activities to the natives of the New World. An interlinear evangelical catechism they prepared for their hopeful converts was full of natural theology followed by evidences for the inspiration of Scripture. The catechism received the imprimatur of the English Puritan Edward Reynolds (1599–1676), bishop of Norwich and also a member of the Westminster Assembly. Practical atheism was among the first themes John Eliot introduced to the Indians. At a 1646 meeting with a group of Indians that was attended by a number of Eliot's ministerial colleagues, the first question he asked the assembled natives was whether they had ever been tempted to think that there might be no God because they had never seen him! When they answered in the negative, Eliot immediately presented them with a simple version of the argument from design in order to strengthen their conviction on this point. Grace renewing and perfecting nature was the Puritan missionary paradigm. As Increase Mather declared, "except men give Credit to the principles of *natural*, they will never believe the Principles of *revealed Religion*."[16]

Long before a current of religious skepticism arose in England during the second half of the seventeenth century, then, the place of natural theology and evidentialism was firmly established among Puritan theologians, and their response to this polemical context followed suit. They published a number of apologetic treatises to combat atheism and disbelief in Christianity. Here, at least on the matter of defending Christianity, Puritans broke with Calvin, who had declared that "those who wish to prove to unbelievers that Scripture is the Word of God are acting foolishly, for only by faith can this be known."[17] There was little if any serious religious skepticism in New England during this period, but at the turn of the eighteenth century Cotton and Increase Mather published apologetic pamphlets directed against

---

15. Barker, *Natural theology*, 40–41.

16. Increase Mather, *Discourse Proving that the Christian Religion is the only True Religion*, 31.

17. Calvin, *Institutes*, 1.9.13.

deism in England and Europe, and when the first reports of American deism appeared on the outskirts of Boston in 1712, Cotton Mather responded in exactly the same way as his counterparts in the mother country, publishing his *Reason Satisfied: And Faith Established*.

As discussed in chapter 4, some English Puritans even asserted that those who had never heard of Christianity could be saved through the knowledge afforded by natural theology—though not, of course, without the regenerating grace of the Holy Spirit. Andrew Willet is an early instance of this opinion. Richard Baxter defended it on numerous occasions, and it was also articulated by Matthew Henry in his sermons and in his devotional expositions of the Bible, which became and have remained one of the best-selling popular commentaries in the English language. John Wilkins and Matthew Barker were explicitly agnostic on the question, and the last of Stephen Charnock's *Discourses on the Existence and Attributes of God* is strongly suggestive of a similar openness.

The Puritans' liberal use of natural theology and evidentialism with believers and unbelievers certainly has a bearing on the debated question of how they viewed the relationship between reason and religion. In chapter 3 I argue that Puritans accorded a large role to reason, and that in terms of its systemic function within their theology and apologetics, there is no discernible difference between English and American Puritanism or between the early and later stages of the movement. However, a comparison of the early seventeenth century to the period after roughly 1640 does reveal a noticeable shift in what I would call the "rhetoric" of reason in certain types of Puritan sermonic discourse, particularly vis-à-vis the doctrines of grace. The evidence for this shift is somewhat fragmentary, but pending a fuller study of Puritan sermons, it seems sufficient for at least a tentative conclusion.

Although the Puritans were rational theologians, they were emphatically not rationalistic. They relished the doctrine of divine incomprehensibility and indeed considered it to be the apex of rational natural theology. As the English Puritan Ezekiel Hopkins put it, "reason itself teaches us, that such a being cannot be God, which may be comprehended by man." Similarly, while they maintained that the inspiration of the Bible could be proved by rational arguments and that nothing in the Bible could be "contrary" to reason, they insisted that it was eminently reasonable to expect that a divine revelation would contain doctrines that were "above" human reason. The difference between the two, as the English Puritan William

Bates explained it, was "between the things which Reason cannot perfectly understand how they can be, and the things which it perfectly understands that they cannot be."[18]

This distinction was hardly peculiar to Puritanism, of course. It was embraced by medieval theologians and was a staple of Reformation theology. It is interesting to note in this connection that when discussing the role of reason in exhibiting the rationality of Scripture doctrine in order to confute heretics and skeptics, the English Presbyterian Puritan Anthony Tuckney (1599–1670), a Westminster Assembly member who occupied the regius chair of divinity at Cambridge from 1656 to 1661, could write, "I fully accord with Aquinas."[19] Whether a given doctrine was "above" or "contrary" to reason could naturally be the subject of vehement debate between Protestants and Catholics and between the various branches of Protestantism. But the availability of the category "above reason" was vital to the theological discourse of the age, and its eventual abandonment by some eighteenth-century theologians would mark a significant transition in the history of Christian thought.

The use of natural theology and evidentialism within seventeenth-century Anglican, or shall we say, non-Puritan Protestantism in England, has yet to receive a full scholarly treatment. But what has been written on the subject indicates, as one might expect, that Anglican divines gave reason as wide a latitude as did Puritans.[20] This in turn raises broader questions about the history of natural theology and evidentialism in Christian thought. Was Anglo-American Protestantism atypical of the seventeenth-century Protestant approach to these issues? What were Roman Catholics doing with natural theology during the sixteenth and seventeenth centuries?[21] And what of Socinianism? For how long, if at all, did its ad-

---

18. Hopkins, *Discourse on the State and Way of Salvation* (*Works*, 3:453); Bates, *Considerations of the Existence of God*, 186.

19. Anthony Tuckney to Benjamin Whichcote, 8 October 1651, in Salter (ed.), *Eight Letters*, 94. Tuckney specifically referred to and quoted from Aquinas' treatment of this issue in *Summa Theologiae*, Ia. 1, 8.

20. See Rivers, *Reason, Grace, and Sentiment*, 1:25–88; the essays by Sarah Hutton and Robert Crocker in Crocker (ed.), *Religion, Reason, and Nature in Early Modern Europe*, 61–96; Gabbey, "'A Disease Incurable': Scepticism and the Cambridge Platonists," 71–91; and Tulloch, *Rational Theology and Christian Philosophy in England in the Seventeenth Century*.

21. For a discussion of arguments for the existence of God in two influential early modern Catholic theologians, Leonard Lessius (1554–1623) and Marin Mersenne (1588–1648), see Buckley, *At the Origins of Modern Atheism*, 42–67.

herents maintain Faustus Socinus' infamous rejection of natural theology in his posthumously published *Praelectiones Theologicae* (1609)? That work provoked a strong reassertion of natural theology from many seventeenth-century divines, especially when some Arminian Remonstrants in Holland adopted Socinus' view.[22] Were the views of John Calvin discussed above broadly representative of sixteenth-century Reformed thought, and if so, what accounts for the shift in emphasis between the sixteenth and seventeenth centuries?

Richard Muller has given some attention to this latter issue in the first of his masterful four volumes on *Post-Reformation Reformed Dogmatics*, but what my research reveals about Puritans (whom Muller includes in the category "Reformed orthodox") is at variance with his conclusions that seventeenth-century Reformed theologians did not view natural theology as a foundation for supernatural revelation and that only Socinians and Arminians attempted to "press this knowledge [of natural theology] into the service of salvation." Indeed, for Muller, the advent of such a foundationalist use of natural theology in the eighteenth century "marks the end of genuine Reformed orthodoxy, or, at the very least, the disruption of the model of orthodoxy and its identification of Scripture alone as *principium cognoscendi theologiae* [principle of knowing theology] with reason as an instrument or *ancilla*."[23]

In arguing that Puritans adopted a foundationalist use of natural theology, I mean that they saw supernatural revelation as building on a foundation of natural revelation—natural revelation being conceived not merely as innate knowledge of God human beings have by virtue of being created in his image, but also in the sense of conclusions derived from reason, contemplation of human existence, and consideration of the works of nature. Similarly, Puritans believed that arguments for both the existence of God and the inspiration of Scripture were not only helpful to doubting Christians but also—by reinforcing the conviction of God's existence, clarifying his attributes, and showing that Christianity was worth being taken seriously—a helpful preparative to conversion. This is not to say that Puritans believed arguments for the existence of God or the inspiration of

---

22. See Platt, *Arguments for the Existence of God in Dutch Theology, 1575–1650*, 202–41; and Platt, "The Denial of the Innate Idea of God in Dutch Remonstrant Theology," 215.

23. Muller, *Post-Reformation Reformed Dogmatics*, 1:270–310 (quotations 286, 307). "One might also conclude," Muller adds (p. 307), "that this shift in perspective also marks the end of the influence of the medieval scholastic model as well."

Scripture could convert people apart from the regenerating work of the Holy Spirit, that they denied the role of Scripture in clarifying the nature and attributes of God, that they substituted rational argumentation for a direct, existential encounter with the preached word, or that they believed arguments for the inspiration of Scripture could produce the same degree of certainty afforded by the inward work of the Holy Spirit.[24] Any of those things would indeed have constituted a departure from Reformed orthodoxy, if not from Reformed theology altogether. But insofar as the history of *orthodox* Reformed theology in the eighteenth and nineteenth centuries is concerned, the departures just outlined seem to be straw men, as no orthodox Reformed theologian would have adhered to them. My contention, then, is simply that eighteenth- and nineteenth-century Reformed theologians were not doing anything different with natural theology and evidentialism than their Puritan predecessors were. Puritans believed the arguments for the existence of God and the inspiration of Scripture were objectively sound. They believed human beings shared a common rational framework for considering the evidences; and their liberal employment of these evidences in catechetical, pastoral, apologetic, and evangelical contexts clearly shows that they believed them to be not only powerful but extremely useful. If anything, Puritans used natural theology and evidentialism *more* than their post-Enlightenment descendants did.

This brings me to a much broader question about the origins of the Enlightenment and its relationship to Christianity. While that question is obviously beyond the scope of this work, my conclusions have a significant bearing upon it. The dominant paradigm governing historians' understanding of the relationship between Christianity and the Enlightenment parallels an old misconception about the relationship between Christianity and the rise of modern science that was enshrined in John Draper's *History of the Conflict between Religion and Science* (1874) and Andrew Dickson White's *A History of the Warfare of Science with Theology in Christendom* (1896). According to this "warfare hypothesis," modern science emerges in opposition to, rather than out of, Christianity, and is then at war with theology in the centuries that follow.

Over the last three decades, the warfare hypothesis has been almost universally rejected by historians of science (with Draper's and White's

---

24. Cf. *Westminster Confession of Faith*, 1.5, which states that the rational arguments for the inspiration of Scripture "*abundantly evidence* [the Bible] to be the Word of God," but also that "our *full* persuasion and assurance thereof, is from the inward work of the Holy Spirit bearing witness by and with the Word in our hearts" (emphases mine).

books frequently serving as their whipping boys). Indeed, the demise of this paradigm is by now a truism in the field.[25] Scholars recognize that while there have been episodes of conflict between Christianity and science, Christian thought has generally lived quite comfortably with, and often contributed to, the rise of modern science. Puritanism itself, as we will see in chapter 3, was markedly enthusiastic about the study of the natural world.

When it comes to Christianity and the Enlightenment, however, the rigidly adversarial paradigm persists.[26] The Enlightenment continues to be seen as a foreign entity to which a fideistic Protestantism either adapted or capitulated (which of the two depends on whether one views this supposed development positively or negatively). This is hardly the place for me to mount an argument against this idea. I simply wish to note that it does not fit with what this book reveals about Puritanism. I suspect it is this mistaken narrative that has caused historians to assume—unaware of the massive evidence to the contrary one finds in the primary sources—that Puritans had little to no use for natural theology and rational apologetics, or that Locke's *Reasonableness of Christianity* (1695) offered a "pathbreaking" proposal for how reason and special revelation should be related,[27] when in fact Locke's stance on that matter was entirely conventional by seventeenth-century standards.

This error involves far more than a simple chronological miscalculation or a mistake about the role of reason in Puritanism. The historian who is committed to the view that natural theology and "reasonable religion" were products of the eighteenth century will miss the richly variegated points of continuity between the Enlightenment and the history of Christianity, as well as the reciprocal influence of the two. The Enlightenment ends up being conceived as an alien movement that gradually infiltrated Christian thought, and the result is a confusion that parallels the distorting effects of the science-religion warfare hypothesis historians have been laboring to correct for the past thirty years.

I have modernized the spelling of quotations from the seventeenth-century sources used in this book (e.g., "persuade" for "perswade"), except

25. For two (among many) helpful correctives to this paradigm, see Lindberg and Numbers (eds.), *When Science and Christianity Meet*; and Ferngren (ed.), *History of Science and Religion in the Western Tradition: An Encyclopedia*.

26. For examples, see Appendix 1, "The Role of John Locke in the History of Natural Theology and Evidentialism."

27. Porter, *The Enlightenment*, 33.

where quoting from modern scholarly editions that preserve the original spelling; and in a few cases I have modified tortuous punctuation. This was done partly for the benefit of my readers, but also because my quotations of Puritans are drawn from both seventeenth- and nineteenth-century editions. Since spelling is corrected in the latter, it made sense to do so in my quotations from the former, otherwise I would have been left with interspersed quotations in which a Puritan uses modern spelling in one breath and antiquated spelling in the next. I have, however, let stand the original capitalization and italics, though readers unfamiliar with seventeenth-century sources should be aware that italics do not always indicate emphasis.

1

Rational Theism and Practical Atheism

> "How do you persuade yourself that there is a God?"
>
> —William Perkins, 1590

> "Many of the children of God . . . feel this temptation, Is there a God? bitterly assaulting them sometimes."
>
> —Thomas Shepard, 1640

While Puritans believed that reason could establish a fairly comprehensive system of theism, they recognized that there was a vast difference between the objective validity (or logical soundness) of the arguments of natural theology and its historical manifestations among ancient philosophers and "heathen" nations who were bereft of special revelation. As the early English Puritan William Pemble (1591/2–1623) put it, "there may be a twofold consideration of [natural theology]: 1. How far the Heathen have gone. 2. How far they might have gone in the knowledge of God and Godliness, if they had carefully used all Nature's helps." The latter of these was the key issue for natural theology, said the nonconformist minister and historian of philosophy Theophilus Gale (1628–79): "For that a thing be called natural, it is not necessary, that it be actually in all men; but it sufficeth if it may be derived from a natural principle."[1] Puritans

---

1. Pemble, *Vindiciae gratiae*, 61; Gale, *Court of the Gentiles: Part IV*, bk. 2, chap. 4, § 5, p. 302.

also extended this distinction to the subjective realities of religious experience among Christians. They frankly acknowledged that doubts about the existence of God, providence, and immortality were common among even sincere believers, and indeed they were keen on pointing out that self-examination uncovered numerous subtle manifestations of this skepticism. But this perception did not in the least diminish their enthusiasm for natural theology. The proper response to this problem, as they saw it, was to reinforce rather than abandon the rational arguments for these foundational religious tenets.

Puritans were especially positive on the objective validity of the proofs for God's existence. If people would simply apply their reason to this question in the same unbiased fashion as they handled the ordinary affairs of life, "they would *conclude* nothing more strongly than that God is," said the English Congregationalist Matthew Barker (1619-98), noting Plato's observation that it was this extreme unreasonableness of atheism that made it so rare, so that the few who indulged it hardly ever retained this opinion into old age. Atheism was thus "not only Impious but *Irrational*." After presenting the argument from design, William Bates (1625-99), an English Puritan who advocated the restoration of Charles II but was swiftly disappointed by the Act of Uniformity, to which he felt unable to subscribe, concluded that the universe was so full of testimonies to the existence of God that "We must pluck out our Eyes, and extinguish common sense, not to see infinite Wisdom, Power and Goodness shining in them, the proper marks of the Deity." "[W]hen we view the variety, harmony, and law of the creation," remarked Ezekiel Hopkins (1634-90), the Bishop of Derry who unlike Bates subscribed to the Act of Uniformity, "our reason must needs be very short, if we cannot from these collect the infinite wisdom, power, and goodness of the Creator."[2]

The same confidence appears as early as 1590 in the work of William Perkins (1558-1602), whom Patrick Collinson calls "the prince of Puritan theologians and the most eagerly read." "How do you persuade yourself that there is a God?" he queried in his catechetical work, *The Foundations of Christian Religion* (1590). "Beside the testimony of the Scripture," came

2. Barker, *Natural theology*, 33-36 (quotations 34, 33). Cf. Plato, *Laws*, book 10, 888a-b. Bates, *Considerations of the Existence of God, and of the Immortality of the Soul*, 50. Not only God's existence, but personal immortality and a future judgment, said Bates, had in this treatise of his "been proved by such invincible Evidence that Reason cannot resist" (Bates, *Divinity of the Christian Religion*, 3). Hopkins, *Discourse Concerning the Use of the Holy Scriptures* (*Works*, 3:360; also see 3:374).

the reply, "plain reason will show it." The pervasiveness of this perspective among Puritan divines is indicated by Thomas Vincent's (1634–78) didactic commentary on the Westminster Assembly's *Shorter Catechism*, a work whose commendatory epistle was signed by no less than forty Puritan theologians. Vincent, an English nonconformist who won widespread respect for his fearless preaching and visitation of the sick and dying during the London plague of 1665, introduced the subject with the following question and answer, and afterwards proceeded to lay out five arguments for God's existence:

> Q. 6. How doth it appear that God is true, that he hath a true being, or that there is a God indeed?
>
> A. By several arguments, sufficient to convince all the Atheists in the world, if they would hearken to their own reason.[3]

While presenting seven theistic proofs in a series of sermons on the *Westminster Shorter Catechism*, Thomas Watson (d. 1686), one of the most prolific devotional writers among the English Puritans, preached that atheism was so irrational that one could only regard it as symptomatic of one who had "sinned away his sense and reason." This was why, said Watson's co-pastor and fellow nonconformist Stephen Charnock (1628–80), in reference to the classic text of the Hebrew psalmist, "no better title than that of a fool is afforded to the atheist.... The demonstrations reason furnisheth us with for the existence of God, will be evidences of the atheist's folly." That God exists, Increase Mather (1639–1723) told his Boston congregation in a 1716 sermon on the divine existence and attributes, "is as Clear to the Understanding of a Rational Creature, as the Light of the Sun at Noon." He considered atheism "the most unreasonable Thing that possibly can be. A man might with a great deal more *Reason* question his own Being, than to question the Being of the God of Heaven."[4]

---

3. Perkins, *Foundation of Christian Religion* (*Workes*, 1:3); Collinson, *The Elizabethan Puritan Movement*, 125; Vincent, *Shorter Catechism of the Westminster Assembly Explained and Proved from Scripture*, 35. Among the signatories were John Owen, Joseph Caryl, Matthew Barker, and the three Thomas's—Manton, Watson, and Brooks. The work was frequently reprinted on both sides of the Atlantic during the eighteenth and nineteenth centuries.

4. Watson, *A Body of Divinity*, 39; Charnock, *Discourses Upon the Existence and Attributes of God*, 1:25–26. The biblical passage is Psalm 14:1, "The fool hath said in his heart, There is no God." Mather, *Discourse Concerning the Existence and Omniscience of God*, 6, 65.

Puritanism and Natural Theology

Richard Baxter (1615–91), who as we will see went through a crisis of doubt regarding the truth of Christianity, yet thought the existence of God a matter beyond all question, arguing like Mather that since it was "the most certain, intelligible verity among all the whole world of Certainties, and Intelligibles," its denial would logically entail the destruction of all human knowledge:

> [N]othing in the world is so illustriously and Eminently Intelligible and Certain, as that there is a God. So that if this principle were denied, I doubt not upon that ground, to deny and destroy all the rest, and to prove that no man knoweth anything: and not only that sense is fallible, but that there is no such thing as a man in the world; nor any other Being, Truth, or Good, if there be not a First Being, Truth and Good.

Perhaps no Puritan theologian asserted the objective validity of the theistic proofs more forcefully than John Owen (1616–83), the dean of Christ Church at Oxford from 1651 to 1660 and a leading advocate of ecclesiastical independency. He viewed their rejection as a species of insanity. The evidences for God's existence from the works of creation, he said, were "infallible," so that "whoever knoweth how to use and exercise his reasonable faculty in the consideration of them, their original, order, nature, and use, must necessarily conclude that so it is." If anyone denied these arguments, he added, "it is a sufficient reply, in case he be so indeed, to say he is *phrenetic*, and hath not the use of his reason; and if he be not so [phrenetic], that he argues in express contradiction unto his own reason, as may be demonstrated."[5]

If some doubt remained after all this, said Charnock (Pascal-like), still only a fool would wager against the possibility of God's existence, for in doing so there was virtually nothing to gain and everything to lose; while conversely, the opposite wager cost little more than a few "sordid lusts" and held out the hope of everlasting bliss: "He is not a reasonable creature, that

---

5. Owen, *Reason of Faith* (*Works*, 4:87, 89); Baxter, *Unreasonableness of Infidelity*, 3:276. Compare chapter three of his autobiography, where Baxter relates his struggle with unbelief regarding Christianity but says he never had any doubt about the existence of God, that being as clear to him as "what the sun is to my eye.... And he seemed mad to me that questioned whether there were a God," since no satisfactory account could then be given for the existence and order of the universe, much less the origin of mind. "These and all the suppositions of the atheist have ever since been so visibly foolish and shameful to my apprehension that I scarce find a capacity in myself of doubting of them" (*Autobiography*, 27).

will not put himself upon such a reasonable arguing." The wager argument was also employed by the scientist and Puritan lay theologian Robert Boyle (1627–91) and by his close friend Baxter, who put more pen to paper than any other Puritan and indeed was one of the most prolific writers in the history of the English language.[6]

In addition to the existence of God, Puritans believed that natural theology could demonstrate his essential attributes of incomprehensibility, eternity, immutability, immateriality, omnipotence, omniscience, and infinite goodness—all of which could be derived once the existence of a most perfect and independent being had been proved.[7] Natural theology also taught that this being was "man's chief end," as the immortal answer to the first question of the *Westminster Shorter Catechism* put it; and from this and the divine perfections followed the human duty of loving and worshipping God. Reason could show the immortality of the soul, a future judgment, and the two great commandments of natural law: to love God with all the heart, soul, mind and strength, and one's neighbor as oneself. Finally, reason could establish the doctrine of divine providence. As we will see later, however, this doctrine proved to be the stickiest issue in Puritan natural theology. While confident they could give sound reasons for believing in God's continuing providential government of the world, Puritans often noted that it was not as easily demonstrable as the other components of natural theology.[8]

Natural theology's dictates regarding both the existence of God and the duty of worship delineated above were succinctly expressed in that quintessential Puritan document, the *Westminster Confession of Faith* (1646):

6. Charnock, *Existence and Attributes of God*, 1:83; Boyle, *Aretology*, in Harwood (ed.), *Early Essays and Ethics of Robert Boyle*, 181; Baxter, *The Saints Everlasting Rest*, in *Practical Works*, 22:209–10; Baxter, *Reasons of the Christian Religion*, 452. Their source for the wager argument, and perhaps Pascal's too, was probably the patristic apologist Arnobius (d. early fourth century). See his *Adversus nationes*, 2.4, which Baxter quoted directly (*Reasons*, 452). On Baxter's voluminous literary output, see Keeble, *Richard Baxter: Puritan Man of Letters*, 2–3; and Orme, *Life and Times of Richard Baxter*, 2:466. For Baxter and Boyle's friendship, see Bates' funeral sermon for Baxter in *Works of the Late Reverend and Learned William Bates*, 800.

7. For two brief statements of this capability of natural theology, see Pemble, *Vindiciae gratiae*, 65; and Charnock, *Knowledge of God in Christ* (*Complete Works*, 4:115–17) which lays out most of these attributes, concluding (p. 117), "All this may be known of God by the creation, and it is a true (though not a full) discovery of God."

8. The two great commandments come from the Gospel of Matthew, 22:35–40, where Jesus says that everything in the "law and prophets" can be reduced to these two precepts.

Puritanism and Natural Theology

> The light of nature sheweth that there is a God, who hath lordship and sovereignty over all; is good, and doeth good unto all; and is therefore to be feared, loved, praised, and called upon, trusted in, and served, with all the heart, and with all the soul, and with all the might.[9]

Barker appealed to Aristotle to make the same point. The philosopher had rightly defined wisdom as "the knowledge of things great and wonderful," and therefore it followed that since nature revealed God as an infinite being and the "Fountain of all Good," it was our reasonable duty "to search after him so far as our finite capacity may extend, and then sit down and leave the rest to an holy admiration." John Owen considered the two great commandments to be "so clear in the light of nature as that no question can be made but that what is required in them is our duty to perform."[10]

Numerous treatises addressed the subject of natural law as a result of the Sabbath controversy that racked the world of English theology for almost the entire seventeenth century, which witnessed the publication of nearly 150 works on the question.[11] Since the command to celebrate the Sabbath was one of the ten commandments, Puritans generally regarded it, like the rest of the Decalogue, as part of the law of God revealed in nature and then seconded by special revelation. Under what authority, then, had the Christian church changed the day of celebration from Saturday to Sunday? Or did one of the ten commandments after all not belong in the catalog of natural law? The majority of Puritans affirmed that it did indeed belong there, and their contributions to the debate clearly demonstrated their belief in natural law.[12]

---

9. *The Westminster Confession of Faith*, ch. 21, art. 1, pp. 89–90. Also note Q. 2 of the *Westminster Larger Catechism* (1647): "How doth it appear that there is a God? A. The very light of nature in man, and the works of God, declare plainly that there is a God" (p. 129). The Westminster Confession was accepted on both sides of the Atlantic and would be the foremost doctrinal standard of American Calvinists during the eighteenth and nineteenth centuries.

10. Owen, *Pneumatologia* (*Works*, 3:635); Barker, *Natural Theology*, 90, 93. Aristotle says something similar in his *Nicomachean Ethics*, VI. 7, 1141b2–4, but the Greek text Barker quotes is drawn from another source I have been unable to find.

11. See Robert Cox's invaluable bibliographical work, *Literature of the Sabbath Question*.

12. For more on the controversy, see Collinson, "The Beginnings of English Sabbatarianism," in *Godly People*, 429–43; Dennison, Jr., *Market Day of the Soul*; Parker, *The English Sabbath*; Katz, *Sabbath and Sectarianism in Seventeenth Century England*; and Ball, *The Seventh-day Men*. Thomas Shepard spilled more ink on the question and dealt

Rational Theism and Practical Atheism

The immortality of the human soul was asserted along rational lines in numerous places, among them *The Immortality of Man's Soul Proved both by Scripture and Reason* (1645), a treatise Thomas Hooker (1586–1647) wrote from his pastorate in Hartford, Connecticut. Puritans fought this battle on two fronts. First, they were concerned to establish the existence of an afterlife in order to combat the widespread religious skepticism they perceived in England during the second half of the seventeenth century. But they also found themselves contending for a particular form of immortality against sectarians such as Hooker's antagonist, the Leveller Richard Overton (fl. 1640–63), who held that soul was simply synonymous for life in the Bible, and that there was no conscious existence after death until the resurrection, when the human race would be raised together with the entire animal creation.

The exchange between Hooker and Overton is interesting on a number of levels. Overton's treatise, first published as *Mans Mortalitie* in 1644 and then in an expanded second edition, *Man Wholly Mortal* (1655), was largely taken up with a discussion of numerous biblical passages bearing on the question, especially Old Testament texts he saw as being flatly at variance with the idea of a soul surviving the death of the body. Surprisingly, only two of Hooker's forty-five pages were devoted to proving the doctrine from Scripture. The rest were taken up with arguments from reason. He cited dozens of ancient philosophers and poets who believed in the soul's immortality. In the second edition of his treatise, Overton quoted a passage from Pliny indicating that there was less consensus in antiquity on this doctrine than was usually supposed. But he was content to grant the general point and indeed used it to explain how the doctrine of an immortal soul had crept into Christianity. The ancients, he maintained, knew that there was a just God yet observed that the righteous often went unrewarded in this life, and the wicked unpunished. Being ignorant of the Scripture doctrine of the resurrection, however, they had no other recourse but to invent the idea of a distinct component of the human person that could survive the dissolution of the mortal frame. One of the classical Christian arguments for an afterlife thus became in Overton's hands a sociological explanation for the origin of "this ridiculous invention of the soul, traduced [by Christians] from the *Heathens*."[13]

---

with it more thoroughly than did any other Puritan. See his 1649 work, *Theses Sabbaticae, or The Doctrine of the Sabbath* (*Works*, 3:7–271).

13. Hooker, *Immortality of Mans Soule*; Overton, *Mans Mortalitie*, "ridiculous

Such, then, were the dictates of the light of nature according to Puritan theology. Reason could demonstrate the existence and attributes of God and give good reasons for believing in providence. It could show that human beings were created to worship and glorify God and had for this and other reasons been endowed with immortal souls. From these followed the legitimacy of natural law: that what one found to be universally and perpetually engraved on the consciences of mankind must be of divine origin.

But for all their confidence in the objective validity of natural theology, Puritan ministers believed that neither they nor their parishioners were exempt from temptations to disbelieve the existence of God. They were generally well aware of the historical ambiguities of the epithet "atheist" and routinely distinguished between three different brands of atheism. The first was "speculative" or "absolute," which meant an outright denial of God's existence. The second was "Epicurean," so named from the ancient philosopher's denial of providence and assertion that the gods were unconcerned with human affairs. Epicurean atheism was thus equivalent to what would come to be known in the eighteenth century as deism. It was also a label for those who attributed the origin of the ordered universe to a chance collocation of atoms. Finally, however, there were "practical atheists," those who believed in God but whose behavior manifested in varying degrees some doubt or denial of his existence.[14]

No theme was more prominent in Puritan discussions of natural theology than this last category of unbelief. Practical atheism did not simply refer to those who lived as if there were no God, sinning riotously without any thought of religion and a future judgment, but to those who led relatively upright lives and even to those who were deadly serious about religion. Near the end of his extraordinarily productive life, Robert Boyle remarked that in discussing religion with "no small variety of persons" over a number of years, he had come across at most two or three flat-out atheists, but many who were only "baptized infidels," and still more who "do rather *take it for granted*, that there is a Deity, than *truly believe it*." This was why

---

invention" quotation on p. 9; Overton, *Man Wholly Mortal*, p. 111 for Overton's belief in animal resurrection, pp. 128–30 for the quotation from Pliny. Cf. Pliny, *Natural History*, Book VII, chap. 56 (55).

14. Charnock (*Existence and Attributes of God*, 1:24), distinguished a fourth category, "skeptical" atheism, referring to those who were agnostic on the question of God's existence.

there was so much vice in the world, and so little fervent piety.[15] Perkins concurred and thus heartily recommended

> the examination of our own hearts, touching this thought, whether it may be found among us or not: doubtless every one will labour to clear himself hereof ... because they never felt in themselves, any such conceits as this, *that there is no God*. But we may easily deceive ourselves herein.... [I]f we examine ourselves ... we shall find this wicked thought to be amongst us.[16]

Richard Capel (1596–1656) classified atheism as "the master-vein in our Original lust," all other sins being "from" and "to" it—from it, in that no one would sin "did he then verily think, that there were a God that saw all, and would punish all; and such a God, God must be, or no God"—to it, in that the more one fell in love with sin, the more one was driven to forget God, lest the remembrance of him torment a guilty conscience.[17] Barker observed that "though men with their tongues say they believe his Being, yet men's actions speak otherwise," lamenting, "I verily believe that there is to be found less sense of a *Deity* upon many Christians so called, that live in the midst of Gospel-Light, than in any part of the world."[18] Before commencing his demonstration of the existence of God, Ezekiel Hopkins (1634–90) addressed the question of whether such a procedure were not altogether out of place in Christian England, replying:

> I heartily wish it were both unnecessary and impertinent; but, truly, if we consider that usually the practices of men are guided and influenced by their principles, we shall find reason enough to suspect that there are some notions of Speculative Atheism that lie at the bottom of that Practical Atheism, which we may observe so generally to prevail in the world: for any considerate person would think it impossible, that men should so daringly rush into all those prodigious crimes and villainies, that every where rage and reign, were it not that they entertain loose and wavering apprehensions

---

15. Boyle, *Christian Virtuoso* (*Works*, 6:757–58).
16. Perkins, *A Treatise of Mans Imaginations* (*Workes*, 2:461–62).
17. Capel, *Tentations*, 153–55, 262. Capel's student William Pemble rang the changes on this theme in a scorching section of the lectures that became his *Vindicae gratiae*, concluding, "You have now here, my brethren, opened unto you that Master-vein wherein runs all that corrupt blood of Hypocrisy and secret Infidelity, wherewith the greatest part of men professing Christianity are infected. This is that bitter root of men's Apostasy and back-sliding from Piety to profaneness" (252).
18. Barker, *Natural Theology*, 49, 56–57. Also see p. 37.

of the existence of a Deity; and encourage themselves in their vices by some unformed and callow thoughts, that perchance all that religion teacheth concerning God and a future state, are only polite devices and fictions.[19]

Watson preached that the world was "full of practical atheism," and he added that he was thankful the unevangelized heathen had more than the example of the average Englishman to commend Christianity to their consideration: "If an Indian who never heard of a God should come among us, and have no other means to convince him of a Deity, but the lives of men in our age, surely he would question whether there were a God."[20] Increase Mather similarly asserted that "although there are comparatively but few *professed Atheists*, and fewer (if any at all) that are direct *Speculative Atheists*; nevertheless, the greatest Part of Mankind are *Practical Atheists*, such as in Works deny God. . . . The World is swarming full of *Practical Atheists*."[21]

Charnock and the early English Puritan John Preston (1587–1628) elaborated at great length on the workings of practical atheism in religious believers. Charnock began his celebrated discourses on God's being and attributes with not one, but two essays on atheism, the first taking the simple title, "On the Existence of God," the second, "On Practical Atheism." To drive home the point, his announced scripture text was the same for each discourse—the aforementioned Psalm 14:1, "The fool hath said in his heart, There is no God." Perhaps not surprisingly, the second essay was some twenty-five pages longer than the first. Its central theme was that the affections and actions of the best of Christians, let alone those of the rest of the world, often reflected a reserve of unbelief regarding the nature and even the very being of God. "Let us labor to be sensible of this atheism in our nature, and be humbled for it," he exhorted his congregation at Crosby Hall shortly before his death in 1680. "All our baseness, stupidity, wanderings, vanity, spring from a wavering and unsettledness in this principle."[22]

As would be the case with Charnock, Preston's final publication was a series of sermons on the divine existence and attributes preached during the last year of his life and published posthumously under the title *Life Eternall* (1631). Preston was a lifelong friend of the American Puritan

---

19. Ezekiel Hopkins, *An Exposition on the Ten Commandments*, in *Works*, 1:279.
20. Watson, *Body of Divinity*, 43.
21. Increase Mather, *Existence and Omniscience of God*, i–ii, 67.
22. Charnock, *Existence and Attributes of God*, 1:167, 85.

John Cotton (1585–1652) and successor to the preacher-poet John Donne at the Honourable Society of Lincoln's Inn from 1621 until his death. He was also the person to whom the early American Puritan Thomas Shepard attributed his spiritual awakening. Thomas Ball (1590–1659) and Thomas Goodwin (1600–1680), the latter of whom was a prominent figure in the Westminster Assembly debates, hailed *Life Eternall* as an invaluable work "that presents to all men's understandings, so clear, evident and immediate expressions of *God; his Name & Attributes*."[23]

This publication is the richest source in early Puritan literature for what Preston called "this untaken-notice-of-Atheism" and a classic instance of how the Puritan penchant for introspection and self-examination could manifest itself in what essentially amounted to a sociological analysis of religion. Consider the following queries Preston propounded to his auditors in these sermons. Why was it, he asked, that people were far more conscientious of others' opinion of them than of God's? How was it that they felt intense shame when their follies became public and yet indulged private sins with hardly any embarrassment at all? Why were they much more solicitous to seek help in their troubles from creatures than from God? Why were they more preoccupied with the transitory present than with the eternal future in which they professed to believe? Why was it that "when men come into the presence of *God*, they carry themselves so negligently, not caring how their souls are clad," whereas, "If you should come before men, you would look that your clothes be neat and decent, and you will carry yourselves with such reverence, as becomes him in whose presence you stand." The grand culprit, replied Preston, was practical atheism:

> And this is the ground of all the difference between men: One man believes it fully that there is such a mighty *God*; another believes it but by halves.... We speak not to Atheists now, but to them that believe *there is a God*, and yet we do not think our labour lost: For, though there be an assent to this truth in us, yet it is such an one as may receive degrees, and may be strengthened: for I know that there are few perfect [i.e., absolute] Atheists; yet there are some degrees of Atheism left in the best of *God's* Children, which we take no notice of.... There are some degrees of doubting in the hearts of all men.[24]

---

23. *DNB*, 45:261–62, 50:232; McGiffert, *God's Plot . . . Being the Autobiography and Journal of Thomas Shepard*, 41–42, 45–47, 73 (hereafter Shepard, *Autobiography and Journal*). Ball and Goodwin, preface to John Preston, *Life Eternall*, iv.

24. Preston, *Life Eternall*, 24–25, 27–28.

But practical atheism and practical disbelief in special revelation were not the only forms of unbelief to which the Puritans thought their parishioners subject. They also addressed themselves to genuine intellectual doubts about the existence of God, his intervention in the world, and the truth of Christianity itself. In dealing with the subject of atheism and natural theology, it is necessary to give some attention in this chapter to Puritan struggles with the trustworthiness of revealed religion, not only because of its importance to our understanding of the whole complex of Puritan doubting, but also because Puritans used natural theology itself, and not just evidential arguments for the inspiration of Scripture, to address this particular species of unbelief. Atheism, as they saw it, was the root of all sin and unbelief. Conversely, the existence of God was the foundation of all religion, and natural theology was the normal preparative to Christianity. Hence, when doubts about the superstructure of revealed religion appeared, it was likely that something in the foundation needed to be addressed as well.

One of the most striking and unnoticed features of Puritanism was its forthright approach to unbelief among Christians. Indeed, not a few Puritan theologians confessed to grappling with these doubts themselves. "The best of God's children," wrote Thomas Manton (1620–77), "are sometimes tried and exercised in the sorest way, and we are apt to doubt sometimes of the supreme truth, whether there be a God or no?" In his *Sincere Convert* (1640), one of the most popular devotional treatises in early New England, Thomas Shepard (1605–49) commenced his proofs for the existence of God with a similar observation, noting that the more introspective one's religious experience, the greater the likelihood of temptations to atheism: "Many of the children of God, who are best able to know men's hearts, because they only [i.e., only they] study their hearts, feel this temptation, Is there a God? bitterly assaulting them sometimes." Shepard's journal entries in the early 1640s reveal that he knew in a very personal way whereof he spoke. On December 4, 1641, he wrote, "I felt a wonderful cloud of darkness and atheism over my head, and unbelief, and my weakness to see or believe God," and he prayed that God would "heal this wound, which was but skinned over before, of secret atheism and unbelief." Seven weeks later came another such entry: "I did not see but doubt of the very being of God, whereby I did bury his glory." He gained some relief over the course of the next year but still felt the cloud had not been completely dispersed, consoling himself on February 12, 1643 with the thought, "I saw the reason why I felt so much blasphemous unbelief, that it might be of God only to try my faith."²⁵

Shepard would have been sympathetic, then, when the eventual successor to his pulpit, Jonathan Mitchell (1624–68), told him in 1648 or 1649 that he had sometimes been "suddenly and strangely filled with my atheistical thoughts about [the] being of God and [the] truth of Scripture." During these same two years the young Robert Boyle was composing his *Philaretus*, a third-person autobiographical account of his early life and religious experience. He related that while studying abroad at the age of twelve or thirteen he had been seized with "strange & hideous thoughts, & such distracting Doubts of some of the Fundamentals of Christianity/Religion." The sentiments soon left him, but "never after" (Boyle was now twenty-one or twenty-two years old) "did these fleeting Clouds cease now & then to darken" his faith.²⁶

Increase Mather and his son Cotton (1663–1728) had similar experiences. Plagued with doubts during the summer of 1664, the twenty-five-year-old Increase wrote in his diary on July 29, "Grieved, grieved, grieved with temptations to Atheisme."²⁷ Cotton's temptations began to assail him in his mid-forties. A "wretched Idea" had entered his mind with "incredible Force" and "Satanic Energy" over the course of the preceding year, he noted in his diary on February 7, 1707. He introduced his veiled discussion of the matter with the remark, "Many poor Servants of God, have been strangely distressed with Temptations to *Atheism* and *Blasphemy*," while noting that his particular temptation was "of another Importance [i.e., import]" and was not any "grosser Pollution." Two years later the dark thoughts were still with him. This time he identified what kind of unbelief was troubling him, although he still could not quite bring himself to utter its name: "I am assaulted with Sollicitations to look upon the whole *Christian Religion*, as—(I dare not mention, what!)." The translation of this still cryptic remark

---

25. Manton, *By Faith: Sermons on Hebrews 11*, 76; Shepard, *Sincere* (1640) (*Works*, 1:9); Shepard, *Autobiography and Journal* (ed. McGiffert), 135, 153, 203. Also see Shepard's entries on November 24, 1641; and on March 9, April 10, June 13, 1642.

26. Boyle, *Account of Philaretus During his Minority*, in *Robert Boyle by Himself and his Friends* (ed. Hunter), 17; McCall, "Thomas Shepard's Record of Relations of Religious Experience, 1648–1649," 456. Shepard's manuscript has Mitchell's words as "truth of God and being of Scripture," but this is almost certainly a miswriting of "*being* of God and *truth* of Scripture."

27. Quoted in Hall, *The Last American Puritan: The Life of Increase Mather, 1639–1723*, 65.

is that he was struggling with temptations to deism. The root cause of this temptation seems to have been his inability to discern any logic in God's providential dealing with him, for he concluded his discussion of the matter with a resolve to no longer be staggered by God's "*dark*" and "*unaccountable*" proceedings, but to "rely upon his unsearchable *Wisdome*" and patiently wait for the unfolding of these mysteries in the world to come: "For, what He does, tho' *I know not now, I shall know hereafter*."[28] Whether Shepard, Mitchell, Boyle, and Increase were experiencing temptations to absolute atheism or—like Cotton Mather—to deism (for which "atheism" could sometimes be shorthand in Puritan literature) is uncertain.

No Puritan spoke more freely of his struggles with unbelief than Richard Baxter. In his younger days all his doubts were concerned with whether or not he had really been born again, but in later years they revolved around the inspiration of Scripture and the truth of Christianity. So severe were these assaults, he wrote, which commenced during the time of his legendary pastoral labors at Kidderminster in the early 1640s, that "had I been void of internal experience, and the adhesion of love, and the special help of God, and had not discerned more reason for my religion than I did when I was younger, I had certainly apostatized to infidelity;" and thus he counted it a mercy that God "let not out these terrible and dangerous temptations upon me while I was weak and in the infancy of my faith, for then I had never been able to withstand them."[29]

Baxter's writings also provide some insight into the extent to which Puritan laity were subject to religious doubting. Of some forty or fifty "melancholy," i.e., clinically depressed individuals he had counseled over several decades, all but four of them had been "hurried with suggestions to Blasphemous thoughts, against God or the Sacred Scriptures."[30] But despondent

---

28. *Diary of Cotton Mather*, 1:585, 2:3. The second entry is dated March 4, 1709. This seems to have been the last of these episodes. "I found a wonderful peace," Mather concluded, "in being thus resolved. I found this Faith, to be my best *Wisdome*. The Damp which there began to grow upon my Piety and Usefulness, vanished. The Flame revived; and I went on with Joy in my usual Methods of flaming Zeal, to do good abundantly."

29. Baxter, *Autobiography*, 109–10, 26.

30. Baxter, *Gods Goodness Vindicated*, 2–3. He makes a similar comment in his 1655 treatise, "The Spirit's Witness to the Truth of Christianity" (*Unreasonableness of Infidelity*, Part 1, p. 62): "I have had multitudes of people come to me for counsel in deep Melancholy, some for their bodies, and some for their minds, and I scarce remember two of them, but they were strongly tempted to deny Christ and Scripture, and many to question whether there were a God. Many that being very godly were well grounded before, and many that were worldlings and never minded it much before, yet now they

individuals were not the only ones so tempted. In a preface to his *Reasons of the Christian Religion* (1667)—appropriately subtitled, "First meditated for the well-settling of his own Belief; and now published for the benefit of others"—Baxter said his pastoral experience had taught him that one of the reasons for the prevalence of practical atheism was that parishioners were usually too ashamed to discuss their doubts, and thus rarely had the opportunity of getting them resolved:

> I perceive, that because it is taken for a shame, to doubt of our Christianity and the Life to come, this hindereth many from uttering their doubts, who never get them well resolved, but remain half Infidels within, whilst the Ensigns of Christ are hanged without [i.e., on the outside]; and need much help, though they are ashamed to tell their needs....
>
> The best complain of the imperfection of their Faith: And too many good Christians, especially if Melancholy surprise them, are haunted with such temptations, to Atheism, blasphemy and unbelief, as make their lives a burden to them! And one that hath heard so many of their complaints as I have done, is excusable for desiring to relieve them.[31]

We now turn to examine how Puritans brought natural theology to bear on these problems, as well as the other contexts in which they employed it.

---

are assaulted with these Blasphemous Temptations."
31. Baxter, *Reasons of the Christian Religion*, title page, "To the Christian Reader," ii–iii. Also see pp. 153, 205, and 454, where Baxter says more about his personal experience.

2

The Role of Natural Theology

"Arm yourself with evident proofs that there is a God."
—Henry Scudder, 1627

"It is very profitable to come to this disjunction."
—John Preston, 1628

So then, could natural theology be of any help in overcoming this practical atheism, and could the rational evidences for Christianity be of parallel assistance in resolving a Christian's doubts about its legitimacy? With a few exceptions, Puritans answered both of these questions with a resounding affirmative. When doubt moved from a pastoral to a polemical context, their answer was the same. But natural theology also fulfilled several positive functions, serving as a tool for catechesis and as an evangelical preparative in their missionary endeavors with the natives of the New World.

Let me begin with the exceptions to this general perspective, however. According to the philosophical William Twisse (1577/8–1646), prolocutor of the Westminster Assembly until declining health compelled him to step down from the chair in January 1646, believers had nothing to gain from studying the rational evidences of God's existence. Christians discovered God experientially in the Bible, and nothing further than this was needed: "For certainly we have no need of it for the fortification of our faith, that being built only upon the word of God."[1] Capel gave a less dismissive assessment. He held that since the evidences for God's existence were so clear, natural theology was a general help against atheistic thoughts. But he urged that when temptations to atheism became "fierce," dabbling with the light of nature would only worsen the situation. Doubting Christians were likely to be staggered by the incomprehensibility of God, and Satan would use this to convince them that a being so far above the reach of their reason was after all a mere fiction:

> [T]hat which must and only will hold us against the tentation [temptation] when it is strongly put to by Satan, is to fly to the Word of God: The Word saith, that there is a God, and therefore I will believe that there is a God: out of tentation other considerations taken from nature and from divers Acts of Divine providence may stop the mouth of our Lust.... [B]ut when once we are set upon with some fierce tentation, I would wish all Christians to do these things. The first is not to enter into dispute with his own reason; for the understanding of man, is too weak, & too short to reach the comprehension of a Deity: he that shall take (in) his own thoughts and muse about the nature and infinite Being of God, shall but let in Satan the more. The counsel then I am bold to give to the poor Christian, is, in any hand not to study this point, but to take his mind off from thinking and disputing this argument, lest he come to say in his heart, I cannot conceive what *God* is, and therefore I doubt me there is no such being. Away then with all reasonings and disputes about that subject.... [C]leave to the word and say, though my reason cannot tell what to make of it, though lust in me say there is no *God* at all, though Satan say that there is no God, and most do live as though there were no *God*: yet because it is in the word, the scripture saith it, I must and will and do believe it; we must see both *God* and Heaven and all in the word.... He that shall go about by the force of his own wit to conquer his Atheism, is in great danger to fall into some degrees of it; for when he sees that reason cannot find out what this God is, he will come to question all, and to think that there is no such being. He then doth best, who doth dispute least, and in the heat of tentation, rests himself wholly on the Word.[2]

---

1. Twisse, *Discovery of D. Jacksons Vanitie*, 45.
2. Capel, *Tentations*, 157–58. This advice is repeated almost verbatim in Samuel Clarke's (1599–1682) *Medulla Theologiæ, or The Marrow of Divinity*, 149–50, a compendium of practical directions given by various theologians.

The English Puritan William Gurnall (1617–79) adopted the same approach. Since reason could demonstrate it, the existence of God was indeed "a piece of natural divinity," and Christians could in general avail themselves of rational argumentation to confirm and strengthen their convictions. But when a temptation to atheism became "furious," the believer was to simply "believe there is a God at the report of God's word" rather than turning to reason. Never at loss for an illustration, Gurnall compared the situation to the most famous story in the Bible: "Let the word, like David's stone in the sling of faith, first prostrate the temptation; and then, as he used Goliath's sword to cut off his head, so mayst thou with more ease and safety make use of thy reason to complete the victory over these atheistical suggestions."[3] How the testimony of the word of God could be of any help when the existence of God itself was in question, Capel and Gurnall did not say. They probably had in mind the doctrine of the Spirit's immediate witness to the believer in Scripture, a point which will be discussed later in this chapter.

In addition to these published remarks of Twisse and Capel, there are indications that a few other Puritans may have had similar reservations about the use of natural theology and the rational evidences for Christianity. In a 1652 preface to the second edition of his runaway bestseller, *The Saints' Everlasting Rest*, Richard Baxter felt compelled to defend himself against several ministers who had taken exception to the proofs of Christianity he had laid out at some length in the first edition of that work (1650). Some had criticized him for making so much use of the argument from miracles, holding that it was "invalid" as a demonstrative proof, "except it be apparent truth which they [the miracles] are brought to confirm." Baxter replied that such an opinion was "striking at the very root" of the Christian cause, and moreover was contrary to the Bible itself: "That which was the great argument used by Christ and his apostles to win the world to believe," he said, citing a host of scripture texts, "should be the great argument now for every man to use to that end with himself and others." Worst of all, however, was a blistering criticism he had received from some who had reproached him for "seek[ing] to satisfy reason so much of the Scripture's authority," on the grounds that this was "too near the Socinian way," and that as a first principle, Scripture was not to be proved. Baxter responded with an adamant defense of the role of reason in religion:

> [W]hat more can be done to the disgrace and ruin of Christianity, than to make the world believe that we have no reason for it? nor

---

3. Gurnall, *The Christian in Complete Armour*, 2:92–95.

are able to prove it true against an adversary? What would these men do if they lived among Christ's enemies, and were challenged to defend their religion, or prove it true? Would they say, as they say to me, 'I will believe and not dispute?' Christ's cause would then be little beholden to them. And how would they preach for the conversion of infidels, if they had not reason to give them, for what they persuade them to?[4]

Another indication of this minority dissent to which Baxter was here responding is indicated in the defensive remarks made by the English Puritan John Howe (1630–1705) in an introductory chapter to his *Living Temple* (1675). Howe complained of those who thought it inconsistent with piety to inquire into the grounds of theism. Such a stance he considered "unmanly and absurd; especially when a gross ignorance of the true reasons and grounds of religion shall be shadowed over with a pretended awe and scrupulousness to inquire about things so sacred; and an inquisitive temper shall have an ill character put upon it, as if *rational* and *profane* were words of the same signification."[5] Who these critics were, Howe and Baxter did not say, and I have been unable to find any published criticisms. It seems probable, however, that they came from some of their Puritan brethren.

But these were rare exceptions. The majority of Puritans thought natural theology and rational evidences were a potent help against the unbelief of believers. It is interesting to compare the previously quoted remarks from Capel's *Tentations* with the approach found in one of the most popular Puritan devotional treatises of the early seventeenth century, Henry Scudder's (d. 1652) *The Christian's Daily Walk* (1627). It was in at least its sixth edition by 1635, which contained a dedicatory epistle by John Davenport, who emigrated to America in 1637 and became a pastor in the town of Quinnipiac, CT (later renamed New Haven). A German translation of *The Christian's Daily Walk* appeared in 1636; and in 1674, by which time the

---

4. Baxter, *The Saints Everlasting Rest* (*Practical Works*, 22:216–17, 220, 221–22, 225). Baxter justified his vehemence on the grounds that "if you heard the accusation, you would excuse my apology." He frequently reiterated this disgust with the view that Scripture was simply to be believed rather than proved, writing in 1655 that it was "so unbeseeming the mouth of a true Christian, that I will not say against it what it deserves, because I know it will exasperate many that do befriend it." *Unreasonableness of Infidelity*, 3:10; also see 4:62.

5. Howe, *The Living Temple* (*Works*, 1:18).

work had gone through some fifteen printings, the leading nonconformist divines John Owen and Richard Baxter added a commendatory preface.[6]

Like Capel, Scudder included a section containing helps against "evil and blasphemous thoughts," the first such being temptations to atheism. His remedy, however, was quite different from the one Capel had proposed. "Arm yourself with evident proofs that there is a God," he counseled, and proceeded to set forth three arguments for God's existence. Those tempted to doubt the divinity of the Scriptures were similarly equipped with six arguments for its divine origin.[7] Scudder was following the path laid out in William Perkins' famous work of casuistry, *The Whole Treatise of the Cases of Conscience* (1596). Perkins had no inclination to enter into dispute with outright atheists, but he was more than ready to present evidences for God's existence and the divine origin of the Bible in order "to remove, or at least help an inward corruption of the soul, that is great and dangerous, whereby the heart and conscience by nature denieth God and his providence."[8]

Thomas Vincent, as we have seen, likewise furnished his catechumens with proofs for God's existence and the divinity of the Scriptures, as did Samuel Willard (1640–1707) during the inaugural year of the weekday afternoon lectures on the *Westminster Shorter Catechism* he delivered to his Boston congregation once a month between 1688 and 1707.[9] Like many Puritans, Willard's primary rationale for proving the existence of God was "because there is so much of *Atheism* in men's hearts naturally, as tacitly to deny it." Vincent and Willard were following the model of the early English Puritan John Ball (1585–1640), who had done exactly the same in his own immensely popular catechism and catechetical commentary.[10] The same

---

6. *Dictionary of National Biography*, 15:267–68; 49:582.

7. Scudder, *The Christian's Daily Walk*, 286–89.

8. Perkins, *The Whole Treatise of the Cases of Conscience* (*Workes*, 2:49 [quotation], 49–52 [existence of God], 57–60 [divinity of the Scriptures]). Also see chapter two of Perkins' *Golden Chaine* (*Workes*, 1:11).

9. Vincent, *Shorter Catechism Explained*, 17–20, 35–38 (recall that this work had a commendatory preface signed by forty Puritan theologians); Willard, *A Compleat Body of Divinity*, 16–19, 37–40 (quotation 37).

10. See Ball, *A Short Catechism*, 2–4; and Ball's commentary on this catechism, *A Short Treatise Contayning all the Principal Grounds of Christian Religion*, 15–43, 60–67. I have been unable to discover the original publication dates for these two works. It would have to be sometime before 1624, since by then Ball's commentary on his catechism was already in its fourth printing. The catechism itself was in its twenty-third printing by 1645. Ball's *Shorter Treatise* had reached its fifteenth printing by 1632 and had even been translated into Turkish. *DNB*, 3:562.

The Role of Natural Theology

approach was taken by the English Puritans Thomas Manton, Thomas Watson, John Preston, and Ezekiel Hopkins, and by the American Puritans Increase Thomas and Thomas Shepard, all of whom followed up their previously quoted remarks on the prevalence of practical atheism with a presentation of the rational evidences for the existence of God.[11] Preaching in the 1620s, Preston dismissed all objections against this procedure:

> And although it may be thought that there are none that doubt of this [the existence of God], yet these proofs are useful, partly because they serve to answer those secret objections of Atheism, which we are all subject to; and partly because they strengthen that Principle in us, *that God is:* which is very necessary to be confirmed, seeing it is the main and principal foundation of all Christian religion, and can never sufficiently enough be rammed down, as being that that must bear all the weight of the building. Therefore let no man think, that those proofs that we shall use for the manifestation of this truth, are a thing altogether needless.[12]

John Owen considered the proofs for the Bible's inspiration to be "of singular use for the strengthening of the faith of them that do believe ... as also for the conviction of gainsayers."[13] The purpose of his *Natural Theology*, said Matthew Barker after lamenting the increase of practical atheism in England, was "to convince Men's Reasons, to awaken their sleepy Souls, to a practical acknowledgment of his Being .... I thought no better way to recover it [the present age], than to set God before Men's view in the Works of his Creation."[14] John Howe offered his treatise on natural theology to, among other things, "reinforce and strengthen" languishing faith and combat practical atheism, as did William Bates, Stephen Charnock, and

---

11. Manton, *By Faith*, 76–77; Watson, *Body of Divinity*, 39–44; Shepard, *Sincere Convert* (*Works*, 1:9–13); Preston, *Life Eternall*, 5–44 (proving the existence of God), 45–91 (proving the divine origin of Christianity and the inspiration of the Scriptures); Increase Mather, *Existence and Omniscience of God*, 13–37; Hopkins, *Exposition on the Ten Commandments* (*Works*, 1:279–92). Also see Thomas Shepard's *Short Catechism*, 1–2, 13–15, which offered proofs for the existence of God, the immortality of the soul, and the inspiration of the Scriptures.

12. Preston, *Sermons*, 65–66. This volume was published after Preston's death in 1628.

13. Owen, *The Reason of Faith* (*Works*, 4:47). Also see 4:20, 71–72; 16:343. On the usefulness of evidential arguments for strengthening the believer's faith in the Bible, also see Cartwright, *A Treatise of the Christian Religion*, 76–77; Adams, *Meditations upon Some Part of the Creed* (*Works*, 3:260); Lee, *The Joy of Faith*, 2–30, 39–41; Baxter, *Christian Directory*, 1.4.1 (pp. 166–71).

14. Barker, *Natural Theology*, iv, vi.

Richard Baxter.[15] Even strong believers, said Howe, would gain satisfaction from studying the rational grounds of their convictions:

> [I]t wants neither its use nor pleasure, to the most composed minds, and that are most exempt form wavering herein, to view the frame of their religion, as it aptly and even naturally rises and grows up from its very foundations—to contemplate its first principles, which they may in the meantime find no present cause or inclination to dispute. They will know how to consider its most fundamental grounds, not with doubt or suspicion, but with admiration and delight; and can, with a calm and silent pleasure, enjoy the repose and rest of a quiet and well-assured mind, rejoicing and contented to know to themselves (when others refuse to partake with them in this joy), and feel all firm and stable under them, whereupon either the practice or the hopes of their religion do depend.[16]

One is not surprised to find, then, in that fascinating document relating one of the religious encounters between Puritans and Native Americans that took place in October of 1646, that when the American Puritan missionary John Eliot brought some of his ministerial brethren along with him to spend a day discoursing with the Indians about Christianity, the first question he propounded to them, after entertaining some of their own inquiries, was whether they were not sometimes "tempted to think that there was no God" because they had never seen him! Apparently this thought had never occurred to his interlocutors, for they said nothing about ever having been tempted to atheism but rather declared their belief that though God could not be seen with the physical eye, "yet that he was to be seen with their soul within." Upon hearing this reply, Eliot immediately presented the classic Ciceronian argument for God's existence in order to strengthen their conviction:

> Hereupon we sought to confirm them the more, and asked them if they saw a great *Wigwam*, or a great house, would they think that *Raccoons* or Foxes built it that had not wisdom? or would they think that it made itself? or that no wise workman made it, because they could not see him that made it? No, but they would

---

15. Howe, *The Living Temple* (*Works*, 1:19); Bates, *Considerations of the Existence of God*, 3–4; Charnock, *Existence and Attributes of God*, 1:26–27, 83–84; Baxter, *Reasons of the Christian Religion*, vi.

16. Howe, *The Living Temple* (*Works*, 1:19). Also see Baxter, *Unreasonableness of Infidelity*, "Epistle Dedicatory," iii.

believe some wise workman made it, though they did not see him. So should they believe concerning God, when they looked up to heaven, Sun, Moon, and Stars, and saw this great house he hath made.[17]

Puritans often spoke of natural theology as foundational to or at least as a preparation for the supernatural revelation of God in the Scriptures. We have already seen this in Preston's comment that the existence of God was "that which must bear all the weight of the building." Perkins wrote that "the light of nature serveth to give a beginning and preparation" to the "light of grace."[18] "Indeed there are many uses of reason," wrote Manton, "partly to prepare and induce us to hearken to the word of God; this is the mind God hath given us to know him, the stock left in nature, upon which he would implant faith." Barker considered natural theology an excellent preparation for the gospel on the grounds that the widespread lack of a firm belief in the reality of God's existence was "one great Reason why Christ is preached so much in vain." Natural theology could serve as a doorway to repentance for the unregenerate and it could deepen the repentance of real Christians, as was the case with Job. The general rule, preached Howe in a 1695 thanksgiving-day sermon, was that people's receptivity to biblical revelation rose and fell with the strength and character of their natural theology:

> For it is to no purpose, when the world is generally atheistical, and have either buried the notion of God, or perverted it; so as that to think there is a God, or that there is none, is all one with them. It is, I say, to little or no purpose for men to go up and down

---

17. *The Day-Breaking, if not the Sun-Rising of the Gospell With the Indians in New-England*, 6. This treatise was anonymously authored by "a Minister of Christ in New England," possibly Thomas Shepard or John Wilson (1588-1667). Cf. Cierco, *Nature of the Gods*, 2.17.

18. Preston, *Sermons*, 65-66; Perkins, *Cases of Conscience* (*Workes*, 2:49). Perkins asserts this again a few pages later where he says that "the light of nature is only a way of preparation to faith," whereas the light of grace actually "begets faith" (52). It is interesting to note in this connection the summary paragraph of theistic proofs Perkins added to chapter two, "Of God, and the nature of God," in the 1595 edition of his *Golden Chaine*. The first two editions (1591 and 1592) had simply launched right into a discussion of the divine attributes, but in 1595 he inserted the following prefatory paragraph, which appeared in all subsequent editions: "That there is a God, it is evident. 1. by the course of nature: 2. by the nature of the soul of man: 3. by the distinction of things honest and dishonest: 4. by the terror of conscience: 5. by the regiment of civil societies: 6. the order of all causes having ever recourse to some former beginning: 7. the determination of all things to their several ends: 8. the consent of all men well in their wits." *Workes*, 1:11.

among such persons, in such a state of things, with a Bible; for they disbelieve such a kind of Deity, as that book reveals. But if the thoughts of God be recovered, and rectified in the minds of men, they are a great deal more susceptible of super-added revelation from heaven.[19]

Increase Mather put this point quite bluntly, asserting that "except men give Credit to the principles of *natural*, they will never believe the Principles of *revealed Religion*." He added that this was why when the apostle Paul was at Athens, "he first instructed them in the knowledge of God *the Creator*, before he declared to them the *Mediator*," i.e., Jesus Christ. Charnock concurred: "The knowledge of God by nature and creatures is necessary, as a foundation for higher apprehensions, and for turning to God. Men without it would be wholly brutish, incapable of instructions in Christianity." Indeed, no less a model of English Puritan piety than Mathew Henry (1662–1714) could preach to his congregation, "Let us be more and more confirmed in our belief of the principles of natural religion, which Christianity supposes, and is founded upon." In the introductory chapter to his *Divinity of the Christian Religion Proved* (1677), Bates remarked (in reference to his *Considerations of the Existence of God*, published the previous year), "Having in some former Discourses established and cleared the Foundations of Religion, I shall now proceed to raise the Superstructure." He took the same approach to the rational evidences for Christianity. These could not in themselves convert a person, but they could bring one to concede the truth of the Christian religion, thus producing "a rational human Faith, grounded on just and powerful motives, which is preparatory for the Divine."[20]

The nonconformist minister and natural philosopher Samuel Lee (1625?–91) concurred in this assessment of "human," or as he called it, "historical" faith, pointing out that while the evidences for Christianity "do not, nor can of themselves directly cause true Faith in the heart, without the Almighty power of God . . . yet are they a strong Foundation for Faith

---

19. Manton, *By Faith*, 91; Barker, *Natural Theology*, 70–75 (quotation p. 70); Howe, *Sermons on Several Occasions*, 2:374.

20. Increase Mather, *Discourse Proving that the Christian Religion is the only True Religion*, 31. Cf. Acts 17 and compare Calvin's comments on v. 22 of this *locus classicus*: "For it was requisite to handle those four points [of natural theology] generally, before he did descend unto the faith of the gospel." Charnock, *Knowledge of God in Christ* (*Works*, 4:118); Matthew Henry, "Faith in Christ Inferred From Faith in God" (1711), in *Complete Works of Matthew Henry*, 2:294; Bates, *Divinity of the Christian Religion Proved*, 3.

to insist upon," inasmuch as they could both "satisfy and confirm weak Believers" and "by the good conduct of God's Spirit . . . influence the minds of Heathen and Atheists, would they but improve the common light of reason, that Candle of the Lord."[21] Few Puritans insisted more strongly on the necessity of improving this candle than did Baxter, who believed not only that natural theology was a useful preparative to special revelation, but that failing to inculcate it in one's parishioners was positively detrimental to faith in the Bible:

> It is a great wrong to the Christian cause, that too many preachers of it have missed the true method, and still begun at supernatural revelations, and built even *natural* certainties thereupon; and have either not known, or concealed much of the fore-written natural verities. And it is an exceeding great cause of the multiplying of Infidels, that most men are dull or idle drones, and unacquainted with the common natural truths, which must give light to Christianity, and prepare men to receive it.[22]

Nowhere did this foundationalist function of natural theology manifest itself more fully than in the catechetical treatise Jonathan Mitchell's brother-in-law and tutor, Abraham Pierson (1608–78), prepared in 1654 for his missionary work with the Quinnipiac Indians on the north shore of Long Island. The title itself was indicative of his strategy: *Some Helps for the Indians; Shewing them how to Improve their Natural Reason, to know the true God, and the Christian Religion*. The first thirty pages of the work were essentially a child's primer in natural theology. "How do you prove that there is a God?" read the first question, followed shortly with, "How do you prove there is but one God?" Pierson went on to raise and then answer a number of objections to classical theism. Since God was by definition an incomprehensible being, did it not follow that no one could demonstrate the fact of his existence? If God created everything, did that not make him the author of evil? Would it not be more reasonable to conclude that there are two ultimate powers, one good and the other evil? What about providence?—"Seeing Jehovah made heaven and earth, and all things in

---

21. Lee, *The Joy of Faith*, 30, vi, 1–2. Cf. Prov 20:27, "The spirit of man is the candle of the LORD."

22. Baxter, *Reasons of the Christian Religion*, 445. Also see his remark in the second prefatory epistle, "To the Doubting and the Unbelieving Readers," ii; and pp. 241, 369, and 273: "For there is no coming to the highest stop of the Ladder, without beginning at the lowest: Men ignorant of things knowable, by *Natural Reason*, are unprepared for higher things." Also see Howe, *The Living Temple* (*Works*, 1:20).

them, does He now leave them and no more look after them, as a carpenter doth leave an house he hath built?" Given the existence of providence, did it extend to all events? And, "If it be so; how then comes it to pass that Sin doth so abound in the world?" This was followed by a discussion of the need for special revelation and its rational evidences: "How do you prove that this Book containeth the word of God?" Only after this did Pierson move on to present the "divine truths necessary to salvation," as the second part of the title read.[23]

But was this use of natural theology perhaps a mere aberration written by a minister laboring far away from the Boston plantation? Evidently not, for Pierson's treatise was soon translated into the Algonquian dialect for the use of Massachusetts Bay missionaries.[24] It was also included in John Eliot's *A further accompt [account] of the progresse of the Gospel amongst the Indians in New-England* (1659). The Puritan bishop Edward Reynolds wrote a preface for this publication, commending Pierson's work as follows:

> It is a work likely to be by the blessing of God of singular use to the natives there, and a very proper and necessary course for those to take who would convert and persuade *Pagans* to believe the Truth .... [C]ertainly here may be much use made of *natural reason*, to demonstrate unto *Pagans* the falseness of the way they are in, and so to prepare a way for entertainment of the Truth.

Reynolds went on to outline the ideal progress of this preparation, which consisted of both natural theology and the rational evidences for the divinity of Scripture, concluding, "these and the like considerations being set on by the finger of the Holy Spirit, he is persuaded to believe the Gospel, and by believing comes to reap those Joys and comforts as make him know whom he hath believed."[25] Certainly Robert Boyle, who was one of the chief benefactors of Eliot's mission to the Indians, would not have objected to

---

23. Pierson, *Some Helps for the Indians*, 5–37, quotations from 21, 25, 34–35.

24. Pierson originally wrote the catechism in the Quiripi dialect in 1654. This version seems never to have been printed, but in 1656 he was asked to assist Thomas Stanton, Sr. in translating the work into Algonquian. This task was completed in 1657. See Cogley, *John Eliot's Mission to the Indians before King Philip's War*, 185. Cogley says the title date for the Cambridge, MA, edition quoted above is erroneous, showing 1658 instead of 1659 as the publication date. This is confirmed by the date and contents of the preface to the 1659 London edition printed by M. Simmons, which evidently was the first copy to come to press.

25. *Eliot Tracts*, 325, 327.

the course Eliot was taking; for according to him, natural theology was "the foundation, upon which revealed religion ought to be superstructed."[26]

This grace-perfecting-nature paradigm also appears in the anonymous authors of *New Englands First Fruits* (1643), who encouraged their readers in England not to be dismayed by the fact that they could not presently relate more instances of Indian conversions, considering not only the language barrier but "their infinite distance from Christianity, having never been prepared thereunto by any Civility at all."[27] Similarly, the twelve Puritans who wrote a commendatory preface for Shepard's *Clear Sunshine of the Gospel* (1648) encouraged Parliament to lend their assistance to the New England missionaries who were "dealing with such whom they are to make men, before they can make them Christians."[28] By this they did not mean that the Indians were a subhuman species (the Puritans frequently referred to their own countrymen in such terms),[29] but rather that the light of reason needed further cultivation before Christianity would be able to make significant progress among them. It may be of interest to note in passing the same paradigm in the influential Dutch Reformed theologian Herman Witsius (1636–1708): "For, as grace supposes nature, and makes it perfect; so the truths revealed in the Gospel are built on those made known by the light of nature."[30]

---

26. Boyle, *Christian Virtuoso* (*Works*, 6:718). For Boyle's connection to Eliot's mission, see Eliot's eleven letters to Boyle between 1664 and 1688 in the latter's *Works*, 1:ccv–ccxiv, 6:509–10.

27. *The Eliot Tracts*, 58.

28. Shepard, *Clear Sunshine of the Gospel Breaking Forth Upon the Indians in New England* (*Works*, 3:449–50). The twelve Puritans included Stephen Marshall, Philip Nye, and Thomas Goodwin. This treatise is also found in *Eliot Tracts*, 101–39 (quotation 106). The one Puritan exception to this preparational use of natural theology I have been able to find is in William Pemble, who rejected it on the historical grounds that in the early centuries of the church, "the Gospel found most resistance and neglect at their hands who seemed to have used their Natural abilities best, as the learned Philosophers, the wise, temperate, just, politic men of the world, who were so far from being the fitter to receive the Gospel, that they cut of pride and fleshly wisdom were its greatest enemies." *Vindiciae gratiae*, 86.

29. See, e.g., Baxter, *Christian Directory*, 1.1.1 (p. 9); Baxter, *Reasons of the Christian Religion*, x., 445; Shepard, *Works*, 1:12; Charnock, *Existence and Attributes of God*, 1:87; and any number of Puritan comments and commentaries (e.g., Matthew Henry, Matthew Poole, John Trapp) on Psalm 49:20, "Man that is in honour, and understandeth not, is like the beasts that perish." Also see *The Day Breaking*, 4, 10.

30. Witsius, *Economy of the Covenants Between God and Man*, 3.5.15 (1:350).

Puritanism and Natural Theology

In speaking of natural theology as foundational to revelation, Puritans did not mean that before people could profitably read the Bible or be converted it was first necessary for them to master the intricate details of the theistic proofs and be well studied in the apologetical arguments for the divinity of Scripture. What they meant was that human awareness of the existence of God came naturally rather than supernaturally, through rational reflection rather than through faith. The task of natural theology was not to introduce its recipients to a line of reasoning to which they were utter strangers but to articulate and reinforce what had on a less conscious level already been deduced from the created order. All Puritans held that true believers encountered God experientially through the Spirit and the Scripture, and that the Bible was itself strong evidence for the existence of God. This latter point was occasionally expressed in the circular style of Capel and Gurnall, though a closer reading of these remarks shows that what was usually intended was not the question-begging argument, "The Bible is the Word of God—The Bible says God exists—Therefore God exists," but rather that the Bible's transformative power as well as its prophecies and record of miracles—the historical factuality of which could be confirmed by rational arguments—demanded a belief in God, since none of these things would be possible without some divine power in existence. Thus in an indirect way, the Bible demonstrated the existence of God, since it was a phenomenon that could not be accounted for on the supposition of atheism.[31]

The arguments that Puritans presented for the Bible's inspiration were three-fold. First, there were the "external" proofs of its divine origin, primarily miracles and fulfilled prophecies. Next came the "internal"

---

31. One might read a Capel-like circularity into the previously quoted remark in Perkins' *Foundations of the Christian Religion*, where in answer to the question, "How do you persuade yourself that there is a God?" the reply is, "Beside the testimony of the Scriptures, plain reason will show it" (*Workes*, 1:3). The only other place I have found it is in Preston's *Life Eternall*, p. 20, where in connection with showing how God's existence is made certain to the believer not only by reason but by faith, he explains this latter route as follows: "I believe the Scriptures to be true, and that they are the word of *God*; now this is contained in the Scriptures, that *God made heaven and Earth*; therefore I believing the Scriptures to be the Word of *God*, and whatsoever is contained in them, my faith lays hold upon it also, and so my consent grows strong and firm, that there is a *God*: After this manner you come to conclude it by faith." But when Preston goes on to expound this point in an entire sermon devoted to the subject (pp. 45–57), his rationale is that the prophecies and internal characteristics of the Bible show that it must have been divinely authored. Ergo, God exists; since one cannot have a divine book without a divine being. The same train of logic appears in Thomas Vincent's *Shorter Catechism Explained*, 37, and in Ezekiel Hopkins' *Exposition on the Ten Commandments* (*Works*, 1:289–91).

evidences, which called attention to the characteristics of the biblical writings: their depth, majestic simplicity, purity, honesty, and above all their immense suitability to the human condition. The third and final proof was taken from the transformative effects of the word in the regenerate.[32] These three made up the Puritan doctrine of Scripture's self-authentication. One should not forget the Roman Catholic polemics in the background. Protestants were at pains to show that the ordinary believer's assurance of the divine origin of the Bible arose out of the Bible itself rather than from the received testimony of an infallible church.[33] That debate was carried on between laity as well as clergy.[34]

The external and internal evidences mutually supported each other. Readers were routinely directed to assume for a moment the negative of the external evidences—that prophecies had merely been passed off as such but were in reality written after the event they claimed to be predicting; that Jesus never performed miracles or rose from the dead and that his apostles were either deceivers or delusional—and then asked if these suppositions agreed with the evident characters of the biblical authors and their writings. The arguments of natural theology were also connected to the internal evidences. When nature's declarations concerning human sinfulness, "man's chief end" and divine justice were duly considered, who could fail to be struck by the sheer sublimity of the biblical revelation of salvation and

---

32. For examples of this three-fold evidence, see Ball, *A Short Catechism*, 1–3, elaborated in his *Short Treatise*, 15–43; Trapp, *Theologia Theologiae* . . . . (London: Printed by K.B. for George Badger, 1641), 12–40; Baxter, *Unreasonableness of Infidelity*, xxvi, and passim; Gurnall, *Christian in Complete Armour*, 2:197–218; Vincent, *Shorter Catechism Explained*, 17–20; Owen, *The Reason of Faith* (*Works*, 4:21–47, 64); Willard, *Compleat Body of Divinity*, 16–19; and Anthony Tuckney to Benjamin Whichcote, 8 October 1651, in *Eight Letters of Dr. Anthony Tuckney, and Dr. Benjamin Whichcote* (ed. Salter), 67, 71–72.

33. See, e.g., Pemble, *Vindiciae gratiae*, 214–16; and Owen, *The Reason of Faith* (*Works*, 4:67): "The scandalous quarrels and disputations of those of the church of Rome against the Scripture and its authority have contributed much unto the ruin of the faith of many . . . . [T]hey seek continually to entangle those of the weaker sort by urging them vehemently with this question, 'How do you know the Scripture to be the word of God?' and have in continual readiness a number of sophistical artifices to weaken all evidences that shall be pleaded in its behalf." Puritans did not, however, consider the testimony of the church to be of no consequence. On the contrary, one almost invariably finds it among their delineations of the external evidences. It was only rejected as a primary ground of faith in the Scriptures.

34. See the two letters between a Catholic and a Protestant layman Baxter printed in his *Certainty of Christianity Without Popery* (London: Printed for Nevil Simons, 1672), v–x.

restoration through the death and resurrection of God incarnate? Puritans insisted that honest and reasonable people would find the combined weight of the "external" and "internal" arguments persuasive even if they had not yet been born again.[35] And once the Holy Spirit had used the word to create new life within them, they would possess the strongest evidence of its divine origin, namely a personal experience of its transformative power.

An occasionally disputed but usually overlooked question at this point was whether Scripture's self-authentication consisted only in this three-fold set of evidences, or whether in addition to these there was, fourthly, an immediate and mystical witness of the Spirit in the minds of believers infallibly assuring them of the Bible's divine origin. John Trapp affirmed the latter in his *Theologia Theologiae* (1641), and Owen argued for it at some length in his *Reason of Faith* (1677), dismayed that it was often neglected by theologians. He conceived this immediate witness as a conviction that was beyond and independent of all internal marks of divinity in the word, akin to the way in which the prophets would have known that the message they carried was from God, or Abraham would have been able to discern that the command to sacrifice his son had a divine rather than (as the content of the message would have otherwise suggested!) a demonic origin. Owen may have had Baxter in mind, who thought this doctrine veered too close to the Spirit-led enthusiastic sects. Trapp's and Owen's reply to this concern was that the immediate witness of the Spirit was only for the use of the individual receiving it, whereas the sects attempted to make their private revelations binding on others.[36]

Given their belief in the Bible's self-authentication and consequent indirect proof of God's existence, as well as their conviction that natural theology taught nothing about God that could not likewise be derived from the Bible, Puritans might have simply left the matter there and bid their parishioners to rest their faith entirely on the revealed word, as Twisse recommended. But most had no desire to drive such a wedge between nature and grace. Faith was imperfect in the best of saints, and the Puritans were ready for it to entertain help from any legitimate corner. Besides, they believed that in the general order of things one's belief in the existence of God was arrived at via reason and the light of nature rather than by revelation—indeed

---

35. Pemble, *Vindicae gratiae*, 227–30; Baxter, *Unreasonableness of Infidelity*, "Preface," xxx; 2:73; Owen, *The Reason of Faith* (*Works*, 4:45, 110).

36. Trapp, *Theolgia Theologiae*, 36–38, Owen, *Reason of Faith*, passim; Baxter, *Reasons of the Christian Religion*, 348; Baxter, *Unreasonableness of Infidelity*, "Preface," xxv–xxx.

that the latter more or less assumed the former. Owen advised his readers that his discussion of the inspiration of the Scriptures presupposed the "τὸ γνωστὸν του θεου, 'whatever may be known of God' [Rom 1:18] by the light of nature, whatever is manifest in or from the works of creation and providence, and necessary actings of conscience, as to the being, rule, and authority of God."[37] Howe put the matter similarly in refuting (perhaps with reference to Capel's previously quoted remarks) those who wanted to lay the case for God's existence on the Scriptures' own testimony:

> It were indeed very unseasonable and absurd to urge *their authority* in the inquiry, whether there be a God or no? For what authority have they more than other writings, but as they are God's word? Therefore to expect, or give, assent to them as such, while yet it remains an undecided controversy, whether there be any such one, or no, for whose sake the assent should be given, were to expose our religion, not to prove it. These writings were not intended, by their affirmation of it, to inform us of God's existence, which they *suppose*, and *do not prove*, as a thing we may otherwise be certain of; but to teach us our duty towards him, and what our expectations may be from him.[38]

As for the proofs of God's existence, Puritans did not think most of them were difficult to apprehend. Their articulation was simply an exposition of what thoughtful people should have concluded from a survey of the theatre of nature and a consideration of their own humanity. Special revelation was given to clear up *what* God was and his relationship to us, not to establish *that* he was. Natural theology could also arrive at most of the divine attributes, but here Puritans were especially conscious of the disjunction between what unaided reason had in the course of ancient history been able to attain and what one recognized it could attain after the light of special revelation had entered the world.

We will return to this last point in chapter four, but to finish out the present subject of the role of natural theology within Puritanism there is one more question to be answered. Puritans believed that natural theology and the rational evidences for Christianity were highly useful in evangelizing pagans, assuaging the doubts of wavering believers, and affording further satisfaction to the unwavering. But did they also think that these arguments should be arrayed against skeptics and attackers of the faith?

---

37. Owen, *The Reason of Faith* (*Works*, 4:109).
38. Howe, *The Living Temple*, (*Works*, 1:207).

As it turned out, history gave them abundant opportunity to answer this question. The second half of the seventeenth century in England witnessed the rise of deism, popular scorn of religion, and even atheism.[39] As early as the late sixteenth century, Richard Greenham (early 1540s–1594), a Puritan minister in London whose death was considered by a contemporary to be "no small wrack to the Church and people of God," had been prescient enough to predict that the Protestant battle against Roman Catholicism would soon be eclipsed by a war against disbelief in Christianity itself. In 1627 Pemble was already speaking of "those monstrous sins of Atheism and Infidelity, wherewith this age is infected as much as any."[40]

The writings of Baxter, whose vigorous efforts to Christianize his entire parish gave him more opportunity than most ministers to take the religious pulse of his countrymen, are a fascinating window into the rising skepticism of the times, none more so than his first full length apologetic work, *The Unreasonableness of Infidelity* (1655). "I find that there are an abundance of young students, and other Christians," he wrote, "assaulted with these Temptations, of which I have heard many complain that dare not make them known to many." Some of his "familiar friends" had completely apostatized to unbelief, and he had himself occasionally fallen into "whole companies of [skeptics] besetting me at once, and with great scorn and cunning subtlety endeavour[ing] to bring my special friends to a contempt of the Scripture and the life to come." When he "stirred sometime further abroad" and discoursed with "some persons of considerable quality and learning" who had "read such Books as *Hobbs* his *Leviathan*," the encounters were even more shocking: "Sometimes they make a jest at Christ: Sometime at Scripture: sometime at the soul of man: sometime at spirits; challenging the Devil to come and appear to them, and professing how far they would travel to see him (as not believing that indeed he is)."[41]

---

39. A helpful general introduction to this issue is Aylmer, "Unbelief in Seventeenth-Century England," 22–46. Also see Berman, *History of Atheism in Britain: From Hobbes to Russell*, 1–67; and Gabbey, "'A Disease Incurable': Scepticism and the Cambridge Platonists," 71–91.

40. "He feared rather Atheism than Papism in the Realm: for many having escaped out of the gulf of superstition, are now too far plunged and swallowed up of profaneness, thinking either that there is no God, or else that he is not so fearful and merciful, as his threatenings and promises commend him to be." Greenham, "Commonplaces" (*Workes*, 3); *DNB*, 23:595; Pemble, *Vindicae gratiae*, 225.

41. Baxter, *Unreasonableness of Infidelity*, 3:8; "Preface," xxvi, vii, ix.

The Role of Natural Theology

The intense appeal Baxter made later in this treatise to those who were on the verge of leaving the church suggests something of the reality of the religious skepticism some English pastors were facing in the 1650s, and it is also a classic illustration of how broadly natural theology and evidentialism functioned within the Puritan framework—as a catechetical tool for grounding the faith of their parishioners, as a refuge for believers who were tormented by doubt, and as an apologetic method of dealing with those who had gone over to skepticism:

> It may be you will say, this is not our first consideration of these things, we have been Christians many a year. *Answ.* But were you not all the while Christians in name only? Did you not take up your Religion merely upon Trust? and believe Scripture to be the word of God merely upon tradition, and the authority of your Teachers? .... The objections of the Devil and heathenish Seducers which have drawn you from Christ and Scripture, have but discovered the sandiness of your former foundation, and weakness of those grounds on which you had so carelessly built your Faith: but they have not discovered the weakness of Religion and the Christian Doctrine itself, nor the weakness of those reasons by which other men can maintain it, though you could not, or cannot. And is it not a desperate betraying of your souls, that you fly discourse with those that have studied more than you . . . ? You think by opening your doubts men will account you blasphemers, and so you shall lose your credit, and you are confident that you are in the right, and you know already all that they can say, and therefore you will not open them to any that are able to judge of them; but you do not know what can be said against them. Ministers do not use to deal with such blasphemous errors ordinarily in public . . . . However tis worthy your trying, to hear the utmost, before you venture on eternal misery.[42]

Baxter apologetic writings also indicate how Puritans perceived a progression of religious skepticism in England from doubts about revealed religion during the 1650s to disbelief in the very existence of God during the following decade. *The Unreasonableness of Infidelity* took theism for granted and was focused on defending Christianity. But twelve years later, when Baxter wrote his magnum opus apologetic treatise, *The Reasons of the Christian Religion* (1667), he felt compelled to defend this foundational tenet at some length. It was the same with Ezekiel Hopkins when he delivered

---

42. *Unreasonableness of Infidelity*, 1:65–66.

his *Exposition on the Ten Commandments* while living at Exeter between 1667 and 1669. Not long before his death in 1680, Charnock would remark that the days when it was needless to demonstrate the existence of God were gone: "The apostles spent little time urging this truth; it was taken for granted all over the world . . . that age ran from one God to many, and our age is running from one God to none at all." Locke's observation in 1689 is also worth noting: "Complaints of Atheism, made from the pulpit, are not without Reason."[43]

By the early 1670s English Puritans were acutely aware that they were living in the midst of an unprecedented environment of deism and unbelief, and they responded with a wave of apologetic treatises. Baxter composed his *More Reasons for the Christian Religion* (1672), a two-fold response to a semi-anonymous skeptical letter he had received and to Lord Edward Herbert's proto-deistic tract, *De Veritate*.[44] The notable English Puritan commentator Matthew Poole (1624?–1679) took time off from his massive *Synopsis criticorum* to write and preach *A Seasonable Apology for Religion* (1673). Over the next nine years came Barker's *Natural Theology* (1674), Howe's *Living Temple* (1675), Bates' *Considerations of the Existence of God* and *Divinity of the Christian Religion Proved* (1676 and 1677), the posthumous publication of Charnock's *Discourses Upon the Existence and Attributes of God* (1682), and John Ray's influential *Wisdom of God Manifested in the Works of the Creation* (1691). John Flavel (1630?–91), whose pastoral labors in the English port town of Dartmouth exposed him to the worst of popular vice and carelessness about religion, capped off the wave with his *Reasonableness of Personal Reformation* (1691), a work that he introduced by remarking that "haply appeals to reason may produce a reformation in some men, sooner than appeals to the scriptures, or principles of faith, especially when the world is so notoriously drenched in practical atheism, that serious religion becomes the common subject of drollery amongst multitudes of men."[45]

---

43. Charnock, *Existence and Attributes of God*, 26; Locke, *Essay Concerning Human Understanding*, I. 4. 8.

44. Baxter, *More Reasons for the Christian Religion, and No Reason Against it*. In *Reliquiae Baxterianae*, Part III, p. 90, § 199, Baxter identifies the correspondent as a "Stranger, calling himself *Sam. Herbert*," which may have been a fictitious pen-name. Written in Latin, Herbert's *De veritate, prout distinguitur a revelatione, a verisimili, a possibili, et a falso* (On truth, as distinguished from revelation, probability, possibility, and error) first appeared in Paris in 1624 and in London in 1633.

45. Flavel, *Reasonableness of Personal Reformation* (*Works*, 6:474).

Across the Atlantic in New England the reaction was delayed, as unbelief had not yet reared its head there. When the Mathers penned their polemics against deism in 1700 and 1702, they both spoke of it as a movement on the mother continent. Cotton Mather, for example, wrote of those "so prone to *Deism*, as we do with Horror see them in the *Baptized Nations* of *Europe*," and his father Increase thankfully remarked that, "There are not as yet many (I wish there were none at all) amongst us in this part of *America*, that avow the *desperate Heresies* of that sort."[46] But it was only a matter of time. Increase warned that "we know not what Changes, nor what Temptations with them [European nations] may overtake us," and thus it was "good for us to be *ready always to give an Answer and a reason of our Christian Hope*, if we should be put upon the Trial."[47] Sure enough, ten years later Cotton received a letter from a Christian living some fifty miles outside Boston informing him that deism had indeed made its way across the water. "I am astonished to hear some of their Discourses," wrote his correspondent. "Had I been to guess, *by them*, where they had been Educated, I should have rather thought of *Turkey* or *China*." He begged Mather to write a short pamphlet against these notions, and Cotton responded with his *Reason Satisfied: And Faith Established*.[48]

Ernest Lowrie is correct to point out that Puritans did not think there were very many absolute atheists in the world, but it is not true that because of this Puritans "seldom" attempted to demonstrate the existence of God, fearing that the use of such "discursive proofs" engendered doubt.[49] On the contrary, said Baxter, "That faith stands but totteringly, that standeth only because men hear not what Infidels say against it."[50] All of these Puritan treatises attempted to prove the existence of God and the truth of Christianity from rational considerations. The arguments that had long been employed against "practical" unbelief were now fully developed and aimed at genuine skepticism. Bates summarized the Puritan perspective on the matter with his confident remark that "with the use of equal Arms,

---

46. Cotton Mather, *Reasonable Religion: Or, the Truth of the Christian Religion Demonstrated*, 18–19; Increase Mather, *Discourse Proving the Christian Religion*, 3.

47. Increase Mather, *Discourse Proving the Christian Religion*, 3–4. Cf. 1 Peter 3:15, "Be ready always to give an answer to every man that asketh you a reason of the hope that is in you."

48. Cotton Mather, *Reason Satisfied: And Faith Established*, iii–iv. Mather printed excerpts from the letter in his preface.

49. Lowrie, *Shape of the Puritan Mind*, 48.

50. Baxter, *Unreasonableness of Infidelity*, 3:10.

Reasons against *Reasons*, the cause of *Religion* will be victorious."[51] Apart from the aforementioned critics mentioned by Howe and Baxter, there was no objection to this course. Increase Mather, who referred to Bates as his "once intimate and never to be forgotten friend," declared in 1716 that "they have done Service for Religion, who have confuted the Cavils of Infidels, and evinced the *Unreasonableness of Atheism*."[52] Skeptics were not only to be boldly preached to, said Owen, but shown "that the *Scripture is true and divine* by rational arguments; wherein some learned persons have laboured, especially in these last ages, to very good purpose." Like efforts were "greatly to be commended," provided that they employed solid reasoning and did not "pretend their rational grounds and arguments to be the sole foundation that faith hath to rest upon."[53]

Perhaps Twisse would have objected had he still been alive, for in connection with his previously quoted remark in 1631 that theistic proofs were needless for believers he had also stated that they were useless to atheists.[54] Mention should also be made here of Cotton Mather, who wondered in 1721 whether it had not after all "been an *inconsiderate* thing to pay so much of a Compliment to *Atheism*, as to bestow solemn *Treatises* full of learned *Arguments* for the Refutation of a *delirious Phrenzy*." Especially unadvisable, he thought, had been the practice of those polemicists who, "that they may have the honour of *laying a Devil when they have raised him*," were so generous as to present the best possible case for atheism before refuting it![55] But Cotton Mather had already entered the fray against both atheism and deism, and moreover, these reservations about proving the existence of God merely stemmed from his conviction that the evidences for God's existence were so patently obvious that atheism was rather to be laughed at than reasoned with; and thus like Twisse he went on give his readers two theistic proofs, justifying his brevity with the remark that even this was

---

51. Bates, *Considerations of the Existence of God*, x.

52. Increase Mather, *Existence and Omniscience of God*, ii, iii. Increase met Bates and other English Puritans during his years in London between 1688 and 1691, during which time he had several audiences with William of Orange. He and Bates visited Baxter together on the day before Baxter's death. See Hall, *The Last American Puritan*, 212–54.

53. Owen, *The Reason of Faith* (*Works*, 4:103; also see pp. 47, 71–72, 110–11).

54. "And as for Atheists, may we not justly say of them, as Abraham saith of the rich Gluttous brethren, *If they believe not Moses and the Prophets, neither will they believe though a man should rise from the dead*." Twisse, *D. Jacksons Vanitie*, 45.

55. Cotton Mather, *The Christian Philosopher*, 308.

"*more* than could be deserved by such an *Idiot*" as the atheist was.[56] Indeed, Cotton Mather expressed this reservation in the middle of a work that was entirely taken up with a rapturous exploration of the wonders of the natural world and whose stated purpose was to show that Christianity was not only an "evangelical" but a "philosophical" religion, commanding respect from educated and uneducated alike. *The Christian Philosopher* drew heavily from the English natural theologians John Ray and William Derham, and from the German Reformed theologian Johann Alsted's *Theologia naturalis* (1614).[57] Neither Twisse nor Mather, then, had any thought of rejecting the objective validity of natural theology; it was merely a question of when and to what extent it should be applied.

Several scholars have interpreted the early English Puritan William Ames' criticisms of the Jesuit philosopher-theologian Francisco Suarez (1548–1617) as a rejection of natural theology.[58] Ames frequently corresponded with New England Puritans, often considered sailing for the New World and as one of his biographers notes, "participated in the New England Way in everything short of actually immigrating."[59] His *Medulla Theologiae* (*Marrow of Theology*, 1623) was a standard divinity textbook at Harvard and Yale and was esteemed by Thomas Hooker and Increase Mather as "next to the Bible . . . the best book in the world."[60] Ames was not opposed to natural theology, however, but merely to what he perceived as Suarez's sharp didactical division between natural and supernatural theology. The degree to which Suarez intended to separate philosophy and theology has been debated by scholars,[61] but the disagreement between him and Ames was only a categorical controversy. Suarez advocated a separate philosophical prolegomena on the grounds that since so many theological

---

56. Cotton Mather, *The Christian Philosopher*, 309. For Twisse's two theistic proofs, see his *D. Jacksons Vanitie*, 48–51.

57. See Solberg's introduction to *The Christian Philosopher*, lxiv–lxvi; and Mather's own introduction, 7–10, where he freely acknowledged his indebtedness to "the Industrious MR. RAY, and the inquisitive Mr. DERHAM; *Fratrum dulce par* [a delightful pair of brothers]" (10).

58. Gibbs, in Ames, *Technometry*, 180–81; Fiering, *Moral Philosophy at Seventeenth-Century Harvard*, 49n83.

59. Sprunger, *The Learned Doctor William Ames*, 200.

60. Increase Mather, "To the Reader," in Fitch, *The first Principles of the Doctrine of Christ*, v.

61. See the translator's introduction to Suarez, *On Creation, Conservation, and Concurrence*, xiv–xxv.

topics demanded recourse to prior questions of metaphysics, it would be easier to treat these philosophical questions separately and previously rather than attempting to handle them piecemeal as they arose in the context of systematic theology. Ames did not deny, but on the contrary affirmed that the book of nature, though more obscure than that of Scripture, could give certain knowledge of God. But since the Bible reiterated everything that could be known of God via the light of nature, he deemed it cumbersome to treat these questions once under the banner of philosophy and then again under the banner of theology, for then "teachings are multiplied . . . without necessity."[62] Ames not only retained the category of natural theology but like so many other Puritans employed its proofs in his sermons.[63]

It is worth mentioning that Puritans did not expect that their apologetic treatises would be very successful in converting hardened atheists and deistic ridiculers of special revelation. They had a Pascalian sense of the general futility of reasoning on religious matters with those who did not even think the existence of God was an urgent question or had reached the point of laughing at Christianity rather than seriously considering it. A rational disputation with such a person, said Howe, was likely "to beget more *wrath* than *conviction*, and sooner to *incense* the impatient wretch than *enlighten* him." Their best hopes of persuasion were the judgments of God to awaken them and the lived examples of Christians to attract them.[64] Baxter introduced his *Reasons of the Christian Religion* by similarly remarking that he was "far from expecting universal success" among skeptics since most of them had "unprepared minds, and will not come up to the price of truth." He was writing for "such as are willing to be *wise* and *happy*, and that at dearer rates than jesting."[65] But as we have seen, the Puritans did not regard unbelief as an either/or affair but as a disease infecting everyone to some degree. It was of little consequence to Puritans, then, if hardened skeptics were not converted by their arguments, because those who felt their faith wavering would be greatly assisted by a confutation of religious skepticism and furnished for their own personal encounters with

---

62. Ames, *Technometry*, theses 111–12 (pp. 112–13).

63. See his sermons on Revelation 4:11 and Romans 11:36, in Ames, *Substance of Christian religion*, 62–77.

64. Howe, *Living Temple* (*Works*, 1:16–17). Also see Lee, *Joy of Faith*, v.

65. Baxter, *Unreasonableness of Infidelity*, "To the Doubting and Unbelieving Readers," ii, v–vi.

The Role of Natural Theology

unbelievers. As Charnock put the matter after presenting his proofs for the existence of God:

> I do not know what some of you may think, but I believe these things are not useless to be proposed for ourselves to answer temptations; we know not what wicked temptation in a debauched and skeptic age, meeting with a corrupt heart, may prompt men to; and though there may not be an atheist here present, yet I know there is more than one, who have accidentally met with such, who openly denied a Deity; and if the like occasion happen, these considerations may not be unuseful to apply to their consciences.... We should never be without our arms in an age wherein atheism appears barefaced without a disguise.[66]

Historian D. A. Walker could scarcely have been more mistaken, then, when he wrote that the pastoral emphasis of Puritans was "one of the strongest restraints" to their development and use of natural theology.[67] On the contrary, it was pastoral concerns that more than anything else drove them to employ natural theology. No movement in the history of Christianity had ever called so much attention to latent atheism and unbelief as did the Puritans, nor would anyone else after them. There are, I think, two explanations for this phenomenon. The first is the introspection that was a hallmark of the Puritan movement, particularly its predilection to examine the dark and sinful side of Christian experience. Thomas Shepard's previously quoted remark that serious believers were more likely to struggle with temptations to atheism because "they only [i.e., only they] study their hearts" was both perceptive and accurate.[68] An older historian of theology has noticed the same thing in Scottish Puritanism, the most striking and pathos-laden instance being that of the covenanting preacher and martyr James Renwick (1662–88), who staring at the mountains while engulfed in doubt declared, "If these were all devouring furnaces of burning limestone,

---

66. Charnock, *Existence and Attributes of God*, 1:83–84. Also see Willard, *Compleat Body of Divinity*, 16–17: "[W]hen *Atheism* begins to put itself forth, and the Scriptures to be reproached, and God blasphemed upon their account, it is requisite that young ones be confirmed in the evidence of this truth"; and Cotton Mather, *Reason Satisfied: And Faith Established*, vi: "And if it [his treatise] prevail not for the Recovery of those who are already *Poisoned*, yet it may help to preserve others from taking in the *Poison* of *Infidelity*."

67. Walker, "Puritanism and Natural Theology After the Restoration of 1660," 74.

68. Shepard, *Sincere Convert* (*Works*, 1:9).

I would be content to go through them, if so be that thereby I could be assured that there is a God."[69]

A second and related explanation lies in what was one of the most distinguishing features of Puritanism, and in terms of practical theology its most distinguishing feature. At the heart of the movement was a driving desire to make religion a deeply personal reality for the average churchgoer. One may love or hate various aspects of the theology that undergirded this reality, but no one who spends much time in the original sources can fail to be impressed with the energy Puritan pastors poured into this task. The first step in this process was making sure their parishioners were fully persuaded of the articles in the Christian creed, and especially the two foundational articles—the existence of God and the divinity of Scripture.

The frequency with which Puritans invited the laity to evaluate the evidences for these tenets and decide whether or not they really believed them is remarkable. Baxter said that while examining the splintered factions of religion in England, he had "found so much latent Atheism and Infidelity, that I think among many (that do not observe it) the true root of all the difference is, Whether there be a God, and a Life to come? And whether the Scriptures be true."[70] Preston forcefully drove his auditors to this very "disjunction" at the conclusion of his discourses on atheism and the truth of Christianity, bidding them to examine his proofs "to the full" and make their decision accordingly:

> It is exceeding profitable to search and examine these truths to the full, not to give over pondering of them, til your hearts be established in the present truth. It is good to do with yourselves, as *Elijah* did in the case of *Baal, Why halt you between two* Religions? Come to that disjunction, *If Baal be god, follow him:* So I say to you in this case. Examine it to the full: if these principles be not true, walk according to your liberty and lusts, take no pains, but live as your nature would have you; but if they be true, then walk so as if thou didst thoroughly believe them so to be. The belief of them is that which will carry us through all losses and slanders, through good report and ill report. If thou didst thoroughly believe them, they would make thee do anything for *God*. I say, it is very profitable to come to this disjunction, and it strengthens our faith much;

---

69. Walker, *The Theology and Theologians of Scotland*, 44. Walker observes that the prominent Scottish Presbyterian divine Robert Bruce (1554–1631) often remarked, "It is a great thing to believe in God," and adds, "I have no doubt what that meant."

70. Baxter, *Reasons of the Christian Religion*, "To the Christian Reader," vi.

The Role of Natural Theology

and this being laid, then draw the conclusion from it, that we thus here must live, and that it is here best for us to do so.[71]

Even more striking was the exhortation of William Pemble in a posthumously published treatise Capel brought to press in 1627, one year before Preston's death. After laying out the proofs for the divinity of Scripture, Pemble proceeded in the strongest language to sting his readers out of a reliance on custom and tradition for their religious beliefs, warning them that they were liable to lose their faith on their deathbeds if they went no further than this:

> [2nd] Admonition is to put you in mind of that danger, wherein careless men, who build, without having laid a sure foundation. Come to most men and ask them, Why do you believe the Scriptures, and these points of religion out of them? Their answer is, Because they be the Word of God. Yea, but what persuades you to think so? Here they are staggered, and have nothing to say, but they are led unto this belief by Custom of Education in a Christian Church, wherein the Scriptures' Divinity is generally received for an undoubted truth, and they believe what they see others doubt not of; else it were a shame for them. But in the mean time themselves have never laboured to get infallible assurance unto their own consciences, from the Scriptures themselves, by prayer, study, & all due observation.... [L]et me tell them thus much, that this loose and unsettled faith, is one of the fiery darts, & forcible engines of Satan, whereby he assaults and overthrows the hope and comfort of many a dying man, who having not strengthened himself on this point by undoubted arguments and experiments, is there laid at, where he lies open and unarmed, by such cunning cavils, shifts, and elusions brought against the authority of Scriptures, that the poor man not able to clear himself from such suggestions, falls into an universal doubting of all Religion, and at last, perceiving his Faith hath only grasped at the air, and embraced the empty shadow of man's authority, instead of the Substance of Divine truth, he is utterly confounded, and sinks down in despair. If I am able to judge anything of the Methods of Satan's temptations, I dare say, that this weapon is reserved usually for the last combat, and that many a man's faith hath perished upon this rock both in life, and especially in the last agonies & conflicts with the powers of death and darkness.[72]

71. Preston, *Life Eternall*, 67–68. For the story of Elijah and the prophets of Baal, see 1 Kings 18:17–40.

72. Pemble, *Vindicae gratiae*, 218–19.

This disdain for religious persuasion rooted in nothing more than socialization was a theme Puritans returned to again and again. The forty-four signatories of the *Westminster Confession*'s "Epistle to the Reader" lamented that "most men take up their religion upon no better an account than Turks and Papists take up theirs, because it is the religion of the times and places wherein they live; and what they take up thus slightly, they lay down as easily."[73] Custom and tradition might well inform the beginnings of our religious knowledge, said Charnock, but in the end we were to "come to know it by its own light."[74] Owen wistfully observed that most people never took this next step. Instead of seriously considering the rational evidences for Christianity, "the truth is, *tradition* and *education* practically bear the whole sway in this matter."[75] Baxter complained that the "way of taking Religion upon trust, without rising up to make it our own, hath filled the church with Hypocrites," and he emphasized to his readers that "Christianity is not in shutting your eyes, and following any teachers blindfold: it is opening your eyes, and using your understanding, and reasoning solidly and rightly that God calls you to." [76]

It should now be clear what a large role Puritan theology accorded to reason and how far that role transcended the mere instrumental function of interpreting Scripture and organizing the data of revealed religion. But while Puritans were rational theologians, they were emphatically not rationalistic. How they related the incomprehensibility of God and the mystery of existence to human learning in general and natural theology in particular is the subject of the following chapter.

---

73. *Westminster Confession of Faith*, "To the Christian Reader," ii. Compare the similar remark in William Bates, *Harmony of the Divine Attributes*, 140–41: "Those that owe their *Christianity* meerly to the Felicity of their Birth, without a sight of that transcendent excellency in our Religion, which evidences that it came from Heaven, do not believe aright.... 'Tis not Judgment but Chance that inclines them to embrace it. The *Turks* upon the same reason are zealous *votaries* of *Mahomet*, as they are *Disciples* of Christ."

74. Charnock, *Works*, 4:101.

75. Owen, *The Reason of Faith*, 46. Also see Howe, *Living Temple* (*Works*, 1:129).

76. Baxter, *Reasons of the Christian Religion*, "To the Christian Reader," iv; Baxter, *Unreasonableness of Infidelity*, 1:64.

3

Reason, Learning, and the Mystery of God

"Yea the truth is, that there never was any man eminently serviceable as a Teacher in the Church since the Apostles, except he were a Learned man.... And it is very worthy the taking notice of, that the Interest of Religion and good Learning, have risen and fallen together."

—INCREASE MATHER, 1672

"There will be a *plus ultra* [further beyond] to the end of the world."

—SAMUEL LEE, 1685

PURITANS BELIEVED THAT REASON had been corrupted by the Fall in two ways. The first was a mere diminishment of its intellectual power that paralleled the physical infirmities occasioned by the Fall. Perry Miller aptly described the Puritan conception of this blow to human reason as "simply the loss of an ability to use the syllogism." This disability could be more or less pronounced in various individuals, and it could be partly remedied in this life by the study of logic. As the early English Puritan Thomas Spencer (fl. 1628–29) put it, one of the chief benefits of learning logic was that "hereby (in some sort) is healed the wound we received in our reason by *Adam's* fall."[1] The second corruption of human reason was moral. Here the problem was not a lack of logical power but an unwillingness to accept the dictates

---

1. Spencer, *Art of Logick,* "To the Reader," iii. Also see Gale, *Court of the Gentiles: Part IV*, p. 4.

of reason when it presented the mind with unpleasant truths. The root of this species of corruption was thus not reason itself but the evil desires of the will, so that, as William Bates put it, "the corrupt Will bribes the Mind to argue for what it desires." The solution to this obstacle was not the study of logic, of course, but rather divine grace, for the problem in this case was not the instrument of reason but a stubborn refusal to acknowledge the truth. The function of grace was not to instill a kind of new logic in the mind of the redeemed but rather to free one's existing logical powers from the distorting influence of evil desires. Hence Thomas Hooker's declaration that once the new birth had removed the obstruction of sin, "the coast is now clear that reason may be heard." While Puritans emphasized both the intellectual and moral corruptions of human reason, they naturally deemed the latter to be more serious and fundamental. As Charnock put it, human reason was merely "dark" with regard to its intellectual disability, but until spiritual rebirth it was "stark blind" with regard to it moral disease.[2]

Nevertheless, this apprehension of a moral corruption in human reason did not, as we have seen, prevent Puritans from using rational arguments with unregenerate souls. And in the life of the redeemed, especially, reason was accorded a prominent role. As Thomas Manton put it in a treatise on the virtue of faith:

> Faith makes advantage of the confessions and acknowledgements of nature: there is no truth we believe, but afterwards we may find excellent advantages to confirm us in it by rational searches. These confirmations of reason are of great use for the quenching those fiery darts which Satan flings into the soul, by which he would bear down all principles of religion.

John Flavel argued that reason led naturally to faith, and that while there were "some mysteries in religion above the sphere and flight of reason: yet nothing can be found in religion, that is unreasonable." Matthew Henry had such a high regard for reason and natural law that he exhorted his congregation to jettison from their Christian creed whatever contradicted them:

> So agreeable is revealed religion to right reason, and the established rules of good and evil, that what contradicts and violates

---

2. Bates, *Considerations of the Existence of God*, vi; Hooker as quoted in Miller, *The New England Mind: The Seventeenth Century*, 202; Charnock, *The Knowledge of God* (*Works*, 4:73).

them, how plausible soever its pretensions may be, ought to be rejected, as no part of Christianity.[3]

As Henry's employment of the term "right reason" suggested, however, Puritans insisted on distinguishing between what was "above" reason and what was "contrary" to reason. "We fully yield," wrote the Presbyterian Puritan Anthony Tuckney (1599–1670), a Westminster Assembly member who occupied the regius chair of divinity at Cambridge from 1656 until Charles II asked him to resign in 1661, "that *materia fidei* [the matter of faith] is not contrary to reason: but then we believe, it is in many things much above it." In New England, Samuel Willard expressed himself in nearly identical terms: "Faith doth not relinquish or cast off reason; for there is nothing in Religion contrary to it, tho' there are many things that do transcend, and must captivate it."[4]

The distinction between the two categories, William Bates explained, was "between the things which Reason cannot perfectly understand how they can be, and the things which it perfectly understands that they cannot be." He saw a sublime compatibility between reason and the biblical revelation and deemed this to be one of Christianity's chief apologetic advantages. While all other religions contained some things "repugnant to the dictates of clear Reason," Christianity had "this noble prerogative above the rest: the more one searches into it, the more its Divinity appears."[5]

The closest one gets to an official Puritan statement on the role of reason is *The Judgment of Non-conformists of the Interest of Reason in Religion* (1676), which was signed by fifteen nonconformist English Puritans and

---

3. Henry, "Faith in Christ Inferred From Faith in God" (*Complete Works of Matthew Henry*, 2:294).

4. Manton, *By Faith*, 91; Flavel, *The Reasonableness of Personal Reformation* (*Works*, 6:472); Anthony Tuckney to Benjamin Whichcote, 8 October 1651, in *Eight Letters* (ed. Salter), op. cit., 68; Willard as quoted in Miller, *The New England Mind: The Seventeenth Century*, 205. Also see Boyle, *Reflections upon a Theological Distinction . . . That Some Articles of Faith are above Reason, but not Against Reason* (*Works*, 5:541–49).

5. Bates, *Considerations of the Existence of God*, 186; idem, *Divinity of the Christian Religion Proved*, 33. Also see Boyle, *The Christian Virtuoso* (*Works*, 6:714, 787), and Bates, *Harmony of the Divine Attributes*, 132–33: "There are some Doctrines in the Gospel, the Understanding could not discover, but when they are reveal'd, it hath a clear apprehension of them upon a rational account, and sees the *characters* of Truth visibly stamped on their Forehead . . . . Now although the *primary* Obligation to believe such Doctrines ariseth from Revelation, yet being ratified by Reason, they are embraced with more Clearness by the Mind." Transubstantiation was the view that the bread and wine of the Eucharist were literally transformed into the body and blood of Christ.

probably drawn up by Richard Baxter. The document had something of an ecumenical bent inasmuch as its stated objective was to show that not only nonconformists but all Protestants were "herein of one mind" against Socinianism on the one hand and enthusiastical fanaticism and Roman Catholicism on the other. Socinians rejected the Trinity "because they think that it is against reason (though in that they err)." Enthusiasts, meanwhile, were deluded into thinking that "the secret impulses of their diseased Fantasies, and Passions, are such motions of God's Spirit as Reason must give place to"; while those "unreasonable renouncers of Common Sense and Reason," i.e., Roman Catholics, demanded belief in "the most stupendous Fiction of Miracles, against *Reason*, and *Common sense*, that ever (to our knowledge) was entertained by any Sect, or Heresy in the World." Reason's proper province was to examine the credentials of any proposed revelation: "Man's *Reason* must by *discerning this evidence*, know its *Divinity* and *truth*." It also belonged to reason to demonstrate and inculcate the truths of natural theology, since these formed the foundation on which supernatural revelation was constructed: "We are Men before we are Christians, in order of Nature at least." It was indeed regrettable that not only were these natural preparatives commonly neglected, but (again this theme appears) that beliefs in the Bible were generally the product of socialization rather than serious personal study:

> It is a great cause of the slight superficial Religion, and weakness of all Grace which abounds among us, that too many taking the *Essentials* of their Religion too much on the *trust* of those that educate them, or with whom they live, do labour *only to build upward* on such an ill-laid Foundation; when (*as Trees* grown *downward* in the Roots as well as upward) they should be all their days still growing *downward* in the confirmation of their Faith, and in the clearer and more orderly discerning of their Fundamentals, and the Evidences of them.

This, the signatories concluded, was where "holy Reason" would find its "most necessary, great and fruitful Work." Indeed, the ideal progress of the Christian life of mind, to be perfected in the world to come, was to more and more discern the "*Reasons*" and "admirable Harmony" of all the truths of religion.[6]

6. Baxter (?), *Judgment of Non-conformists of the Interest of Reason in Matters of Religion*, 1–3, 18, 9–10, 14–15. The writing style is very much that of Baxter, who was at any rate one of the signatories, along with Thomas Manton, William Bates, Thomas Case, Gabriel Sangar, Matthew Pemberton, Matthew Sylvester, Henry Hurst, Roger Morrice,

But how should the historian interpret and place that panegyric to reason published in 1718 by a man who was arguably the last American Puritan? The stated intent of Cotton Mather's *Man of Reason* was to establish the doctrine that "*Men ought to hearken to Reason.*" Evidently he saw some humor in putting the matter that way, remarking that "it seems a strange, and a sad Thing, and little short of a *Satire* upon Mankind," that one would have to argue such a patently obvious point. It was not his first foray into this territory. Mather had already published, as we have seen, his *Reasonable Religion* and *Reason Satisfied* in 1700 and 1712, respectively; and while *Man of Reason* argued the same position as these earlier treatises, namely that the religious life, and belief in Christianity in particular, were entirely consonant with and indeed demanded by the dictates of reason, its main focus was not apologetics but rather an exhortation to Christians to be fair and considerate in their dealings with each other by following the golden rule known by both Scripture and reason. But in introducing his subject Mather spoke more glowingly of reason than perhaps any Puritan had ever done, declaring that it was a divinely instituted tribunal and that to disobey its dictates was to defy God himself:

> GOD sets up *Reason* in Man. If we do not keep *Reason* in the *Throne*, we go to *Dethrone* the Infinite GOD Himself. The voice of *Reason*, is the *Voice of GOD*. GOD speaks, as often as *Reason* and *Wisdom utters its Voice*. GOD who has furnished us with *Reason*, has required us, to be obedient unto the *Dictates of Reason*. To Man, He says, *Let Reason be thy Guide; Never go against thy well-enlightened Reason*. We have received this Order from GOD our Maker; Isaiah 46.8. *Show yourselves Men*. That is to say, Act *Reasonably; Do* like *Reasonable Men*. How many *Appeals to Reason*, do we find in the Word of God .... Such Things had never been spoken, if this were not incontestable; That if we shake off the *Government* of *Reason*, we shake off the *Government* of our Great *Creator*, who has put *Reason* into us, as the *Grand Instrument* of His *Government* over us. When we don't *Hearken to Reason*, we say, *GOD Himself shall not Reign over us*! A *Rebellion*, Horrible to be thought upon![7]

Edward Lawrence, Benjamin Agas, James Bedford, Samuel Fairclough, John Turner and Joseph Read. "Nonconformists" were those who refused to subscribe to the 1662 Act of Uniformity and were accordingly ejected from their pulpits and forbidden to preach within five miles of any town.

7. Cotton Mather, *Man of Reason*, 1, 7–8. Mather had expressed these ideas in his diary seven years earlier and it was at this time that he penned *Man of Reason*. The

Certainly this sounds like something worlds away from the picture presented in John Morgan's study of pre-revolutionary Puritanism in England, which asserts that Puritans believed "only faith could comprehend grace" and accordingly "sought to demonstrate that when reason looked upwards, towards God, it superseded its proper calling and became a reprehensible enemy, indeed an ally of Satan." While conceding that Perry Miller "still towers over all approaches to the Puritan use of reason," Morgan has criticized him for projecting more rationality onto the Puritan mind than was in fact there. "The prime message of puritan Reformed protestantism," he contends, "was irrational: the free grace of God made available to his chosen, dependent upon nothing that people did in their own lives."[8]

It is impossible to accommodate Morgan's assessment of the role of reason within Puritanism to the discussions of reason that appear in Puritan literature or to the various ways in which Puritans used rational argumentation, even if we confine ourselves to the period before 1640, the terminus of his study. But Morgan has put his finger on a motif of earlier Puritanism that is noticeably diminished in Puritan writings of the second half of the seventeenth century. Perkins, for example, preached that a person intent on becoming a Christian had to "reject his own natural reason, and stop up the eyes of his natural mind, like a blind man, and suffer himself wholly to be guided by God's Spirit in the things of God, that thereby he may be made wise unto salvation." "Bid battle then to reason, if you will fight against sin," counseled Richard Greenham. "Those (I say) which mean to inherit the kingdom of heaven, must renounce their own reason, and fight against their own judgment." The prominent preacher Richard Rogers (1551–1618) spoke similarly of the unregenerate sinner in *Seven Treatises* (1603), a popular devotional book of the early seventeenth century: "For (to speak of the actions of the mind) what are his cogitations about heavenly matters, but errors, falsehood and lies?"[9] The strongest such statement occurs in a passage of Richard Capel's *Tentations* [Temptations] that also

---

treatise was subsequently lost on its way to England but was eventually returned to him. In 1718 he preached it to "a religious Society of young men" and then committed it to the press. See the entries for December 16, 1711 and June 1, 1718 (*Diary of Cotton Mather*, 2:144, 541–42).

8. Morgan, *Godly Learning*, 55, 4.

9. Perkins, *Treatise of Mans Imaginations* (1607) (*Workes*, 2:464). He was commenting on 1 Corinthians 3:18, "If any man among you seemeth to be wise in this world, let him become a fool, that he may be wise." Greenham, *Exposition of the 119. Psalme* (*Workes*, 467); Perkins *Ninth Sermon* (*Workes*, 298); Rogers, *Seven Treatises*, 4.

appears almost verbatim in a posthumously published devotional treatise written by Robert Bolton (1572–1631), who like Greenham was highly esteemed as a counselor of troubled souls. Wrote Capel:

> [R]eason can do nothing; (as it is natural) it is vain, and doth no good. The Temptation is a spiritual thing; *reason*, a natural weapon. Now a natural thing can have neither stroke nor force against a spiritual [thing], & therefore reason is a false weapon. And (as our reason is carnal) it is a secret friend to Satan, takes part with him against us.... We must not then consult with flesh and blood; down with reason, away with our own wit; let faith do all, else faith will do nothing; faith never works so well, as when it works alone.[10]

Caveats about the dangers of reason do occur in Puritan literature after 1640, but they do not exhibit such a stark dichotomy between faith and reason as one finds in the early seventeenth-century sources just quoted. Samuel Lee, for instance, commenting on what he or someone else had once heard muttered by a parishioner at the close of a sermon—"My Religion is my Reason, and my Reason is my Religion"—remarked, "If this be not *cum ratione insanire* [to be mad with reason], to dote upon that withered hag of corrupt reason and its dangerous fables: then commend me from these giddy Christians, to the more noble *Heathens* of former ages," such as the Platonists, Stoics, and even Epicureans, many of whom, he claimed, had derived from the mere light of nature "more generous principles" regarding the mystery of the divine being and had taught the world "not to think so strange of matters of Faith." Cotton Mather, too, in the same treatise in which he sang the praises of reason, reminded his hearers to distinguish between what was above reason and what was contrary to reason and to

---

10. Capel, *Tentations*, 63; Bolton, *The Carnall Professor*, 214–15. *Tentations* was first published in 1633, two years after Bolton's death. Capel may have had access to Bolton's manuscript, or it may be that both men derived the quotation from another source. For a similar though less severe comment by Bolton, see Morgan, *Godly Learning*, 51. Morgan (52n63, 53n71) provides references to five supposedly similar statements made by the early Puritans Thomas Adams, Thomas Hooker, Samuel Wright, Thomas Taylor, and John Preston. None of these five passages, however, express the kind of faith-reason dichotomy that appears in the above quotations. In fact, only two of them contain anything that even remotely bears on the relationship between faith and reason, Hooker commenting that "the poorest humbled sinner" knows more spiritual truth than "the most wise and learned in the world that are not humbled," Taylor remarking that while the godless are puffed up with a little knowledge, the righteous remain humble and recognize how much they still have to learn. Hooker, *The Soules Vocation*, 108; Taylor, *Principles of Christian Practice*, 432.

remember the naturally "darkened" state of the human mind: "We must *Hearken* to *Right Reason*: but beware, Lest we ascribe too much, to our own *broken Faculties*."[11]

Now, in terms of the catechetical use of natural theology and evidentialism, there is little if any difference between early and later Puritanism, though their apologetic use, as we have seen, became much more pronounced after the rise of religious skepticism in post-revolutionary England. Nor is there any discernible shift in the way reason functioned within the systematic theology of Puritanism. We will seriously misunderstand Puritanism if we make either late or early Puritan caveats about reason the basis for locating it within a "Protestant epistemology" that held "the essentials of Redemption" to be "foolish, absurd, and impossible," believed that "the cognitive faculties could perform no autonomous function," and accordingly confined reason to the bare instrumental function of interpreting, organizing and applying the data of biblical revelation.[12] Perkins himself followed St. Anselm in using the incarnation as an example of how reason confirmed the truths of revelation, and on the opening page of his 1598 treatise on predestination, he announced that that doctrine was not only taught in the Scriptures but "agree[d] with the grounds of common reason, and of that knowledge of God which may be obtained by the light of nature."[13] Greenham went on to explain his disparaging comment about reason just quoted by giving his parishioners as an example their impulse to irrational anger and the fighting it occasioned among them. To "overcome reason" in this case, he informed them, was to come to rightly understand "what things to be angry for, and what things to be patient in, what to love,

---

11. Cotton Mather, *A Man of Reason*, 15–16; Lee, *The Joy of Faith*, 216–17. Lee went on to quote Plato, Theophrastus, Galen, and Pliny to this effect.

12. Bozeman, *To Live Ancient Lives*, 53 (cf. 69). "Foolish, absurd, and impossible to reason" is Luther's description of the doctrine of justification by the imputed righteousness of Christ. See *Luther: Selections From His Writings*, 128.

13. Perkins, *A Christian and Plaine Treatise of the manner and order of Predestination*, "Master Perkinses Epistle to the Reader," i; also see pp. 58–59. First published as *De praedestinationis modo et ordine* (1598). For Perkins' remarks on the rationality of the incarnation, see his *Cases of Conscience* (*Workes*, 2:54–55): "For in natural understanding, God is not all justice, and no mercy. But if there were no Redeemer, then should God be all justice without mercy. Now because he that revealed himself to be as well merciful, as he is just, reason concludes that there is a Redeemer. Again, that this Redeemer should be God and man, is above reason, yet not against it. For reason teacheth, he must be God, that he might satisfy the infinite justice of God for sin; which none but God can do. Again, that he must be man, because man having sinned, man must be punished for the sin of man."

and what to hate." It was thus not reason *per se* that Greenham had in view; the problem was rather that "our reason is unreasonable."[14]

Nevertheless, there does seem to be a noticeable shift during the course of the seventeenth century in the rhetoric of reason vis-à-vis the doctrines of grace. Sharp pronouncements against reason such as those quoted above from Perkins, Greenham, Rogers, Capel, and Bolton are hard to find in post-1650 Puritanism. By the same token, it is difficult to imagine a Puritan minister of the early seventeenth century uttering Cotton Mather's words, "Let reason be thy guide," even taking into account the qualifier he immediately subjoined—"*well enlightened* reason." The same might be said of the latter clause of the following declaration Matthew Henry made to a London congregation in 1711: "Let the dictates of the light and law of nature be always sacred with us, and have a commanding sway and empire in our souls."[15]

The difference between earlier and later Puritanism on this matter, I think, does not lie in the theoretic function of reason within Puritan theology but rather in the parish context of late sixteenth- and early seventeenth-century England. As Patrick Collinson remarks, early Puritans "were essentially pastors, faced with blank irreligion and ignorance in the souls under their care." Some indication of this environment, at least as the Puritans perceived it, occurs in a preface William Perkins wrote for his 1590 catechetical work, *The Foundation of Christian Religion*, a valuable document for the sociological dimensions of the Reformation and especially the history of popular religion. Adorned with the unflattering subtitle, "To All Ignorant People that desire to be instructed," it rattled off thirty-two of "those your common opinions" about religion Perkins promised to overthrow if they would persevere with him through the work.[16]

While Puritans believed their doctrines of grace were rational, they also regarded them as counter-intuitive and disagreeable to fallen sinners. In polemical debates, whether against skeptics on the one hand or Arminians, Catholics, and heretics on the other, early Puritan theologians were no less prone to justify their tenets by reason than were later Puritan divines. In the pastoral context, however, early Puritans were more likely to

14. Greenham, *Ninth Sermon* (*Workes*, 298–99); Greenham, *First Sermon* (*Workes*, 242–43).

15. Henry, "Faith in Christ Inferred From Faith in God" (*Complete Works of Matthew Henry*, 2:294).

16. Collinson, *The Elizabethan Puritan Movement*, 128; Perkins, *Foundation of Christian Religion* (*Workes*, 1:i–ii).

direct their parishioners to abandon their common-sense opinions about religion and submit their judgments to the bare authority of the written and preached word. But this note was sounded less frequently and less sharply as the seventeenth century wore on and they increasingly found themselves preaching to more Christianized congregations. Even Capel seemed to moderate his stance on the faith-reason relationship during the last years of his life. Not long before his death in 1656, he spoke of the evidences for the divinity of Scripture as a "preparation" for the work of the Spirit, and even went so far as to assert that "we cannot ordinarily look for faith infused [i.e., by the Spirit], but by the way of this faith which is gotten by the arguments, reasons, considerations, convictions, and helps wrought by the Argumentations."[17] Perhaps early Puritans saw their parishioners as being too religiously illiterate to follow rational arguments for the doctrines of grace, though evidently they did not regard them as too dull to apprehend rational arguments for the existence of God and the divinity of the Bible.

The Puritans' enthusiasm for the gift of reason went hand-in-hand with their adamant insistence that ministers not only be trained in the Scriptures and in systematic theology but also have "humane learning," as they liked to call it—the study of logic, philosophy, and the classics. Samuel Eliot Morison pointed out long ago how remarkably rapid was the development of intellectual life in New England compared to that of other European colonies, a phenomenon he attributed to the strong religious drive of Puritanism and its demand that learning accompany this religion.[18] Here again was a matter on which Puritans found themselves contending against sectarianism, the classic New England response to which on this issue was a 1655 sermon delivered by Charles Chauncy (1592–1672) the day after commencement at Harvard College, where he served as president from 1654 to 1672. Chauncy pointed out that the Bible itself quoted pagan authors favorably, that all truth came from God, whatever its origin, and that since there were "many excellent & divine moral truths in *Plato, Aristotle, Plutarch, Seneca, &c.* . . . to condemn all pel-mel, will be an hard censure."[19] Remembering the generous donation of John Harvard to the college that

---

17. *Capel's Remains*, 72.

18. Morison, *Intellectual Life of Colonial New England*, 1–56.

19. Chauncy, *Gods mercy shewed to his people*, 36. The biblical texts Chauncy appealed to were Titus 1:12, Acts 17:28, and 1 Corinthians 15:33, the same ones William Perkins had laid out while discussing the matter in his classic preaching manual of the late sixteenth-century, *The Arte of Prophecying*, 98. It was first published in Latin as *Prophetica, sive, De sacra et unica ratione concionandi tractatus* (1592).

subsequently bore his name, the authors of *New England's First Fruits* related in 1643 that as soon as they had finished building homes, churches, and providing for the bare necessities of survival, "One of the next things we longed for, and looked after was to advance *Learning* and perpetuate it to Posterity; dreading to leave an illiterate Ministry to the Churches, when our present Ministers shall lie in the Dust."[20]

Eliot was intent on upholding the same standard in his missionary endeavors. In a 1670 letter on the progress of his work with the Indians, he wrote that one of his "chief cares and labours" was to train Native American pastors (whom he considered far more suitable missionaries than Englishmen) by teaching them "some of the Liberal Arts and Sciences," especially logic and rhetoric, and he accordingly published two years later his English-Algonquian interlinear *Logick Primer*.[21] The same year Increase Mather was instructing the members of Boston's Second Church not to choose an unlearned man as his replacement when he was dead and gone, on the grounds that "there never was any man eminently serviceable as a Teacher in the Church since the Apostles, except he were a Learned man," and that "the Interest of Religion and good Learning, have risen and fallen together."[22] Thomas Manton was sounding the same theme on the other side of the Atlantic:

> [R]eligion is not illiterate. Grace doth not make men simple, but rather perfects human learning. None discern truths with more comfort and satisfaction than a believer; it solves all doubts and riddles of reason. *Quod ratio non capit, fides intelligit* [what reason cannot contain, faith understands]. Simple men despise learning, and carnal men despise grace, both on the same grounds. Faith and reason must go together, though reason must be subordinate. We should not despise the help of human learning, neither should we despise grace, as if it did make men dull, and blunt the edge of their parts [i.e., talents]. Reason and faith, when kept in their proper place, are of excellent advantage. Join faith with your study, and all will be more clear, otherwise we shall stumble at truths. When these three lights are in conjunction, the light of parts, the light of refined reason and the light of grace, they bring forth admirable

---

20. *The Eliot Tracts*, 67. For the early history of Harvard College, see Morison's two works, *The Founding of Harvard College*, which covers the period from 1636–50, and *Harvard College in the Seventeenth Century*, which carries the history up to 1708.

21. *The Eliot Tracts*, 402.

22. Increase Mather, *Some Important Truths About Conversion*, "To the Second Church," xiv–xvi (unpaginated). Mather's preface is dated April 13, 1672.

and happy effects. But on the other side, the decay of learning hath been the sensible abatement of religion. Religion hath never lost more than when outward helps have been despised, which men do to hide their own ignorance.[23]

Indeed, since most of the ancient philosophers believed in God and inclined towards monotheism, Puritans considered them allies in the war against atheism and especially popular religious skepticism, and they frequently referred to them in order to demonstrate that true philosophic wisdom always led to religion. As Matthew Poole put it, to laugh at religion was to "confront all the wisdom of former Ages, and the concurring votes of the most learned Philosophers."[24] "[S]ome have thought," remarked Hopkins, "that reason and philosophy are great enemies to religion, and patrons of atheism: but, in truth, it is far otherwise; and the atheist hath not a more smart and keen adversary, since he will not submit his cause to be tried by Scripture, than true reason and profound philosophy."[25] Poole, Hopkins and other Puritans fondly quoted the maxim of Francis Bacon that "a little philosophy inclineth man's mind to atheism, but depth in philosophy bringeth men's minds about to religion," and Bates pointed out that if nothing else, philosophy awakened its students to the wonder of existence and prevented them from leading dull, inobservant lives: "A Philosopher asked by one, What advantage the instructions of Philosophy would be to his Son? replied, If no other, yet that when he is a spectator in the Theatre, one Stone shall not sit upon another."[26]

As a number of scholars have noted, Puritans similarly befriended natural philosophy. The extent of this kinship and the precise reasons for it have been the subject of much debate that need not concern us here, but

---

23. Manton, *By Faith*, 92.

24. Poole, *Seasonable Apology for Religion*, 51.

25. Hopkins, *Exposition on the Ten Commandments* (*Works*, 1:284).

26. Bates, *Considerations of the Existence of God*, 110 (the reference is to the stone seating of ancient amphitheatres). Bacon, "Of Atheism" (*Essays*, 44). Bacon seems to have had natural philosophy, i.e., natural science, primarily in view, for he continued, "For while the mind of man looketh upon second causes scattered, it may sometimes rest in them, and go no further; but when it beholdeth the chain of them, confederate and linked together, it must needs fly to Providence and Deity." For Puritans quotations of this line, see Poole, *Seasonable Apology*, 60; Hopkins, *Exposition on the Ten Commandments* (*Works*, 1:284); Gale, *Court of the Gentiles: Part IV*, bk. 2, chap. 2, § 1, p. 218; Boyle, *Usefulness of Natural Philosophy* (*Works*, 2:57).

the basic fact seems to be well established.[27] An aspiring man of science would not have had to search long in Puritan writings before discovering ample justification and indeed inspiration for a career in natural philosophy. In 1629 Thomas Adams (1583–1652), whom the poet Robert Southey deemed "the prose Shakespeare of Puritan theologians," was hailing nature as "God's epistle to the world," "Man's primer," and a "large theatre, wherein every creature is either an actor or a spectator." Adams lamented the fact that most human beings, who were created to be both actors and spectators, were only the former, were so "dull and non-intelligent [as] to see an excellent work without minding it."[28]

In the same year, which proved to be his last, the English Puritan and logician Alexander Richardson (d. 1629), wrote that since God was the creator of all things, "this teacheth man thus much, that he is to seek out, and find this wisdom of God in the world, and not to be idle; for the world, and the creatures therein, are like a book wherein God's wisdom is written, and there must we seek it out." Richardson influenced many Puritans through the private school he established in Barking, Essex in 1607 for the purpose of preparing graduates for their MA examinations. Among his pupils were future prominent divines like William Ames, John Barlow, Charles Chauncy, and Thomas Hooker, who remembered his teacher as "a man of transcendent Abilities and a most exalted piety."[29]

Bates complained that insufficient investigation of the natural world caused even "the most learned Professors . . . to take refuge in occult qualities when pressed with difficulties." Without this knowledge we were like those acquainted with the various parts of a musical instrument but without any experience of music:

> . . . 'tis not the sight of the mere outward frame of things, but the understanding [of] the intellectual Music, that springs from the just Laws of Nature, whereby they are perfectly tuned, and the

---

27. For two compilations of a number of key contributions to the debate, see Cohen, *Puritanism and the Rise of Modern Science*, and Webster, *The Intellectual Revolution of the Seventeenth Century*. Also see Abraham, "Misunderstanding the Merton Thesis," 368–87. For more recent contributions, see Morgan, "The Puritan Thesis Revisited," in Hart and Noll (eds.), *Evangelicals and Science in Historical Perspective*, 43–74; and Brooke, *Science and Religion*, 109–16.

28. Adams, *Meditations Upon Some Part of the Creed* (*Works*, 3:120–21); Southey as quoted in John Brown, *Puritan Preaching in England*, 89.

29. Richardson, *The Logicians School-Master*, 48–49. On Richardson's academy, see Webster, *Godly Clergy in Early Stuart England*, 29–30.

conspiring harmony of so many mixed parts without the least harsh discord, that ravishes the Soul with true pleasure.[30]

Charnock extolled the study of nature as one of the most satisfying human activities: "What a sweetness is there in knowing the secrets of nature, and the phenomena in the world!"[31] But he also commended it as a religious duty:

> Study God in the creatures as well as in the Scriptures. . . . The world is a sacred temple; man is introduced to contemplate it, and behold with praise the glory of God in the pieces of his art. As grace doth not destroy nature, so the book of redemption blots not out that of creation. . . . [T]he least creature speaks to man, every shrub in the field, every fly in the air, every limb in a body; Consider me, God disdains not to appear in me; he hath discovered in me his being and a part of his skill, as well as in the highest.

To be sure, there was more clarity in the book of Scripture than in the book of nature, but why put asunder what "the Author of both" had joined together? "God must be read wherever he is legible . . . . Though the appearance of God in the one be clearer than in the other, yet neither is to be neglected."[32] Indeed, Charnock averred that it was nothing short of a gross insult to God to pay so little attention to the things he had made. The animals could not do it, and therefore, "If man regard it not, what becomes of it?" One of the chief ends for which the world was created would be thwarted. God himself had paused after the days of creation to contemplate his works of art, and we were to "follow his example" in this:

> In vain would the creatures afford matter for this study, if they were wholly neglected. God offers something to our consideration in every creature. . . . Shall we be like ignorant children, that view the pictures, or point to the letters in a book, without any sense and meaning? How shall God have the homage due to him for his works, if man hath no care to observe them?

Since the complexity and richness of the created order could not possibly be exhausted by human beings in their brief lifetimes, this activity would

---

30. Bates, *Considerations of the Existence of God*, 111, 112 (also see 108–9).
31. Charnock, *Knowledge of God* (*Works*, 4:95).
32. Charnock, *Existence and Attributes of God*, 1:86 (also see 1:61).

continue in the world to come, "when the fountains of the depths of nature" would be opened.³³

Baxter wrote in similar terms, strongly commending the study of the works of creation alongside the mysteries of redemption on the grounds that one of the primary purposes of the latter was to restore mankind "to see, and love, and honor his Creator, as beholding him in the face of this glorious Creation." He considered it "a great sin of many, and most Christians, that they forget this, or make so little conscience of it"; and to those who disparaged the value of this knowledge he replied, "Why man, darest thou say, that God hath made any thing, which it is a dishonor for us to study (and know), except his Secrets, which we cannot know?"³⁴

No treatment of Puritanism and nature would be complete without a mention of the cleric-naturalist John Ray (1627-1705), who according to one historian of science "revolutionized" botany and zoology, "almost single-handedly moving [them] from a medieval to a modern mode."³⁵ Ray seems to have been a moderate English Puritan, but he was strict enough to refuse the Act of Uniformity in 1662 and was accordingly ejected from his living along with some two thousand other ministers. Shortly thereafter he left for a three-year tour of Europe to gather specimens. He spent the rest of his life observing animal behavior and expanding and organizing his invaluable catalogs of plants, birds and reptiles, scouring ancient and contemporary literature in order to avoid unnecessary multiplication of species. To the end of his life he remained a theologian. He was admitted to the Royal Society in 1667 but a decade later declined an offer to become its secretary, explaining, "Divinity is my profession." His mutual interests culminated in *The Wisdom of God Manifested in the Works of the Creation* (1691) and *Three Physico-Theological Discourses* (1693). In 1700 came a purely theological treatise, the practical *Persuasive to a Holy Life*. Both Ray's scientific and theological treatises were translated into French, Dutch and German, but the *Wisdom of God* was his most popular work. He published expanded editions three times before his death in 1705, and by 1735 a tenth edition had appeared. William Derham gratefully acknowledged its role in his Boyle Lectures of 1711-1712, and William Paley plundered its

---

33. Charnock, *Existence and Attributes of God*, 1:595-98 (quotations from pp. 596, 598). For a similar rebuke of ignoring the natural world, see 1:525.

34. Baxter, *Unreasonableness of Infidelity*, 2:165-66. Note that Baxter was here engaged (pp. 163-87) in giving twenty reasons why "humane learning" should be pursued by Christians. Also see Watson, *Body of Divinity*, 118.

35. Thomson, *Before Darwin*, 73.

riches for his *Natural Theology* (1802). "Paley seldom quotes it by name," writes Ray's biographer, "but repeatedly borrows from it without acknowledgment: indeed almost its whole contents are found rewritten but easily recognizable in his pages."[36]

The Puritan penchant for investigating nature prompted the Mathers, Samuel Willard and several other Puritans to establish the Boston Philosophical Society in 1683. Like the Royal Society in London after which it was patterned, its purpose was to present and discuss the latest developments in natural science. In 1713 Cotton Mather became a fellow of the Royal Society itself, and he contributed numerous papers to its annual gatherings. All of this would eventually lead to that counter-intuitive scenario in which the Mathers and a number of other Boston ministers found themselves imploring the opposed physicians of the town to employ inoculation as a remedy for a smallpox epidemic that struck the city in 1721 and killed over 800 people. So great was the popular ire against the Puritans on this matter that one furious citizen tossed an iron ball loaded with turpentine and gunpowder into Cotton Mather's bedroom. Its poor construction prevented it from exploding and also preserved an attached note that read, "Cotton Mather, You Dog; Dam you: I'll inoculate you with this, with a Pox to you."[37]

While Puritans believed that reason could demonstrate the existence of God, they emphasized that proving his existence did not mean comprehending him. Their favorite pithy line in this connection was that while nothing was easier to know than *that* God was, nothing was more difficult than determining *what* he was; and they liked to relate in this connection a passage from Xenophon's *Hiero* quoted in Cicero's *De natura deorum*, where the poet Simonides, being asked by Hiero, ruler of Syracuse, to say what God is, requests a day to consider before answering, then two more, then eight, then sixteen, and finally informs the exasperated tyrant that

---

36. Raven, *John Ray, Naturalist*, 57–61, 72–108, 452 (quotations 59, 452). Also see Ford, "John Ray's Life and Legacy," 5–22. For the publication and translation history of Ray's works, see Keynes, *John Ray, 1627–1705: A Bibliography, 1660–1970*.

37. On the smallpox affair, see Hall, *The Last American Puritan*, 166, 357–60; and Vaughn, *The Puritan Tradition in America*, 285. After the plague had run its course, Benjamin Colman (1673–1747) collected statistics on the epidemic and sent them to England as a vindication of the usefulness of inoculation. For more on Mather's induction into the Royal Society, see Kittredge, "Cotton Mather's Election into the Royal Society" and Kittredge, "Further Notes on Cotton Mather and the Royal Society," 81–114, 281–92.

the longer he thinks about the question, the more he despairs of finding an answer.[38]

Puritans seemed, in fact, to relish every opportunity to speak of the incomprehensibility of God. "Nothing is more present than God," said Charnock, "yet nothing more hid . . . . He is known by faith, enjoyed by love, but comprehended by no mind." One of their favorite metaphors in this connection was that of someone standing on the edge of an ocean. Expecting to fully comprehend the mystery of this "*I am that I am*," said Preston, was as absurd "as if a man should think to hold the whole sea in the hollow of his hand." Matthew Barker's *Natural Theology* broke out into a rhapsody on this theme, quoting the Christian Neoplatonist Pseudo-Dionysius and exclaiming, "While the Soul is admiring God, it is as it were gone out of its own *finiteness* into his infiniteness; where it is gone beyond its depth; as in the *deep* Ocean where men may swim but cannot wade." Thomas Shepard exhorted his readers to "wade through all creatures, until thou art drowned, plunged and swallowed up with God." "A spoon or shell may as well contain the whole Ocean," wrote Baxter, "as our narrow understandings comprehend the counsels of God."[39] Puritans thought this was so far from being an irrational belief that on the contrary, reason showed that if there were a God, such a being had to be an ultimate, essential mystery. As Ezekiel Hopkins put it, "reason itself teaches us, that such a being cannot be God, which may be comprehended by man."[40]

A champion of the Baconian scientific method like Samuel Lee called in nature itself in support of this point. Like John Ray, Lee took a strong an interest in natural science after refusing to subscribe to the Act of Uniformity. After the Declaration of Indulgence he ministered alongside Theophilus Gale in London, and in 1686 he set sail for America, where he pastored a newly organized congregation in Bristol, Rhode Island. In 1715 his daughter Lydia became the third wife of Cotton Mather, who remarked

---

38. See the American Puritan John Norton's (1606-63) *Orthodox Evangelist*, 1; Willard, *Compleat Body of Divinity*, 40; Charnock, *Knowledge of God* (*Works*, 4:97). Cf. Cicero, *Nature of the Gods*, 1.60.

39. Preston, *Life Eternall*, 102 (cf. Exod 3:14); Charnock, *Existence and Attributes of God*, 1:395 (also see 1:182, 1:200-201; *Knowledge of God* [*Works*, 4:97]); Barker, *Natural Theology*, 91; Shepard, *Sincere Convert* (*Works*, 1:13); Baxter, *Unreasonableness of Infidelity*, 4:50.

40. Hopkins, *Discourse on the State and Way of Salvation* (*Works*, 3:453). On the reasonableness of divine incomprehensibility, also see Charnock, *Existence and Attributes of God*, 1:81; Gale, *Court of the Gentiles: Part IV*, bk. 2, chap. 4, § 4, p. 294; Poole, *Seasonable Apology for Religion*, 61; Bates, *Harmony of the Divine Attributes*, 135.

of Lee that "hardly a more universally learned person trod on the American strand." Observing how far the science of his day had advanced beyond that of the ancients, Lee remarked that the complexities of the natural world were ever unfolding before us, so that however many of them we resolved, there would always be more. After discussing Boyle's recent elaboration of these unresolved issues, he predicted that future scientists—and even theologians!—would one day smile condescendingly on the mistakes of their late seventeenth-century predecessors:

> Indeed so may posterity deride at these our ages, and the more ingenious of future times, may stand amazed at our dullness and stupidity about minerals, meteors and the cure of diseases, and many thousand things besides, about the luster of stars and precious stones, which may be as easy to them as letters to us: which was so wonderful a mystery at first, and is so still to the *American* Heathens, to form the fleeting breath of our lips into painted scrawls upon paper. To them the longitude may be as easy as the Latitude to us, and that by methods, we yet do not dream of. Such rare inventions may be given in of [i.e., by] God to beautify the glory of the latter days. All our writings in Divinity, will be like insipid water, to what shall then appear upon the Stage, when the Jews come in .... The superfine Wisdom and Learned Wits of these acute times will discover vast regions of darkness and ignorance. There will be a *plus ultra* [further beyond] to the end of the world.

So much, by the way, for historian Richard Greaves' claim that Puritans' "deterministic philosophy coupled with their knowledge of God's past dealings with man made any hope of progress futile." On the contrary, the doctrine of predestination was what supported the optimism of post-millennial Puritans, because it meant that the future of religion did not hinge on the whims of human free will.[41] At any rate, Lee concluded that "if in millions of things we are stunted and fooled at every turn" in our investigations of the natural world, nothing could be more foolish than to refuse to acknowledge any mystery in the transcendent ground of nature and being itself. If the creation was inexhaustible, how much more the Creator.[42]

---

41. Post-millennial Puritans believed that history would culminate in a long period of unprecedented spiritual enlightenment and prosperity that would take place prior to Christ's return. See Iain Murray's helpful study, *The Puritan Hope*.

42. Greaves, "Puritanism and Science," 349–50 ("deterministic philosophy"); Lee, *Joy of Faith*, 213; *DNB*, 33:109–10. Lydia experienced severe mental derangement for six years but eventually recovered. See Mather's various diary entries on the matter between 1718 and 1724. "When the Jews come in" refers to a belief that the Jews would convert

Bates, Baxter, Boyle, Charnock, Gale, and Mather all repeated this idea. Baxter, for example, scornfully dismissed the objection that it was irrational to believe in the existence of a being that was by definition incomprehensible with the reply, "I am confident that there is not the least fly or worm or pile of grass (much more the Sun and other Planets), but that which we know of them, is much less than that which no man knows."[43] This was not a stupefied but a "learned ignorance," said Boyle after a lifetime of scientific experimentation; "wherein a man, after having taken pains to be instructed, is, by the utmost knowledge he has attained, made sensible, that that knowledge is but imperfect, and very disproportionate to the admired object." Our loftiest conceptions of God, or rather, the "least unlike idea" we could frame of him, came up "extremely short of being worthy of the incomprehensible God." Had they been able to read it, Puritans would have laughed—from the point of view of both natural and special revelation—at Isaac Newton's private reflection in the early 1690s that "in the conception of God [mystery] is dangerous, and conduces to the rejection of his existence," and that our notion of God should accordingly be "made as easy and agreeable to reason as possible."[44]

There was nothing new in these assertions of God's incomprehensibility. Rooted in the philosophical axiom *finitum non capax infiniti* [the finite cannot contain the infinite], the doctrine was older than Christianity itself, and no less a friend of reason than Thomas Aquinas (1225-74) had reminded his readers at the outset of his *Summa Theologiae* that "we cannot know what God is, but only what He is not."[45] But it is worth taking

---

to Christianity *en masse* prior to the end of history, triggering a period of unprecedented happiness and achievement for the human race. This view was largely derived from an interpretation of Romans 11, especially v. 15, "For if the casting away of them [the Jews] be the reconciling of the world, what shall the receiving of them be, but life from the dead?"

43. Baxter, *Unreasonableness of Infidelity*, 4:51; Bates, *Divinity of the Christian Religion Proved*, 189; Boyle, *Of the High Veneration Man's Intellect owes to God* (*Works*, 5:148-57); Cotton Mather, *Christian Philosopher*, 117-19; Charnock, *Knowledge of God* (*Works*, 4:97; also see p. 122); Gale, *Court of the Gentiles: Part IV*, bk. 2, chap. 4, § 5, p. 295.

44. Boyle, *Christian Virtuoso* (*Works*, 6:761); Boyle, *Of the High Veneration Man's Intellect Owes to God* (*Works*, 5:155). Newton's comment is from an unpublished manuscript dated c. 1692-93, as quoted in Turner, *Without God, Without Creed*, 58.

45. Aquinas, *Summa Theologiae*, Ia. 2, 3 (cf. 1a. 12, 1). The rationale for this essential divine incomprehensibility is further elaborated in Aquinas' *Summa Contra Gentiles*, 1.14.2-3, a passage Theophilus Gale quoted with admiration (*Court of the Gentiles: Part IV*, bk. 2, chap. 4, § 5, p. 303).

notice of because historians have sometimes mistakenly read Puritan assertions of this doctrine as concessions extorted from an ambivalent quest for a reasonable system of religious belief.[46] From the Puritan point of view, however, the incomprehensibility of God was the very capstone of rational religion. Reason demonstrated the existence of an infinite, intelligent being "than which nothing greater could be conceived," to use Anselm's classic terminology. Much could be learned about this being via natural and especially special revelation, but God would by definition always remain an essential, inexhaustible mystery.

Reason was not only prominent in Puritan theology but its starting point insofar as the foundational truths of the divinity of the Scriptures and especially the existence of God were considered by them to be postulates of reason. Yet Puritan reason was not a cold and detached rationality operating with little or no reference to the existential dimensions of religion or to the mysteries of God and nature. The Puritan mind considered it utterly unreasonable to ignore such phenomena; but it was equally unsatisfied with the idea that they could not be included within a holistic rational system. One gets a feel for the extent to which Puritan theologians were intent on integrating the intellectual and affective aspects of religion in reading a work like Charnock's *Existence and Attributes of God*, which moved from one to the other and back again with an ease that could only have come from a mind regularly exercised in both worlds. Reason led the mind to the existence of a knowable yet essentially mysterious God, and Puritanism was so far from refusing this mystery that it rather demanded it as reason's final point of termination. Reason also led to the acknowledgement of this God's written revelation; and by the aid of the Spirit's transforming work this revelation in turn corrected, refined and elevated reason by healing corrupt affections and showing it sublime truths it could not have arrived at of its own accord but which it would afterwards come to admire. As Bates put it:

> If any Divine Mystery seems incredible, 'tis from the corruption of our Reason, not from Reason itself, from its darkness, not its light. And as Reason is obliged to correct the Errors of Sense . . . so 'tis the office of Faith to reform the judgment of Reason, when either from its own weakness, or the height of things Spiritual, 'tis mistaken about them. For this end *supernatural* Revelation was

---

46. See, e.g., Sargent Bush, Jr., *Writings of Thomas Hooker*, 308; Holifield, *Theology in America*, 71.

given, not to extinguish Reason, but to redress it, and enrich it with the discovery of Heavenly things.[47]

Puritanism was thus a multi-dimensional movement marked by a determination to unite and harmonize the various spheres of human knowledge and experience. Religion would not be bracketed off from science, logic, philosophy, and politics; and it was this resolution that helped set the stage for the intriguing interaction between these fields that would become a standing feature of American society and intellectual life in the eighteenth and nineteenth centuries.

---

47. Bates, *Harmony of the Divine Attributes*, 139–40. Also see Charnock, *Existence and Attributes of God*, 1:525: "grace doth not destroy nature, but elevate it."

4

The Limits of Natural Theology

"Though men know God by the light of nature, yet they cannot come to God by that knowledge."

—John Owen, 1669

"Those over-doing divines who pretend to be certain that all the world are damned that are not Christians, do add to God's word, and are great agents for Satan to tempt men to infidelity, and to atheism itself, and to dissuade mankind from discerning the infinite goodness of God."

—Richard Baxter, 1673

FOR PURITANISM, THE PRIMARY shortcoming of natural theology was its inability to discover the Trinitarian nature of God, whether this being was interested in engaging in intimate communion with human beings; and most importantly, the method of redemption from sin through the incarnation, death and resurrection of Christ. In addition, natural theology did not reveal the full extent of mankind's depraved and damnable condition; nor did it offer sufficient comfort and peace of mind against the miseries of human life. Even the essential attributes of God that were in theory discoverable by natural theology had rarely been apprehended by those bereft of special revelation. The same was true of the Christian doctrine of *creatio ex nihilo*. That the world had been created by God was evident to any reasonable person who gave the question a moment's consideration; but discovering that it had been created from nothing was more difficult. While most Puritans believed reason could demonstrate the impossibility of eternal matter, they were well aware that the Platonic tradition had fallen short of this realization and that Aristotle had flatly asserted the exact opposite on the grounds of the axiom, *ex nihilo nihil fit* (from nothing, nothing comes). Finally—and this point belongs to a peculiar aspect of Puritan ecclesiology—natural theology was insufficient because it inculcated the duty of worshipping God but failed to disclose what rituals and activities were to be employed in that worship. Many Puritans (just how many depends on one's definition of Puritanism) followed Calvin in insisting that liturgical worship was to be limited to the ordinances found in the New Testament church, namely prayer, the reading and preaching of Scripture, the singing of praise (usually without instrumental music), and the sacraments. One of the fundamental planks of this reform platform was the contention that it was God's prerogative alone to determine the manner in which he was to be worshipped. This compelled them, of course, to deny that natural theology could provide much help in this matter.[1]

Matthew Barker's *Natural Theology* covered just about all of these deficiencies and is as representative as any Puritan work on this subject. To begin with, Scripture cleared up all confusion as to the divine attributes, which were "more clearly revealed in the Word of God, than in any Evidence of Nature." "The Mystery of Man's Redemption by Christ," moreover, was "not made known by the Works of Creation." Reason indeed taught pagans "the necessity, or at least the expediency of going to God by some Mediator," as is witnessed by the fact that they often employed their inferior deities to precisely this end. But the mediatorship ordained by God was beyond anything that the light of nature could have led reason to expect: "Where is *Socrates* and *Plato*? Where is *Xenophon* and *Aristotle*? Where is *Seneca* and *Cato*? Where is *Demosthenes* and *Cicero*? How is all their Wisdom baffled and non-plussed by the foolishness of Preaching? wherein the way to Man's true Felicity, which they so *anxiously* sought after, is declared to be a *Crucified Christ*," and at that "the Son of God, in the Nature of Man." It was because they lacked the knowledge of this path of reconciliation and union with God that the ancient philosophers disagreed so much among themselves as to what the chief good was or how to attain it: "There was

---

1. See, e.g., *Westminster Confession of Faith*, 21.1; Barker, *Natural Theology*, 120–21; Reynolds, "To the Christian Reader" (*The Eliot Tracts*, 326); Charnock, *Knowledge of God* (*Works*, 4:28).

nothing [that] did more exercise the Minds of the wiser Heathens than this; to find out and enjoy this Good; and nothing were they more divided in their Judgments about." Nor did their ethics penetrate deeply enough to the root vices that underlay human sinfulness: "[T]he *radical* [i.e., root] Corruptions of Man's Nature, which especially are Self-exaltation and Self-sufficiency, they rather did cherish than extirpate." Thus, while many of them correctly ascertained that the chief good was conformity to the image of God, "the way of growing up into this Likeness they did not understand." The light of nature taught them to patiently bear the evils of life as the common lot of the human race and even as heaven-sent trials of their virtue, "But, alas, the *Bed* they made was too short for the Soul to repose itself upon," because it did not clearly reveal the everlasting bliss of heaven and could not have dreamed of the consolation of an incarnate God becoming our fellow sufferer. "We may hence evince," he concluded, "the *absurdity* of casting off Scripture-Light, and betaking ourselves to the Light of Nature."[2] Those who did so, said Boyle, were like "flying fishes," whose wings enable them to elevate above the water for a little while but in the end "are able to carry them to no great height, nor keep them long from descending again."[3]

Could natural theology, notwithstanding these shortcomings, ever prove sufficient for salvation, or were those ignorant of the gospel doomed to perish however much they used and improved the light of nature? The question was not whether there was some other, non-Christological avenue of salvation for such persons. Few Christian theologians of the time would have considered that possibility. Nor was the question whether salvation was possible without the renewing grace of the Holy Spirit, an idea that would have been anathema to Puritans. Rather, the question was whether those unacquainted with Christianity or (in the case of those living before the time of Christ) Judaism might be regenerated by divine grace acting on their natural knowledge of God and thus come to share in the benefits of Christ's redemption.

This was not such a cut-and-dried issue in pre-modern Christian theology as is commonly thought, especially in the wake of the Protestant Reformation, whose severance of the long accepted ties between the

---

2. Barker, *Natural Theology*, 125, 111, 113–15 (cf. 1 Cor 1:20–25), 119, 122–23, 126. One finds some if not all of these themes in almost every Puritan treatment of natural theology. See, e.g., Charnock, *Knowledge of God* (*Works*, 4:72–75)' Charnock, *Knowledge of God in Christ* (*Works*, 4:118–30); Gale, *Court of the Gentiles: Part III*, bk. 1, chaps. 3–4, pp. 45–96; Trapp, *Theologia Theologiae*, 100–103 (also see his commentary on Genesis 1:1).

3. Boyle, *Christian Virtuoso* (*Works*, 6:714–15).

sacraments and salvation opened the way for a new consideration of the problem. Several prominent Reformers, Ulrich Zwingli (1484–1531), Heinrich Bullinger (1504–75), and Jerome Zanchi (1516–90), believed that pagans might occasionally be regenerated by the Spirit and thus brought to genuine faith and repentance through their natural knowledge of God.[4] Nevertheless, most Puritans rejected this possibility. Owen's remark in 1669 summed up the majority opinion: "Though men know God by the light of nature, yet they cannot come to God by that knowledge." Manton flatly stated that "the heathens had never light enough for salvation," and the father of English Presbyterianism, Thomas Cartwright (1534/5–1603), expressed it more severely in his *Short Catechisme*, which claimed that without the gospel the light of nature "serveth rather for further condemnation."[5] One could read the *Westminster Confession* as having left the question open, but if its key clause is interpreted in light of the Assembly's *Larger Catechism*, it has to be concluded that the Westminster divines did not think salvation was possible without the knowledge of Christ, except in the cases of infants and mentally handicapped adults.[6]

4. See my "Salvation for the Unevangelized in the Reformed Tradition" (forthcoming).

5. Owen, *Exposition Upon Psalm CXXX* (*Works*, 6:428); Manton, *By Faith*, 91; Cartwright, *A Methodicall Short Catechisme*, 7. For similar statements, see the American Puritan James Allen (1632–1710), *Man's Self-Reflection*, 18; Willard, *Compleat Body of Divinity*, 12–13, 34; Cotton, *Briefe Exposition with Practical Observations upon the Whole Book of Ecclesiastes*), 2; Adams, *Main Principles of Christian Religion*, 143.

6. See *Westminster Confession of Faith*, 10.3: "Elect infants, dying in infancy, are regenerated and saved by Christ through the Spirit, who worketh when, and where, and how he pleaseth. So also are all other elect persons, who are incapable of being outwardly called by the ministry of the word." The question is whether these "other elect persons" who were "incapable of being outwardly called by the word" referred only to the mentally handicapped or also to those who could not be so called because of their *geographical location*. One might think that the following section (10.4) automatically ruled out this latter possibility inasmuch as it asserted, "much less can men not professing the Christian religion be saved in any other way whatsoever [i.e. "by Christ through the Spirit," 10.3], be they ever so diligent to frame their lives according to the light of nature." But this language only demanded that all the elect, whether capable of hearing the gospel or not (as in the case of infants, the insane, and perhaps those living outside Christendom), were saved on the basis of Christ's atonement and made the subject of the regenerating work of the Spirit, even though in the nature of these cases such individuals would in this life be ignorant of these doctrinal truths underlying their salvation. However, Q. 60 of the Assembly's *Larger Catechism* (submitted to Parliament the following year, 1647) shut the door against this possibility by asserting, "They who, having never heard the gospel, know not Jesus Christ, and believe not in him, cannot be saved, be they never so diligent to frame their lives according to the light of nature." Perhaps the omission of the words

Owen had forcefully argued the case earlier in his *Display of Arminianism* (1643), where unlike Cartwright he at least affirmed that those among the lost who improved the light of nature received both temporal and eternal benefits in the form of greater happiness in this life and "a diminution of the degree of their torments" in hell. But if one went further than this and granted the possibility of eternal life to those who had not heard the gospel, he said, "it will naturally follow that the knowledge of Christ is not absolutely necessary to salvation, and so down falls the preeminence of Christianity; its heaven-reaching crown must be laid level with the services of dunghill gods." This did not mean, Owen emphasized, that no one outside Christendom was ever saved, for nothing was to say that God did not occasionally reveal the gospel by an extraordinary private revelation to some of the heathen:

> But the question is not, Whether a Gentile believing in Christ may be saved? or whether God did not reveal himself and his Son extraordinarily to some of them? for shall we straiten the breast and shorten the arm of the Almighty, as though he might not do what he will with his own; but, Whether a man by the conduct of nature, without the knowledge of Christ, may come to heaven? the assertion whereof we condemn as wicked, Pelagian, Socinian heresy, and think that it was well said of [i.e., by] Bernard, "That many labouring to make Plato a Christian, do prove themselves to be heathens."[7]

The early English Puritan Andrew Willet (1562–1631), a prolific author especially noted for his *Synopsis papismi*, a massive survey of the controversies between Catholicism and Protestantism that was republished in ten volumes as late as 1852 by the British Society for Promoting the Religious Principles of the Reformation, had been willing to be as generous as possible with this logic. He held that God would certainly reveal the knowledge

---

"in any other way" after "cannot be saved" was intended to prevent this more generous interpretation of 10.3–4.

7. John Owen, *Display of Arminianism* (*Works*, 10:112, 110, 111). The reference is to Bernard of Clairvaux's criticism of Peter Abelard in an 1140 AD letter to Pope Innocent II. See Leclercq et al. (eds.), *Sancti Bernardi Opera*, 8:26. Bernard said this only of Abelard, however, not "many": "Ubi dum multum sudat, quomodo Platonem faciat christianum, se probat ethnicum." ("Here, while he labors to make Plato a Christian, he proves himself a heathen.") The context was Abelard's attempt to draw some correspondences between the Holy Spirit and Plato's *anima mundi* (soul of the world).

of the gospel to those who made good use of the light of nature, perhaps as late as "the very instant of the passage of the soul" from this life to the next.[8]

While Willet insisted that regeneration by the Spirit of God was of course essential for salvation in such cases, he did not broach the question of whether the spiritual rebirth of these individuals would precede or coincide with this special divine revelation of Christ. This was a critical issue for two reasons. If one adopted (as would seem natural) the position that regeneration occurred earlier in the life of these individuals and was what drove them to seek God through the light of nature in the first place, it would have followed that the knowledge of Christ was not necessary to salvation. This was because regeneration implied, for Calvinism especially, an immediate, supernatural transition from spiritual death to spiritual life in which a person became a temple of the Holy Spirit. So it would have been impossible, indeed absurd, to conceive of a situation in which someone was regenerated but not yet saved, that is, still lying under the wrath and curse of God. But if this point was conceded, the last-minute special revelation of the gospel would now seem unnecessary. If God had waited this long to communicate it, why could it not wait until after death? This was, as we will see momentarily, precisely the position that was adopted by several prominent later Puritans.

If however, a theologian was uncomfortable with that conclusion and accordingly affirmed that such persons were unregenerate until Christ was revealed to them, it would have the raised the question of how, given the Calvinist doctrine of total depravity, it was possible for a spiritually dead soul to make such good use of the light of nature. One might resolve that matter by appealing to the Calvinist notion of "common grace," i.e., a general and universal activity of the Holy Spirit present in all individuals. But on this assumption it might seem that there was some sort of congruous merit in the good works of the unregenerate, a merit moving God to bestow salvation on them, and most Calvinist theologians would have been averse to that idea.

Once one allowed, as Willet had done, for a last-minute revelation of Christ to pagans who responded positively to the light of natural theology, the internal logic of Calvinism tended to drive one to the position that salvation was possible without the knowledge of Christ. In fact, from

---

8. Willet, *Hexapla*, 66. Cf. p. 65: "[I]t is not to be doubted, but that, if the Gentiles had thankfully acknowledged their Creator, and not abused their natural knowledge, God would have given them further instruction." *DNB*, 59:26–29.

the point of view of the history of theology it is interesting to note, as the Dutch Reformed theologian Herman Bavinck (1854–1921) observed, that whatever its severity on other issues, on the question of salvation for those ignorant of the gospel Calvinism was actually in a better position to be generous than was any other brand of Christian theology.[9] If (contra Catholicism) salvation did not depend on baptism or any other sacrament; and if (contra Arminianism) it was bestowed by a sovereign God as an utterly gratuitous gift without any regard to the merits or previous good works of its recipients; and if (per the Calvinist doctrine of total depravity) all genuine seeking of God and true charity were invariable marks of regeneration; it followed, as Zwingli and Bullinger rightly recognized, that nothing but the free decision of God stood in the way of salvation for those lying outside the pale of the gospel, and that wherever in the world there was sorrow for sin, love to God and love to others, there was spiritual life and salvation in Christ.

Lying in the background of this debate was the question of just what one was to think of the eternal fate of the ancient philosophers Puritans insisted on studying. It was not a new problem in the history of Christianity. Many patristic theologians had grappled with the issue, some coming down positively on the question, others negatively, and others somewhere in between. I have already noted the Puritan habit of appealing to the ancient philosophers in defense of the legitimacy of religious belief, and in general one finds that the positive references Puritans made to them far outnumbered the negative ones. This was especially true of the Platonic tradition. Indeed, it was his amazement at that school's theological and philosophical insights that prompted Theophilus Gale to compose his four-volume *Court of the Gentiles* (1669–77), an erudite encyclopedia of philology and classical philosophy that attempted to trace the origin of these insights and then construct a "Reformed Philosophy," that is, a Christianized Platonism. But Gale was not intent on exaggerating the historical achievements of natural theology. He argued that these insights were corrupted versions of ideas the Greeks had derived from their acquaintance with the Jews and from the remnants of the original oral revelation made to Adam and passed down through Noah's descendants. Gale was not the first to make this case. As he himself noted in the introduction to his book, it had been advanced by other seventeenth-century theologians and by ancient Jewish and Christian apologists as well. But no one had ever poured so much scholarship into the argument.

9. Bavinck, *The Last Things*, 165.

The Limits of Natural Theology

Gale did not address the question of whether salvation was possible for those bereft of special revelation, and given his mixed assessment of the morals of Socrates and Plato, he probably considered it doubtful. There was much to be commended in Socrates' character, but alas, some reason to believe that he "was not exempted from that great Gentile uncleanness," namely pederasty, "which the wisest and best of those Gentile Philosophers were guilty of." As for Plato, his ethical character was variously reported by ancient writers, and there was reason to suspect that he was a proud and covetous man.[10] Willet reached a similar conclusion, noting the reports of some of the church fathers that neither Socrates, Plato, Xenophon or Seneca had made a clean break with the heathen gods. Some of the ancient philosophers might have been saved, he said, but there was insufficient evidence to positively conclude that it was so.[11]

Barker preferred to leave the whole issue an open question, as did the English theologian-scientist John Wilkins (1614–72), whose verdict will be of interest to those who place him within the Puritan fold. Since God had "not thought fit to tell *us* how he will deal with such persons," wrote Wilkins, "it is not fit for us to tell *Him* how he ought to deal with them." The fact that William Bates remained utterly silent on the matter in his discussion of the ancient philosophers and in his defense of eternal punishment indicates a similar disposition on his part, but also suggests that he probably felt it was better not to say anything at all about it.[12]

But Baxter, who here as on other topics proved himself *sui generis* as a Puritan theologian, thought this silence a grave mistake. He had publicly

---

10. Gale, *Court of the Gentiles: Part II*, bk. 3, chap. 1, § 7, p. 233 (Socrates); bk. 3, chap. 3, § 7, p. 255 (Plato).

11. Willet, *Hexapla*, 66: "If this were the behaviour of the most famous Philosophers, who contrary to their own judgment worshipped idols, what is to be thought of the rest? and what argument can we have of their salvation, who both lived, and died for ought we know, in so gross idolatry?"

12. Bates, *Divinity of the Christian Religion Proved*, 75–79, 229–30, 263–65; Bates, *Considerations of the Existence of God*, 245–57; Wilkins, *Principles and Duties of Natural Religion*, 396–98 (quotation 397); Barker, *Natural Theology*, 117–18: "And what respect God may have to some among the *Gentiles* that best improved that Light, and had recourse to his general Mercy, without the distinct knowledge of a Saviour, which they had not means to attain, I shall rather leave it amongst the *Secrets* of God's Counsel, than make determination therein." Bates' silence is noteworthy because he was an intimate friend of Richard Baxter, whose views on this subject differed from those of most Puritans. For a discussion of Wilkins' status as a Puritan, see Shapiro, *John Wilkins, 1614-1672: An Intellectual Biography*, 18–20, 61–80, which maintains that "the answer to the question was Wilkins a Puritan is both yes and no" (67).

disagreed with Owen over this point while debating the terms of ministerial concord during the Protectorate, and he also directly addressed the question in a number of his writings.[13] The prospect of so many souls perishing without any possibility whatever of salvation was "one of the greatest difficulties of Faith," he said, and needlessly so, since there was no reason to shut the gates of heaven against those who never heard the gospel. He thought it "incredible" to suppose that God would ever damn someone who repented for sin, loved him and led an upright life, for "God cannot but take complacency in them that love him, and bear his Image: And those will be happy that God taketh complacency in."[14]

Just about any Puritan, of course, would have been willing to grant this. The question was whether someone could ever be brought to such a state without the knowledge of Christ the Redeemer. But even this question did not quite hit the mark, for Puritanism had already affirmed that it could indeed be so in the cases of infants and the mentally handicapped.[15] Their Calvinist soteriology easily allowed for this since it affirmed that the new birth produced deep within the human soul by an irresistible act of the Spirit of God was the first and fundamental moment of salvation. Regeneration did not follow faith and repentance but rather preceded and produced them. Ordinarily this act of regeneration was accomplished via the means of the preaching of the gospel, but it could be otherwise when God deemed it proper, at the time of an infant's baptism, for instance.

The real question, then, was whether the subjects of such alternative methods had to be limited to those who were mentally incapable of understanding the intellectual contents of the gospel. Baxter saw no reason why it should be so. One reason some theologians did so limit it was their belief that the light of nature showed the goodness of God but failed to communicate anything of his willingness to forgive. Natural theology could convict of sin, but because it disclosed nothing of God's readiness to forgive the penitent, there was no way for it to melt the sinful heart into a genuine remorse for sin. Thus it led only to despair.[16]

---

13. See his *Reasons of the Christian Religion*, 184–202, 359, 393–400; *Gods Goodness Vindicated*, 67–82; *More Reasons for the Christian Religion*, 83–116; *Christian Directory*, Part III, ch. 11, questions 156–57 (pp. 719–21); *Autobiography*, 117–18; and his Latin systematic theology, *Methodus Theologiae Christianae*), Part III, disput. 1–2, pp. 17–29. The argument with Owen is recorded in the *Autobiography of Richard Baxter*, 139.

14. Baxter, *Reasons of the Christian Religion*, 399, 184–85.

15. *Westminster Confession of Faith*, 10.3. Also see Calvin's *Institutes*, 4.16.19–20.

16. For a classic Reformed statement of this perspective, see Calvin's *Institutes*, 2.6.1.

The Limits of Natural Theology

Not every Puritan concurred with this dismal assessment,[17] but Baxter was one of the few to argue vigorously against it. Such a conception, he said, would "turn the Earth into a hell." Were we really to hold that the most reasonable conclusion for sinful souls under the light of nature to reach was that the many blessings they received in this life amounted to nothing more than an utterly irreconcilable Deity fattening them for an inevitable divine slaughter? On the contrary, said Baxter, "Experience assureth all the Earth, that Great Mercy is still continued to them, and they have to do with a Most Merciful God." Natural law's command that we should forgive one another reinforced this apprehension by intimating to us "that mercy and forgiveness are agreeable and pleasing unto God." Besides, how could the agreed upon dictate of natural theology to love, adore and live for the Creator be binding on the human race if that object of worship wore nothing but an angry and unforgiving frown?[18]

The only remaining obstacle, then, was the belief that in the case of sane, adult persons Scripture demanded, both before and after the advent of the gospel, a knowledge of Christ's incarnation and atonement for human sin as a condition of salvation. Baxter dismissed this notion as unscriptural. How had the disciples responded when Jesus told them he must suffer and die on the cross? They were incredulous, and were so far from expecting this fate for their master that when it finally befell him they inferred that he was not the promised Messiah after all! "You may conjecture by this," he concluded, "what the common Faith of those before Christ's coming was,

---

Also see Owen, *Exposition Upon Psalm CXXX* (*Works*, 6:427–31).

17. See, e.g., an ambivalent Barker in his *Natural Theology*, 117; Perkins, *Cases of Conscience*: "For in natural understanding, God is not all justice, and no mercy" (*Workes*, 2:45); Henry, "A Sermon Concerning the Forgiveness of Sin as a Debt" (*Complete Works of Matthew Henry*, 2:327); but especially Stephen Charnock, who at first toed the standard Puritan line but later argued strongly for the opposite opinion. Compare his *Knowledge of God in Christ* (*Works*, 4:141, 324) with the last of his theistic discourses, "On God's Patience" (*Existence and Attributes of God*, 2:500–504). Like Bates, however, Charnock said not a word as to whether this natural knowledge alone might have ever been instrumental in leading those ignorant of the gospel to true repentance, though this section of his treatment of divine patience makes it nearly certain that he was at the very least open to the possibility. He did everything but actually say so, and he could not have been unaware of the deeper theological question that lay just behind his remarks. Also see Witsius, *Economy of the Covenants*, 3.5.10 (vol. 1, p. 347): "But God not only invites men by the light of nature to seek him, but also gives some hope of enjoying him. For why else should he forbear sinners with so much long-suffering, unless he had decreed to take pity on some of them?"

18. Baxter, *Reasons of the Christian Religion*, 186, 182, 184, 400.

who were saved."¹⁹ Moreover, salvation under the Old Testament economy was not limited to the Jews, as appeared by the examples of Melchizedek, Job and his friends. Under the New Testament economy, the degree of knowledge was to be commensurate with what had been revealed. To demand such specific knowledge of Christ among heathens who had never heard the gospel was in effect to put them in a worse condition than they had been in prior to the incarnation.

But in the last analysis, said Baxter, no knowledge whatever of Christ was absolutely necessary for salvation. In order to turn to God, one only had to know or at least think it probable that God was willing to forgive—that neither the religious commands of the light of nature nor the joys of human life had been given in vain. Since Scripture so clearly revealed the nature of God, disclosed the depth of human sinfulness and the necessity of heart religion, and moreover proclaimed and demonstrated God's willingness to forgive, those living in Christendom had an incomparable advantage over the heathen, so that salvation would be far more common there.[20] But that was the most that could be said. The only faith absolutely necessary for salvation was the generic form laid down in Hebrews 11:6—"He that cometh to God must believe that he is, and that he is a rewarder of them that diligently seek him"—and this much could be learned from natural theology alone.[21] In sum, "No one ever perished in any Age or Nation of the World, who by *believing in a merciful, pardoning, holy God, was recovered to love God above all.*"[22] Baxter was even willing to extend this salvation, theoretically at least, to the Muslim world. In reply to Lord Herbert's *De Veritate*, he wrote:

> Do we not then grant you as much as you can reasonably desire? Tell us but what Heathen or Mahometans are *Holy, truly penitent for all sin, and devoted to God in obedience and love*, and we will grant you that they shall all be saved.[23]

All the elect were saved by Christ and regenerated by the Spirit, but the effects and extent of this salvation outstripped the knowledge of it: "There

---

19. Baxter, *Reasons of the Christian Religion*, 399. Cf. Mark 8:31–33, Luke 24:21.
20. Baxter, *Reasons of the Christian Religion*, 197; Baxter, *Gods Goodness Vindicated*, 79.
21. Baxter, *Gods Goodness Vindicated*, 71.
22. Baxter, *Reasons of the Christian Religion*, 398.
23. Baxter, *More Reasons for the Christian Religion*, 110–11.

The Limits of Natural Theology

is no salvation but by Christ the Saviour of the world; though there be more mercy from Christ, than there is faith in Christ."[24]

I am not aware of any Puritan who specifically criticized Baxter on this matter in print, even though he expressed these views in a number of works spanning the last quarter-century of his life, so that many of his fellow ministers would have been aware of them. Nor, surprisingly, does the subject appear in any of the numerous surviving letters of his collected correspondence. But Baxter must have taken his lumps from some quarters, for after laying out the case again in his *Christian Directory* (1673), a massive practical guidebook to the Christian life, he wrote as follows regarding the critics of his position:

> Those over-doing divines who pretend to be certain that all the world are damned that are not Christians, do add to God's word, and are great agents for Satan to tempt men to infidelity, and to atheism itself, and to dissuade mankind from discerning the infinite goodness of God; and occasion many to deny the immortality of the soul, rather than they will believe, that five parts in six of the world now, and almost all before Christ's incarnation, have immortal souls purposely created in them, to be damned, without any propounded means and possibility natural of remedy; and as I know they will pour out their bitter censure on these lines, (which I could avoid if I regarded it more than truth,) so with what measure they mete, it shall be measured to them; and others will damn them as confidently as they damn almost all the world; and I will be bold to censure that they are undoers of the church by over-doing.[25]

It is perhaps worth noting that Increase Mather and the great late English Puritan preacher and biblical commentator Matthew Henry both commended Baxter's apologetic work without any caveat regarding his view on this matter.[26] How much if anything to make of Mather's endorsement is hard to say, but Henry at least came to share Baxter's opinion. Henry's persuasion on this matter is noteworthy since his six-volume *Commentary on*

---

24. Baxter, *Christian Directory*, Part III, ch. 11, Q. 157, § 13, p. 721.

25. Baxter, *Christian Directory*, Part III, ch. 11, Q. 157, § 18, p. 721. For Baxter's correspondence, see Keeble and Nuttall (eds.), *Calendar of the Correspondence of Richard Baxter*.

26. See Henry's 1714 preface to his commentary on the New Testament, in *Matthew Henry's Commentary on the Whole Bible*, 5:viii; Increase Mather, *Existence and Omniscience of God*, iii.

the Whole Bible became and has remained one of the most popular devotional commentaries in the English language. By 1855 it had gone through at least twenty-five editions, and it has been frequently reprinted since. In 1711, three years before his death, Henry was preaching to his London congregation that with regard to those who had never heard the gospel, "we cannot say, it is impossible for any of them, though they live up ever so closely to the light they have, to be saved by Christ they never heard of. It is out of our line to judge concerning them, for it is not in our Bibles."[27] Three years later, when he penned the last of his published works, he expressed himself in more positive and confident terms, asserting that God "never did, nor ever will, reject or refuse an honest Gentile . . . who fears God, and worships him, and works righteousness . . . who lives up to the light he has." Such a life, Henry reasoned, could only be the fruit of the Spirit's regeneration, and God would accept such persons through the merits of the Christ they were ignorant of in this life:

> But, where these [fruits] are predominant, no doubt is to be made of acceptance with God. Not that any man, since the fall, can obtain the favour of God otherwise than through the mediation of Jesus Christ, and by the grace of God in him; but those that have not the knowledge of him, and therefore cannot have an explicit regard to him, may yet receive grace from God for his sake, *to fear God and work righteousness*; and wherever God gives grace to do so . . . he will, through Christ, accept the work of his own hands.[28]

---

27. Henry, "Faith in Christ Inferred From Faith in God" (*Complete Works of Matthew Henry*, 2:283). There is probably an allusion here to the *Westminster Confession of Faith*, 10.4 ("be they ever so diligent to frame their lives according to the light of nature'). See above, n. 6. Also see Henry's commentary on John 12:47: "Those shall not be condemned for their infidelity that never had, nor could have, the gospel."

28. Henry, Commentary on Acts 10:35 (op. cit., 6:107–8); cf. Psalm 138:8. The fifth volume of Henry's commentary, on the four gospels and Acts, was in press when Henry died in 1714. Seven years later sixteen of his colleagues completed the rest of the New Testament, availing themselves of his hearers' notes from his congregational and family expositions of the Epistles. *DNB*, 26:583; *Henry's Commentary*, "Preface" (6:vii–ix).

5

Arguments for the Existence of God

"Say with yourself, *Somewhat now is*, therefore *somewhat hath ever been.*"

—John Howe, 1675

"*Atheism* is now for ever chased and hissed out of the World, every thing in the World concurs to a Sentence of *Banishment* upon it."

—Cotton Mather, 1721

The essential components of Puritans' natural theology were the existence of God, the human duty of loving and living for God, natural law, divine providence, and the immortality of the soul. Many of the arguments they used to support these conclusions were not new. Greco-Roman philosophy had tread these paths ages before, and the Puritans were heirs of this tradition.[1] Two significant areas in which Christian theology had advanced the discussion were the absolute independence of God from other existents, and the concept of divine timelessness. From the point of view of the history of philosophy, nothing is more strikingly absent from ancient discussions of natural theology than their failure to consider the possibility of a transcendent God entirely independent of the cosmos—independent enough to simply speak the world into being. It was the Judeo-Christian

---

1. Gerson, *God and Greek Philosophy*.

tradition that bequeathed this idea to the West.² In some ways, this new concept did not affect the method of proving the existence of Deity. Many of the arguments that Christian and Puritan theologians advanced to demonstrate the existence of God remained largely the same as they had been in the classical world, though the evidences Puritans adduced from the natural world were reshaped in various ways by the rise of modern science. But the concept of a transcendent Creator did fundamentally change how one conceived the nature of that proved Deity and its relationship to the universe, and the Augustinian concept of divine timelessness opened up an avenue for philosophers to resolve Aristotle's conundrum of how the universe could have existed from past eternity despite various absurdities that seemed to follow upon the supposition of the real existence of infinite quantities—in this case the number of events in the history of the world.³

There were three main theistic proofs that Puritans drew from antiquity, and they routinely cited various ancient philosophers in support of them. There was the argument from universal consent, the argument to a First Cause, and the argument from the order of the universe. The first of these was based on the simple assertion that there never had been a people anywhere in the history of the world who did not believe in some kind of Deity. This proof *ex consensu gentium* was, as Gerson has pointed out, "the single most widely used argument by Greek philosophers for the existence of gods."⁴ Cicero had employed it in his *Nature of the Gods* and the *Tuscullian Disputations*, and almost every Puritan presentation of the argument quoted or at least alluded to the latter of these two passages.⁵

---

2. The first place one finds *creatio ex nihilo* clearly articulated is in the second-century church fathers Theophilus (*Ad Autolycum*, 1.4, 2.4, 2.10) and Tatian (*Oratio ad Graecos*, 5). On this whole subject, consult the valuable study by May, *Creatio ex Nihilo*.

3. For a helpful discussion of Aristotle on this point, see Hasper, "Aristotle on Infinity."

4. Gerson, *God and Greek Philosophy*, 297n81, noting occurrences in Plato, *Laws*, 886a; Aristotle, *De Caelo*, 1.3.270b5-8; Plutarch, *De St. Repug.*, 1051d; Plutarch, *De Comm. Not.*, 1075e. For a brief but excellent discussion with further references to the argument's use in antiquity, see Arthur Stanley Pease's annotated edition of the Latin text of Cicero's *De Natura Deorum*, 1:294-95.

5. Cf. Cicero, *Nature of the Gods*, 1.43; Cicero, *Tuscullian Disputations*, 1.13.30. For Puritan presentations of the argument from universal consent, see Perkins, *Cases of Conscience* (*Workes*, 2:52); Ball, *Short Treatise*, 65-66; Preston, *Life Eternall*, 13-15; Hopkins, *Exposition on the Ten Commandments* (*Works*, 1:280-81); Vincent, *Shorter Catechism Explained*, 37; Gale, *Court of the Gentiles: Part IV*, bk. 2, chap. 2, § 2, pp. 223-24 (also see § 6, p. 234); Barker, *Natural Theology*, 14-15; Howe, *Living Temple* (*Works*, 1:24); Bates, *Considerations of the Existence of God*, 82-101; Charnock, *Existence and Attributes of*

Arguments for the Existence of God

As for the reports of a few stray atheists here and there, they were of no more consequence than the rare instances of other forms of mental derangement were against the obvious dictates of reason and experience. And besides, when reading of these rare instances of unbelief one always had to remember the ancient observation of Plato and Socrates that atheism was merely an occasional luxury of youth, hardly if ever to be found in the seasoned and ripened judgment of old age.[6] Robert Boyle was open to the possibility that reports of natives in Brazil and other parts of the Indies who worshipped no Deity at all might in fact prove to be correct. But even if this were so, he added, it could only be because such peoples were "brute, and irrational barbarians" whose ignorance of God would doubtless be found to parallel their ignorance of nature. Their atheism merely resulted from a "want of contemplation of the world," and the apologist would only need to modify the argument from universal consent so as to allow for this exception regarding certain tribes who lived more on the level of animals than human beings.[7]

Belief in God thus met the established criterion of natural law (in the ethical rather than physical sense of that term): that what was universally and perpetually engraved on the human consciousness had to be true. As Thomas Hooker remarked in an attempt to prove that the soul was a separate substance from the body on the basis of the universality of that notion, "what the God of nature hath taught to all men by nature, is, and must needs be a truth." The only alternatives, Puritans maintained, were to deny the idea and legitimacy of natural law or to proclaim that the only real natural law was the ultimacy of power—that might made right. Refusing the argument from universal consent thus entailed a refusal of natural law itself, which would have a nihilistic effect on human society. As Stephen Charnock put it, "Nature cannot plant in the minds of all men an assent to a falsity, for then the laws of nature would be destructive to the reason and minds of men." To deny God was to deny natural law; and to deny natural law was to destroy the very foundation of human society.[8]

God, 1:35–42; Watson, *Body of Divinity*, 42; Increase Mather, *Existence and Omniscience of God*, 31–33; Cotton Mather, *Reasonable Religion*, 9–12. Calvin also quoted Cicero in presenting this argument. See his *Institutes*, 1.3.1.

6. Xenophon, *Memorabilia*, 1.4.16; Plato, *Laws*, Book 10, 888a–b.

7. Boyle, *Usefulness of Natural Philosophy* (*Works*, 2:56).

8. Hooker, *Immortality of Mans Soule*, 9; Charnock, *Existence and Attributes of God*, 1:33. The origin of natural law as an ethical concept is typically attributed to Aristotle, but Helmut Koesler argues that in Greek literature it does not clearly emerge until

Puritanism and Natural Theology

Neither the Puritans nor the classical Greco-Roman tradition were strangers to the idea of a sociological or psychological explanation for this widespread belief in the existence of God. The Puritan acquaintance with such theories, in fact, probably owed more to their reading of ancient philosophy than to real-world encounters with sophisticated unbelievers like Baxter occasionally experienced. The primary psychological explanation was that the gods were a projection of human fear. The sociological explanation was that the idea of God was a political expediency invented by rulers as a means of sanctioning the established civil order and thereby discouraging their subjects from revolting.[9]

It is important to recognize that the Puritans were by no means entirely hostile to such accounts of religion. As we have seen, they frequently engaged in such critiques themselves and could occasionally prove remarkably trenchant sociologists of popular religion.[10] If this appears strange one need only recall the grand Puritan project of replacing what they considered to be outward and external Christianity with an inward, spiritual faith. The prosecution of this task naturally involved them in an attempt to show how heart religion was derived from genuine encounters with God while nominal faith was the product of custom, education, and superstition—in short, of sociological factors.

Nevertheless, the Puritans were not about to class the most fundamental religious conviction of all in this latter category. Their standard answer to the idea that wily despots had invented the concept of Deity in order to keep their citizens in subjection was that history contained no record of any such act, and that even if there had been such an invention, who could imagine that after all these long ages its falsehood would have remain undiscovered? Surely the discontented masses, or at least the philosophers, would have found out a way to overturn it. Besides, if belief in God were a mere political fiction, why was it that history recorded so many instances of civil

---

the first century BC writings of Philo, though there is an earlier and independent origin of the parallel *lex naturalis* in Latin literature. See his "ΝΟΜΟΣ ΦΥΣΕΩΣ: The Concept of Natural Law in Greek Thought," 521–41.

9. See the illuminating discussion in Jaeger, *Theology of the Early Greek Philosophers*, 172–90. Jaeger perceptively notes (p. 175) that "the real fathers of rational anthropology are the fifth-century Sophists. In this respect they resemble the philosophers of the modern Enlightenment, who perform a similar function and have many close points of contact with them."

10. See especially Matthew Barker's discussion of twelve causes of atheism in his *Natural Theology*, 39–56, discussed below in chapter 6.

Arguments for the Existence of God

rulers being terrified of Deity? And why was it that belief in Deity was found among remote tribal peoples that had scarcely any form of civil order?

As for the psychological account of the origin of belief in God, Charnock replied that there was indeed a connection between fear and religion, but that the objection had reversed the correct order. Fear did not create the idea of an offended Deity, but belief in Deity combined with a knowledge of sin gave rise to fear of God. Indeed, said Ezekiel Hopkins, since for most people religion consisted of sordid and superstitious fear rather than peace and comfort, who could imagine that the inhabitants of the world would not have long since thrown off the shackles of such an oppressive belief if it had been at all possible for them to erase this conviction from their minds?[11]

But was Christianity undermining monotheism by adopting this argument from universal consent? Given the widespread prevalence of polytheism, would not the same train of reasoning that compelled us to believe in the existence of Deity also compel us to believe that there were many gods? Not so, said William Bates, for polytheism had not prevailed universally in history but was rejected by the Jews and wiser pagans. He pointed out that even the pagan masses, as the church father Tertullian observed, displayed a root monotheism when in distress they cried out to "God" in the singular rather than "gods" in the plural. That polytheism was only a distorted version of natural law was further evinced by the fact that it had been entirely extirpated in many parts of the world: "Time, the wise discerner of Truth from Falsehood, abolishes the fictions of fancy, but confirms the uncorrupted sentiments of Nature."[12]

In Puritan discussions of the argument from universal consent, there occasionally surfaced the deeper and more fundamental question, related to the moral argument for God's existence, of whether there could be any ultimate foundation for morality in a world bereft of a Creator. If one granted the fact that everyone everywhere believed in God or gods but explained this belief away on psychological or sociological grounds, what would then become of the rest of natural law's dictates? The Dutch Protestant jurist

---

11. Hopkins, *Exposition on the Ten Commandments* (*Works*, 1:280–81); Charnock, *Existence and Attributes of God*, 1:41. On the prevalence of fear as a motive for religion, also see Howe, *Living Temple* (*Works*, 1:10), where he remarks that "it is plainly to be seen, that the great principle which hath mostly animated religion in the world hath not been a generous love, but a basely servile fear and dread."

12. Bates, *Considerations of the Existence of God*, 78–101 (quotation p. 101). See Tertullian, *Ad Scapulam*, 4 (*Ante-Nicene Fathers*, 3:107).

Hugo Grotius (1583–1645), whose *De veritate religionis Christianae* (1627) was among the most widely read apologetic works of the seventeenth century, had remarked in his influential treatise on international relations, *De jure belli ac pacis* (1625), that (ethical) natural law "would have a degree of validity [*locum aliquem haberent*] even if we should concede that which cannot be conceded without the utmost wickedness, that there is no God, or that the affairs of men are of no concern to Him."[13]

The Puritans who addressed this question did not agree. Hopkins opined that belief in God was "almost the only thing which gives authority to the law of nature." Gale, Baxter, Charnock, Willard, and Increase Mather declared that it was the only thing; that the idea of moral obligation simply lost its meaning in a universe devoid of any supreme moral entity. If there were no God, said Baxter, then those who proclaimed that might made right were correct. Granted that human beings might in that state form social compacts for their mutual protection; the fact remained that these compacts were entered into in the name of self-interest and could therefore be exited on the same terms. To be sure, one could reply that those abandoning the social compact would suffer negative consequences. But this was difficult to prove as a universal rule, and moreover, it missed the more fundamental fact that even if it were granted, such violations could only be considered self-injurious, not immoral. Nothing, in the last analysis, would have to be avoided "as a *fault*, but only as a *folly*, exposing the person himself to danger," which hardly accorded with the nature of our moral experience.[14]

---

13. Grotius, *De jure belli ac pacis*, "Prolegomena," § 11. The translation above is taken from Kelsey's translation, *The Law of War and Peace*, 13. Grotius' ambivalence on this question has frequently been overlooked by both ancient and modern commentators who have represented him as granting a wholesale emancipation of natural law from theology. See, e.g., Pierre Bayle, *Continuation des Pensées diverses sur la comète* (1704), in *Oeuvres Diverses*, § 152 (3:409–10); Haggenmacher, *Grotius et la doctrine de la guerre juste*, 468; Lagrée, "Grotius: Natural Law and Natural Religion," in *Religion, Reason and Nature in Early Modern Europe* (ed. Crocker), 21. It was only a partial validity that Grotius granted to natural law on the hypothesis that God did not exist: "Et haec quidem quae iam diximus, locum *aliquem* haberent etiamsi . . . ," lit., "And what we have been saying [about natural law] would have *some* place, even if . . ." (emphases mine). For the scholastic background of this discussion, see Haggenmacher, 482–96.

14. Hopkins, *Exposition on the Ten Commandments* (*Works*, 1:281); Baxter, *Reasons of the Christian Religion*, 51–53, 58–59 (quotation p. 53); Gale, *Court of the Gentiles: Part IV*, bk. 2, chap. 2, § 6, p. 233; Charnock, *Existence and Attributes of God*, 1:69, 78; Willard, *Compleat Body of Divinity*, 40; Increase Mather, *Discourse Proving the Christian Religion*, 32.

Arguments for the Existence of God

The argument to a first cause, or as Kant would later term it, the cosmological proof, was occasionally articulated by Puritans in the form of the "first mover" proof that had been set forth by Plato and Aristotle in antiquity and in the Middle Ages by Maimonides, Aquinas and others. It did not demand the temporal origin of matter (for Plato and Aristotle thought matter was eternal) but merely contended that the motions and causes in the universe could not regress infinitely but must at some point terminate in a primary uncaused cause, the ultimate reality on which the world depended. More commonly, however, Puritans argued against the eternity of the world by using the contingency version of the cosmological argument. Unlike Leibniz, who would use this argument only to show that there had to be a non-contingent, necessary being on whom the world—eternal or not—depended for its existence, Puritans tried to argue that contingent beings could not be eternal.

John Howe's argument to a First Cause serves as a good example. It began with the simple assertion, "*Somewhat now is,*" therefore "*somewhat hath ever been,*" since it would have been impossible for something to spontaneously spring into being if there had ever been no reality whatever (divine or otherwise) in existence. No entity could make itself *ex nihilo*, for making was an action, and a being could not act without already existing. From this it followed that there was some eternal, uncaused, independent and necessary being. Either the world was that being, or God. It could not be the world, said Howe, for what was more obvious than that material reality was dependent, imperfect, and subject to perpetual change? To object that all beings were mutually dependent on one another would not serve the turn, for there would still remain the question of what the whole complex of dependent reality depended on for its existence.[15] There was thus no way to avoid dividing all being into two categories, dependent and necessary: "all things that are, or ever were, must be of these two sorts, *viz.* what was of itself, and what was not of itself, but from another." Perkins and Preston contended that to eternalize matter was to deify it. That matter had simply sprung into existence of its own accord was absurd, for *ex nihilo nihil fit* [from nothing, nothing can come], unless there were a pre-existing power sufficient to perform such a stupendous act. Howe criticized Spinoza for following some of the ancient Greeks in accusing Christians of contradicting themselves because they simultaneously believed in *creatio ex nihilo*

---

15. One of the key points on which twentieth-century debate on this argument has turned. See Rowe, *The Cosmological Argument*, 151–67.

and *ex nihilo nihil fit*. The latter, he explained, simply meant that "a being could never arise out of *no-being, of itself*, without a pre-existent, creative cause," not that "what once was not, could never be produced into being by a pre-existent, omnipotent Cause" possessed of infinite power.[16]

Puritans like William Twisse, Stephen Charnock, and William Ames also urged an enduring philosophical objection to an eternal cosmos, namely that it was logically impossible for an infinite span of past time to have elapsed. Augustine's belief that God's eternity consisted in timeless existence rather than everlasting duration naturally suggested this line of argument, since, combined with the Christian doctrine of *creatio ex nihilo*, it implied that time was not, in fact, eternal in the past. Aristotle had argued in his *Physics* that an infinite magnitude could be approached but never actualized, and he sought to create an exception for time in order to preserve the eternal universe he believed in. But it was the medieval Muslim theologian and philosopher Al-Ghazali (1058–1111) who fully developed the case and pressed it against the possibility of a past-eternal universe. Al-Ghazali's arguments were subsequently advanced by the Augustinian scholastic theologian Paul of Venice (1369–1429), whom Twisse specifically acknowledged, and they would later reappear (partly) in the first of Kant's famous antinomies. Al-Ghazali's argument and its subsequent variations attempted to prove that the supposition of an infinite past led to absurdities. Is the number of days in the history of the universe odd or even? Or take the part-whole objection: if the span of past time is infinite, an infinite number of years has elapsed, but also an infinite number of days. There is thus an equal number of days and years, which is absurd, since for every year there must be 365 days. Al-Ghazali offered an astronomical variation (geocentric, of course) on this theme. For every revolution Saturn completes, the Sun completes thirty, so that as time goes on the Sun becomes further and further ahead of Saturn in terms of the number of orbits completed. Yet if the universe is eternal, Saturn and the Sun have completed

---

16. Howe, *Living Temple* (*Works*, 1:29–36, 123, 195–205; quotations from pp. 203–4, 197); Perkins, *Cases of Conscience* (*Workes*, 2:49–50); Preston, *Life Eternall*, 8. For other Puritan statements of the cosmological argument, see Ames, *Substance of Christian Religion*, 63–64; Ball, *Short Treatise*, 60–61; Twisse, *D. Jacksons Vanitie*, 48–49; Hooker, *Exposition of the Principles of Religion*, 1–2; Baxter, *Reasons of the Christian Religion*, 9–32; Hopkins, *Exposition on the Ten Commandments* (*Works*, 1:288–89); Gale, *Court of the Gentiles: Part IV*, bk. 2, chap. 2, § 3, pp. 228–29; Vincent, *Shorter Catechism Explained*, 36; Charnock, *Existence and Attributes of God*, 1:44–52; Barker, *Natural Theology*, 19–21; Bates, *Considerations of the Existence of God*, 63–66; Willard, *Compleat Body of Divinity*, 37–38; Increase Mather, *Existence and Omniscience of God*, 14–15.

an identical number of revolutions, which is absurd. When we attempt to work out the implications of an eternal past, concluded Charnock, we "run into inconceivable labyrinths and contradictions."[17]

There was also a historical argument against the eternity of the world. Preston pointed out—and this would be repeated by numerous Puritans—that if the world had always existed one would expect that we should have some records of its history. But as the case stood, no ancient historian recorded anything before roughly two thousand years before Christ. Why was it, moreover, that all the arts and sciences were relatively recent inventions? Could one imagine that the human race had existed for innumerable eons without discovering writing, mathematics, philosophy, astrology, printing, etc., all of which dated back no more than several thousand years?[18] Evolutionary theory would later provide potent replies to these queries, but in the seventeenth century they were difficult to resolve on atheistical terms.

But the grand Puritan argument for the existence of God took its rise from the order and complex harmony of the world rather than from the bare existence of material substance.[19] "The Philosopher conjectured truly," wrote Bates, "who being shipwrecked on the Island of *Rhodes*, and come to the shore spying some Mathematical figures drawn on the Sand, cried out with joy, *Vestigia hominum video*, I see the footsteps of men, and comforted his despairing companions, that they were not cast into a Desert, or a place of Savages, but of Men civil and wise." How much easier was a similar inference from the theatre of nature, whose divine footprints plainly showed it

---

17. Twisse, *Discovery of D. Jackson's Vanitie*, 47–52; Charnock, *Existence and Attributes of God*, 1:44–46 (quotation 45); Ames, *The Substance of Christian Religion*, 64; Immanuel Kant's *Critique of Pure Reason*, A426-33/B454-61 (pp. 396–402). For Al-Ghazali's argument, see his *Incoherence of the Philosophers*. The "kalam" cosmological argument, as it has now come to be known, was given new life with the advent of big-bang cosmology and continues to be advocated by some philosophers of religion. See Craig, *The Kalam Cosmological Argument*, and more recently, Koons, "A New Kalam Argument."

18. Preston, *Life Eternall*, 11–13.

19. For the argument from design, see Perkins, *Cases of Conscience* (*Workes*, 2:50); Willet, *Hexapla*, 63–64; Ball, *Short Treatise*, 61; Scudder, *Christian's Daily Walk*, 286–87; Preston, *Sermons Preached Before his Majestie*, 66–76; Shepard, *Sincere Convert* (*Works*, 1:10–11); Pierson, *Some Helps for the Indians*, 17–18; Baxter, *Reasons of the Christian Religion*, 22–23; Vincent, *Shorter Catechism Explained*, 34–37; Barker, *Natural Theology*, 18–32, 163–67; Howe, *Living Temple* (*Works*, 1:36–82); Gale, *Court of the Gentiles: Part IV*, bk. 2, chap. 2, § 2, p. 226; Bates, *Considerations of the Existence of God*, 5–70; Charnock, *Existence and Attributes of God*, 1:52–67; Manton, *By Faith*, 76–77; Willard, *Compleat Body of Divinity*, 38–39; Increase Mather, *Existence and Omniscience of God*, 6–12; Cotton Mather, *Reasonable Religion*, 12–13.

to be "the work of a designing & most wise Agent." If someone objected, as Hume later would, that perhaps that agent was not God but merely some finite creator, this was merely to push the problem back one step further, said Baxter. For either that creator was eternal and self-existent, in which case it was God, or it was a being of magnificent power whose origin had to be accounted for in some way.[20]

The instances of design to which Puritans appealed roughly fell out into four categories: the original formation of the universe, particularly the solar system; specific instances of design in the various life forms on earth; the rational-like activity of seemingly irrational creatures; and the ordered harmony of the whole. These arguments were affected by the revival of Epicurean cosmogony and the rise of mechanical philosophy, so a brief account of these developments is necessary in order to appreciate the context of the evidences for God's existence Puritans drew from the natural world.

The sixteenth, seventeenth, and early eighteenth centuries witnessed the gradual downfall of the Aristotelian science that had dominated European universities since the thirteenth century. The ancient rival to Aristotle's physics had been the atomism propounded by Leucippus (fl. c. 400 BC), Democritus (c. 460–c. 370 BC) and Epicurus (341–270 BC). There were many points of divergence between the Aristotelian and atomistic systems of nature. Of particular importance for theism, however, was the Epicurean cosmogony, according to which the formation of the universe was attributed to a chance or natural arrangement of indivisible particles of matter over which the gods exercised no superintendence. Although Plato himself endorsed an atomic theory of matter, he and Aristotle and Cicero rejected the idea that the marvelous order of the universe could have come about in such a way, and Christian theologians naturally followed them in this. Given Epicurus's rejection of providence and the immortality of the soul, together with a misunderstanding of his theory of pleasure that persists to this day, Epicureanism essentially became synonymous, in Greek philosophy but especially Christian theology, with hedonistic atheism. However, the late fifteenth-century recovery of two ancient writings that expounded the Epicurean system of nature, Lucretius' *De rerum natura* (On the Nature of Things) and Diogenes Laertius's *Lives of the Philosophers*, gradually led

---

20. Baxter, *Reasons of the Christian Religion*, 19; Bates, *Considerations of the Existence of God*, 6–7. Bates' reference is to the Socratic philosopher Aristippus, who is reported by Vitruvius to have said this when shipwrecked off the coast of Rhodes. See the opening sentence of the preface to book six of his *De Architectura*: "Vestigia enim hominum video" ("I indeed see the footsteps of men").

Arguments for the Existence of God

to new theistic formulations of atomist cosmogony, and this, together with a myriad of other factors, contributed to the rise of the mechanistic natural philosophy that would become a hallmark of the Scientific Revolution.[21]

There were three significant ways in which mechanical philosophy influenced Western theology. First, by laying out a program in which all natural phenomena could prospectively be explained on the basis of immutable scientific laws interacting with matter and motion, it compelled Christians thinkers to more clearly define the line of demarcation between ordinary and extraordinary divine action in the world—that is, between providence and miracle. The mechanistic conception of nature made it easier to define what a miracle was, namely an event where the natural causes operative at the particular time and place of the event were insufficient to produce it. But it also made it more challenging to understand God's role in the ordinary phenomena of nature. Second, mechanical philosophy allowed deists and religious skeptics to deny divine providence. Although this would continue to be a critical problem in the history of Christian thought, just as the prospect of a universal material determinism would be in the subsequent history of philosophy, it was not a significant deterrent to Christian theologians, most of whom believed that providential activity and natural law were not mutually exclusive and sought some way of embracing both.

Nevertheless, the transition to this new vision of nature undoubtedly occasioned some cognitive dissonance for some theologians. One prominent example of this is found in the sermons preached in New England in the days following the great earthquakes of 1727 and 1755, many of them delivered while the earth was still trembling and groaning from the aftershocks. Nineteen of twenty-seven such sermons I have examined distinguished between natural and supernatural causes, and thirteen of those nineteen included a specific discussion of the natural causes of earthquakes and attempted to relate their natural causes to the question of divine providence. This is itself significant in that it indicates how much the topic was on the radar screen of New England ministers. When Cotton Mather addressed the shaken citizens of Boston the morning after the 1727 quake, he felt compelled to remark that it was "no fond *Superstition*" to think that an earthquake "usually carries in it, some intimation of the *Divine Displeasure*." He briefly instructed his audience in three main theories about the

---

21. See John Henry, "Atomism," Lisa Sarasohn, "Epicureanism," and Osler, "Mechanical Philosophy," in *History of Science and Religion in the Western Tradition* (ed. Ferngren), 122–27, 128–31, 149–54.

physical causes of earthquakes before moving on to the main business of his sermon:

> But it must be something more *Theological*, that you are now to be treated with. Let the *Natural Causes* of *Earthquakes* be what the *Wise Men of Inquiry* please. *They* and their *Causes* are still under the Government of HIM that is the *GOD of nature*. Shall we say, All this is but a *Chance that happens to us*, or the meer unguided *Motion* of *Matter*? . . . . A *Christian* cannot speak so.[22]

All the ministers agreed that God was the ultimate cause of earthquakes, and most believed that the New England quakes were in some way connected to human sin and should be considered a special providence, that is, an event that had been sent by God for a particular reason. But there was variety and above all ambiguity in the way they connected this theological interpretation of the quakes to the question of their natural causes. Eleven ministers maintained that there was some element of immediate divine intervention involved in the production of earthquakes, several of them reinforcing this view by emphasizing the inability of natural philosophers to fully explain their physical causes. But none of these eleven ministers indicated whether this interventionist view of earthquakes was necessary to their being regarded as special providences.

Thomas Prince (1687–1758), the pastor of Boston's Old South Church, seems to have felt the tension between natural and divine causality most keenly. His discourse, which was preached in 1727 and republished after the 1755 quake, was the only earthquake sermon to essentially deny the reality of natural (physical) laws. Prince asserted that natural causes were not real properties of material substances but merely a human construct for representing God's usual method of manipulating and moving matter: "what we call the *Laws of Nature*, are only the usual Methods in which [God] is pleased to Work in the World; and from which He sees not cause to depart, but in some extraordinary Cases where his usual manner of working cannot reach his Designs."[23]

Several scholars have mistakenly interpreted Increase Mather's *Kometographia* (1683) as manifesting a parallel aversion towards the idea that comets might be governed by natural law. Robert Middlekauff, for instance, has written that Mather was "appalled" by the idea that "the path of a comet was predictable and the return of comets could be precisely calculated"

22. Cotton Mather, *The Terror of the Lord*, 15, 9.
23. Prince, *Earthquakes the Works of God*, 12–13.

Arguments for the Existence of God

because he believed that it would destroy divine concursus and severely compromise the sovereignty of God. David D. Hall and Michael G. Hall have similarly represented Mather as hopelessly conflicted by his desire to assimilate modern astronomy while continuing to view comets as providential signs of impending doom.[24]

It is true that Mather did not think the date of a comet's arrival could be exactly calculated, but this conviction was driven by his science, not his theology. Because comets were "generated in the *Æther*" as opposed to being of perpetual duration like other heavenly bodies, and because they were sometimes absent from the sky for as long as a hundred years, it was from a practical point of view impossible to predict the precise time of their arrival so far in advance. He was nevertheless willing to concede "that a *probable conjecture*, as to the year of a Comet's appearance, may be made from the conjunction of the superior Planets." Mather nowhere expressed dismay at the idea that comets operated according to natural law. In fact, he plainly stated that this had no bearing on the question of whether they should be interpreted as divine messengers:

> There are those who think, that inasmuch as Comets may be supposed to proceed from natural causes, there is no *speaking voice of Heaven* in them, beyond what is to be said of all other works of God. But certain it is, that many things which may happen according to the course of nature, are portentous signs of divine anger, and prognostics of great evils hastening upon the world.[25]

The critical variable for Mather's theological comet-scheme was *concurrence with remarkable events*. And the basis for this scheme was not his conception of nature but his completely uncritical acceptance of the terrible historical events that were reported to have followed on the heels of the hundreds of comets that had appeared over the last several thousand years. 106 of *Kometographia*'s 143 pages were devoted to discussing these coincidences, which Mather drew from various chronographers, crediting them in the margin next to each entry. Among the most bizarre of these was his entry for a comet that reportedly appeared in 423 AD, "after which Prodigious showers of Blood were rained down upon *Tholous* in *France*

---

24. Middlekauff, *The Mathers: Three Generations of Puritan Intellectuals*, 141–42; Hall, *Worlds of Wonder, Days of Judgment*, 170–73.

25. Increase Mather, *Kometographia*, 16–18 (quotations 16, 16, 18). An abbreviated list of these concurrences appears in Samuel Danforth (1626–74), *Astronomical Description of the Late Comet*, 16–18.

for a whole day together."[26] However, most of the historical concurrences noted by Mather had to do with ordinary calamities such as war, famine, and natural disasters.

Increase did not publish anything more on comets for the remaining forty years of his life. Perhaps he felt there was nothing left for him to say about it, or perhaps he learned to be more skeptical of ancient history from his older brother Nathaniel, who wrote Increase from his parish in Dublin telling him that he was "perswaded Comets doe no more portend than Eclipses, and Eclipses no more than the constant conjunctions of the sun & moon, that is, just nothing at all."[27] Increase's son Cotton likewise began at this time to adopt a more skeptical attitude toward reports of prodigies (bizarre natural phenomena); and even where such prodigies were verified, as in the case of "monster" births (deformed babies), he was more hesitant to interpret them as special divine messengers. But the logic for this latter move remained the same as it had been for his father in 1683. One ought not to "be too ready to imagine that *monsters* carry *omens* in them," he wrote in 1716, yet "*Monsters* may no doubt be sometimes attended with such circumstances that they who are more nearly concerned may do well to be sensible of a voice from Heaven therein unto them."[28]

One reason for the Puritans' receptivity to the new science, I think, was their belief that God had, as their *Westminster Shorter Catechism* put it, "foreordained whatsoever comes to pass," a crucial doctrine that is often overlooked by scholars focusing on what was merely one of its subsets: their Calvinistic doctrine of election. This eternal decree embraced every event in history, however small or insignificant, and no matter what its immediate cause. As William Ames put it, "God's will determines all things without exception: the greatest, the least, the contingent, the necessary, the free." Increase frequently reminded his readers of Jesus' saying that not

---

26. Increase Mather, *Kometographia*, 49.

27. Quoted in Hall, *The Last American Puritan*, 383n69. Harvard tutor Thomas Robie (1689–1729) expressed the same sentiment in 1719 while commenting on the *aurora borealis*: "As to prognostications from it, I utterly abhor and detest them all, and look upon these to be but the effect of ignorance and fancy, for I have not so learned philosophy or divinity as to be dismayed at the signs of heaven. This would be to act the part of an heathen, not of a Christian philosopher. See Jer. 10:2." Quoted in Vaughan (ed.), *The Puritan Tradition in America*, 295. Jeremiah 10:2 reads, "Learn not the ways of the heathen, and be not dismayed at the signs of heaven; for the heathen are dismayed at them."

28. Winship, "Prodigies, Puritanism, and the Perils of Natural Philosophy," 92–105 (quotation from Mather on p. 100, from a manuscript draft of his July 3, 1716 letter to the Royal Society).

Arguments for the Existence of God

even a sparrow fell to the ground "without your Father," remarking, "He would not be God if the least thing in the world should happen without him."[29] Since the Puritan mind already conceived of the universe in terms that were ultimately deterministic, it was often of comparatively small importance whether various events proceeded from an immediate exercise of divine power or from the general course of nature. Either way the event was what God had foreordained. This made it legitimate to inquire into the possibility of a special divine message in unusual occurrences. Puritans were not, of course, open to a non-interventionist conception of nature, which indeed they saw as the high road to irreligion. Providence had to retain a prominent active element if their relational, covenant-making God was to be preserved.

But mechanical philosophy did become a real threat to Christianity, and indeed to theism itself, when it reverted to ancient Epicureanism and attempted to explain not just the *workings*, but the very *formation* of the cosmos, on the basis of natural law alone. Ironically, it was a sincerely religious philosopher who became the first modern thinker to present such a cosmogony to the western world. In his *Le Monde*, posthumously published in two parts between 1662 and 1664, René Descartes (1596-1650) proposed that given matter, motion, and the laws of nature, the primeval mass could have fallen into its present order entirely on its own. God was not altogether exiled from this system. He had created matter, established the laws of nature and then set the inherently inert material components of the universe into motion. But from that point on, his immediate power was no longer needed:

> From the first instant of their creation, He causes some to start moving in one direction and others in another, some faster and others slower (or even, if you wish, not at all); and He causes them to continue moving thereafter in accordance with the ordinary laws of nature. For God has established these laws in such a marvellous way that even if we suppose that He creates nothing more than what I have said, and even if He does not impose any order or proportion on it but makes it of the most confused and muddled chaos that any of the poets could describe, the laws of nature are sufficient to cause the parts of this chaos to disentangle themselves

---

29. *Westminster Shorter Catechism*, Q. 7; Ames, *Marrow of Theology*, 1.7.45 (p. 98); Increase Mather, *Doctrine of Divine Providence Opened and Applied)*, 11-12 (cf. Matt 10:29). Also see Wilkins, *Discourse concerning the Beauty of Providence*, 33: "There is no event in the world but it is ordered both according to God's *will*, and by his *counsel*."

and arrange themselves in such a good order that they will have the form of a most perfect world, a world in which one will be able to see not only light, but all the other things as well, both general and particular, that appear in the actual world.[30]

Or as Voltaire satirically summed it up, "Give me matter and motion, and I will make a world."[31]

Aram Vartanian's classic and masterful study has shown how eighteenth-century philosophes were all too happy to "develop the physical at the expense of the theological portion" of Descartes' system on their way to a wholesale scientific materialism.[32] Response to Cartesian physics was largely unfavorable until the early eighteenth century when it began to be widely taught in French universities, but its ascendancy there was short lived. By the 1730s it had been displaced by the scientifically superior system of Isaac Newton (1642–1727).[33] Newton was well aware of the naturalistic tendencies of Descartes' cosmogony and urged that matter, motion, and the laws of nature were by no means sufficient for the making of a world.[34] Voltaire himself—no Christian, but a firm theist nonetheless—heaped scorn on the cosmogony of the philosophes and others who believed in "animals formed from mud by chance, and a thousand other idiocies put forth with confidence."

> Each destroys and rebuilds the earth in his fashion, just as Descartes fabricated it; for the majority of philosophers have put themselves without ceremony in God's place, and think of creating a universe by use of words.[35]

---

30. Descartes, *The World and Other Writings*, 23. Descartes began working on this project in 1629 but abandoned it in 1633 after hearing of the condemnation of Galileo, since his own system was also heliocentric. The work has two parts: *The Treatise on Man* (published as *Renatus Descartes de Homine* in 1662) and *The Treatise on Light* (published under the title *Le Monde* in 1664).

31. "Donnez-moi de la matière et du mouvement, et je ferai un monde." Voltaire, *Les Systèmes* (1772), in *Oeuvres Complètes*, 10:169n3 ('M. de Morza' is Voltaire's pseudonym). This was a near-verbatim repetition of what he had said of the Cartesian cosmogony decades earlier in the opening pages of his *Eléments de la Philosophie de Newton* (1738): "Donnez-moi du mouvement et de la matière, et je vais faire un monde" (*Oeuvres Complètes*, 22:404).

32. Vartanian, *Diderot and Descartes*, 11.

33. Descartes, *Philosophical Essays and Correspondence*, xvii.

34. Thayer (ed.), *Newton's Philosophy of Nature: Selections*, 42, 47–49.

35. Voltaire, *Dialogues d'Évhémère* (*Oeuvres Complètes*, 30:502); Voltaire, *Précis du siècle de Louis IV* (*Oeuvres*, 15:433–34); as quoted in Vartanian, *Diderot and Descartes*, 80, 125.

Arguments for the Existence of God

This fragmentary sketch of an immensely complex development indicates something of the broader scientific context of seventeenth-century natural theology. The issues it raised would not come to the forefront of theistic discourse until the mid-1700s, but by the 1670s the scent of non-theistic cosmogonies was very much in the air, and the transitions that modern science would effect were plainly visible. As an instance of the latter, consider a series of theistic proofs offered by William Perkins in 1596 that were modeled on a distinctively pre-modern conception of nature. How was it, Perkins had asked, that food, a lifeless entity, maintained life? How was it that clothing, having no heat in itself, was able to preserve heat? How did the lifeless sun and the lifeless rain bring forth vegetative life? How did a fully formed chick emerge from the relatively undifferentiated mass of its embryonic form, given that its only impetus was the heat of the mother hen? From the tiny, neglected seed of the silkworm fly came the silkworm, which eventually weaved a cocoon for itself, emerged a fly again, laid its own seed, and died. Who could think that such potential was wrapped up in the seed itself? In all these cases, concluded Perkins, one had to suppose an active divine power that imparted life, being, and propagation.[36]

Thomas Hooker employed the same line of reasoning in one of his arguments for the immateriality of the soul. Confronting the mortalist position that just as the faculty of sight belonged to the eyes, and the power of hearing to the ears, so the power of thought rested in the brain rather than in the soul, Hooker replied that eyes and ears were merely instruments of the soul's capacity for seeing and hearing, and he proved it by asking, "if the eye be the thing that seeth, and the ear the thing that heareth, why do we not see things double, and hear sounds double, seeing we have two eyes & two ears? It is the soul, then, that seeth & heareth."[37]

These and the like phenomena would continue to strike later theistic naturalists with wonder, but there would be an intermediate step for them between phenomena such as Perkins observed and the God he saw behind, or rather *in* them, namely an identification of the astounding complexity within nature that effected these transformations. When anatomists discovered the complicated process by which two eyes relayed a single image, an observation that had once served as an argument for the existence of the soul would instead become part of the argument from design. Perkins simply could not *imagine* a train of natural causes sufficient to account for

---

36. Perkins, *Cases of Conscience* (*Workes*, 2:50–51).
37. Hooker, *Immortality of Mans Soule*, 23 (also see 27).

these phenomena; hence he inferred an active divine power that filled in the gaps where nature appeared to perform so far beyond its powers. In the 1650s Pierson was propounding a similar argument to the American Indians in which he maintained that whereas the natural properties of fire and water were to respectively ascend and descend, God overrode both of these in causing lightning to fall downward and water to rise upward in the process of evaporation.[38] Shortly thereafter, however, the world of nature would open up in such a way that theologians or scientists could readily imagine (even if they could not yet identify) a train of such natural causes, and their admiration of God would flow from their discovery of these complex relations. The emphasis would shift from a divine activity mysteriously intertwined with nature to astounding divine workmanship.

One can also see this issue being worked out in Puritan writings on the curious question of how to account for the seemingly rational behavior of certain animals. When King James paid a visit to Cambridge University in March of 1615, he was entertained by a debate on the question, "Whether brutes had reason, and could make syllogisms." John Preston was appointed one of the disputants and is said to have dazzled the king by offering a brilliant argument in favor of the affirmative, pointing to "the case of a hound," who "when he comes to a place where three ways meet, he tries one, then another; but finding no scent, runs down the third with full cry, concluding that as the hare is not gone in either the first two ways, she must necessarily be gone in the third."[39]

It is not clear if Preston concluded from this that hounds really did have the capability of reasoning, however, for among his stated evidences for the existence of God were "the reasonable actions of creatures, in themselves unreasonable," the idea apparently being that there had to be a higher intelligence that guided animals in these inferences.[40] He was referring to the remarkable animal activities to which many Puritans drew attention in their writings on natural theology: the ingenious architecture of spider webs, beehives, anthills and beaver dams, and the navigational and seasonal instincts of birds. These things could not be, argued Matthew Barker, unless such creatures were "guided and acted by some other *principle* than their own respective Natures." Even if one granted a certain capacity of reasoning

---

38. Pierson, *Some Helps for the Indians*, 22.

39. Brooks, *Lives of the Puritans*, 2:353.

40. Preston, *Life Eternall*, 5. The argument is further developed in his *Sermons Preached Before his Majestie*, 70–72.

to these animals, what was to be said of similar phenomena in the plant world?—ivy winding itself around walls and trees "as if it did know it was a weak Plant," trees stretching their branches upwards toward the light and their roots downward into the earth beneath them with such an engineering skill "that no man can imagine how it could be done better." Whether the *immediate* cause of such activities was divine or natural, Barker was content to leave an open question. Perhaps all these things were done by bare instinct. But that mattered little, he said, for one still had to account for the origin of these instincts that so obviously exceeded the intellectual capacities and nurture of such creatures. We were constrained to acknowledge, concluded Charnock, "a higher being ... who hath planted that genius in them." Bates seemed to think it was a combination of both instinct and immediate providence, commenting that "'Tis evident from their constant and regular actings, that an Understanding above man's ... impressed their unerring instincts, and directs their motions."[41]

Puritans abreast of the new science harnessed their newfound knowledge of nature in the service of apologetics. The pious Robert Boyle is a prime example. The international prestige of his scientific writings made his experimental laboratory a must-see attraction for tourists and gained him the title of "the English philosopher." Boyle never so much as mentioned the name of God "without a Pause and a visible stop in his Discourse," and his writings are replete with reminders that the wonders of the natural world everywhere pointed to its divine origin.[42] Not only the starry heavens above, he said, but "all the rest of creatures do in their courses fight against the atheist, by supplying an unprejudiced considerer of them with weapons fit to overthrow his impious error." The complex workings of animal and especially human bodies were so astounding that it was almost impossible for those who had never witnessed a dissection to imagine "how much excellent workmanship" was contained in them. The design of the most inconsiderable living creatures far excelled anything human ingenuity had ever able to produce. No watch or clock was "in any way comparable, for exquisiteness of mechanism, to the body of even an ass or a frog." As an exuberant Cotton Mather proclaimed in 1721 near the end of his treatise

---

41. Barker, *Natural Theology*, 28–29, 30; Charnock, *Existence and Attributes of God*, 1:60–61; Bates, *Considerations of the Existence of God*, 33–34; Also see Ames, *Substance of Christian Religion*, 73–74; Boyle, *Disquisition about the Final Causes of Natural Things* (1688) (*Works*, 5:429-31).

42. *DNB*, 7:104; Hunter (ed.), *Boyle by Himself and his Friends*, lxxii, 48, 67.

on nature, "*Atheism* is now for ever chased and hissed out of the World, every thing in the World concurs to a Sentence of *Banishment* upon it."[43]

Few theologians of the time developed this theme to greater effect than John Howe, an English Presbyterian who was Oliver Cromwell's domestic chaplain from 1656 to 1659 and thereafter a minister at Great Torrington until his ejection in 1662 upon refusing the Act of Uniformity. Adorned with wit and occasional splashes of brilliant satire, Howe's *Living Temple* (1675) was perhaps the most sophisticated and polished treatise on natural theology published in the English language during the seventeenth century. It anticipated and attempted to answer many of the objections that would later be posed by the skeptical philosopher and historian David Hume (1711–76), and Howe managed to pull it off in such a manner that he was able to delve into contemporary European cosmogony and the more obscure points of the theistic proofs without making the book inaccessible to the common reader. In fact, he included a sort of plain-man's summary of his arguments, which he prefaced with an encouraging directive to uneducated readers to remember their noble endowment of a rational mind and not succumb to mental sloth or impatience: "Do not despair as not to make an attempt; you know not the strength of your own mind till you have tried it."[44]

Apologetic use of the divine-design metaphor of a clock goes back as far as Cicero, and the related metaphor of a watch receives a passing mention as early as the 1620s in John Preston's sermons.[45] But Howe was— so far as I have been able to tell—the first English writer to employ the watch analogy in the rhetorical narrative style that would later appear in the Dutch scientist and mathematician Bernard Nieuwentyt's (1654–1718) widely read *Religious Philosopher* (1714, trans. 1718–19), the likely source for the identical argument in William Paley's *Natural Theology* (1802).[46]

---

43. Boyle, *Usefulness of Natural Philosophy*, First Part (1663) (*Works*, 2:56); Boyle, *Of the High Veneration Man's Intellect Owes to God* (*Works*, 5:136); Cotton Mather, *Christian Philosopher*, 308; also see p. 212: "O *Unbelief*, I command an *eternal Silence* to thee!"

44. Howe, *Living Temple* (*Works*, 1:200–212, quotation 201).

45. Cicero, *Nature of the Gods*, 2.87; Preston, *Sermons Preached Before his Majestie*, 70.

46. LeMahieu, *The Mind of William Paley*, 60; Nieuwentyt, *The Religious Philosopher: Or, the Right Use of Contemplating the Works of the Creator*, trans. John Chamberlayne, 1:xlv–xlvii. The original Dutch title of the work was *Het regt gebruik der werelt beschouwingen* (The Right Use of the Contemplation of the World, 1714). It was also translated into French and German and went through multiple editions. Paley made specific reference to Nieuwentyt in his *Natural Theology* (see chap. 9) and also listed *The Religious Philosopher* as one of many sources he had used. See Eddy, "The Rhetoric and Science

Suppose a person were shown a watch for the first time. The mere sight of its "curious workmanship" would immediately lead him to conclude that it had been designed by some intelligent being, and this apprehension would be reinforced all the more once he had been made to understand the use and purpose of a watch, how its every mechanism concurred to the end of precisely measuring and dividing time. With this preface Howe introduced an Epicurean cosmologist onto the scene:

> But now if a bystander, beholding him in this admiration, would undertake to show a profounder reach and strain of wit, and should say,—Sir, you are mistaken concerning the composition of this so much admired piece; it was not made or designed by the hand or skill of anyone; there were only an innumerable company of little atoms, or very small bodies, much too small to be perceived by your sense, that were busily frisking and plying to and fro about the place of its nativity; and by a strange chance (or a stranger fate, and the necessary laws of that motion which they were unavoidably put into, by a certain boisterous, undesigning mover,) they fell together into this small bulk, so as to compose it into this very shape and figure, and with this same number and order of parts which you now behold: one squadron of these busy particles, little thinking what they were about, agreeing to make up one wheel, and another some other, in that proportion which you see: others of them also falling, and becoming fixed in so happy a posture and situation, as to describe the several figures by which the little moving fingers point out the hour of the day, and the day of the month: and all conspired to fall together, each into its own place, in so lucky a juncture, as that the regular motion failed not to ensue which we see is now observed in it;—what man is either so wise or so foolish, (for it is hard to determine whether the excess or the defect should best qualify him to be of this faith,) as to be capable of being made [to] believe this piece of natural history? And if one should give this account of the production of such a trifle, would he not be thought in jest? But if he persist, and solemnly profess that thus he takes it to have been, would he not be thought in good earnest mad?

What "unspeakably more manifest madness," then, Howe concluded, drawing the expected analogy, should we attribute to those who "suppose this

---

of William Paley's *Natural Theology*," 9. For the history of the clock metaphor in non-apologetic religious contexts, see Otto Mayr, *Authority, Liberty, & Automatic Machinery in Early Modern Europe*, 28–101.

world, and the bodies of living creatures, to have fallen into this frame and orderly disposition of parts wherein they are, without the direction of a wise and designing cause?" How ironic and absurd, Matthew Poole added with reference to the Epicurean cosmogony, that these skeptics should balk at the mysteries and miracles of Christianity, "when the wit of man cannot devise more incredible things than those which atheistic and irreligious men do swallow."[47]

That anyone should come to such a conclusion about even the solar system was to Howe a strange thing, and doubly so on account of recent developments in astronomy that had revealed so much more of its admirable harmony and precise balance. He attributed this "philosophical deliration" to three factors. The first was a simple lack of imagination. Suppose that you were walking through the fields one day and suddenly began to witness the formation of a miniature universe in the air before your eyes; that you watched a glowing ball of fire emerge out of a small chaotic mass, and around this ball little planets taking shape, all of them endowed with regular motion and one of them adorned with trees, rivers, lakes and flowers. Would you have possibly concluded that this phenomenon was the effect of mere chance? Nor would you have so reasoned had you witnessed our own universe come into existence. We need only exercise a little imagination and transport ourselves back in time to see that we would be awestruck by the power and wisdom that could produce such a scene: "It speaks not want of evidence in the thing, but want of consideration, and of exercising our understandings, if what were *new* would not only convince but astonish; and what is *old*, of the same importance, doth not so much as convince!"[48]

A second cause of atheism (or at least of atheistic cosmogonies), Howe maintained, was plain ignorance of the wonders of the created world. If the above were true of the solar system, how much more of the various forms of life on earth. Howe gave special attention, as did most Puritans, to the human body. Here again they drew from their stock of classical learning, fondly relating how the renowned second-century Greek monotheist, physician and anatomist Galen of Pergamum could not refrain from breaking out into a hymn of praise to God when he discovered the remarkable workings of the human body.[49] Most people, said Howe, "little know or think what

---

47. Howe, *Living Temple* (*Works*, 1:43); Poole, *Seasonable Apology for Religion*, 61.

48. Howe, *Living Temple* (*Works*, 1:45–46).

49. Galen's admiration of the Deity is mentioned in Hopkins, *Exposition on the Ten Commandments* (*Works*, 1:283); Baxter, *Reasons of the Christian Religion*, 98; Barker,

prints and footsteps of a Deity" they carried around with them in their own physical frames. As a program for future endeavors, Howe recommended exactly the kind of treatise Nieuwentyt and Paley would subsequently undertake: a detailed elaboration of the marvels of the human body. For now he contented himself with a five-page overview of the matter, drawing much of his material from the Danish and French anatomists Thomas Bartholin (1616–80) and Jean Riolan II (1580–1657). Howe discussed the human hand (especially the fingers and opposable thumb), the various ways in which bones were joined together in order to allow for different types of motion, the "sundry little engines" of the eye, the digestive system, an epiglottis to prevent swallowed food from going into the windpipe, the intricate networks of our circulatory and nervous systems, and "the curious artifice of the brain," which had scarcely begun to be understood. He went on to note the astonishing phenomena that the scientist and inventor Robert Hooke (1635–1703) had recently unveiled in his *Micrographia* (1665), a landmark work that launched the field of microscopy. To contemplate these and innumerable other marvels of nature and then conclude that they were all a production of chance was to speak without any real conception of what we were affirming. Once again Howe asked his readers to exercise their imaginations and consider what their apprehension of these things would be if the covering of the human body were transparent instead of opaque, allowing us a direct view of what was going on just underneath our own skin. Who could gaze at such a fantastic scene and not exclaim with the psalmist, "I am fearfully and wonderfully made"? There was "no man sober, who would not, upon such a sight, pronounce that man mad, that should suppose such a production to have been a mere undesigned casualty." And this was to say nothing of nature's organismic powers of nutrition, growth and reproduction. The greatest machines built by human ingenuity not only paled in comparison to the machines of nature from a mechanical point of view but were inevitably subject to breakdown and decay, whereas the divinely constructed organisms of nature were able to maintain and reproduce themselves. The Oxford bishop Samuel Parker (1640–88) had well noted, Howe concluded, the absurdity of those who would not hesitate

---

Natural Theology, 165; Charnock, *Existence and Attributes of God*, 1:64; Lee, *Joy of Faith*, 217–18; Increase Mather, *Existence and Omniscience of God*, 11; Cotton Mather, *Reasonable Religion*, 13; Willard, *Compleat Body of Divinity*, 40. Cf. Galen, *On the Usefulness of the Parts of the Body*, 3.10 (vol. 1, p. 189); also see 17.1 (vol. 2, pp. 728–32).

to admire and praise the skill that went into a mere statue or painting of a man, and yet failed to do the same when it came to the real thing.[50]

After elaborating on the human body, Howe moved on to discuss the intellectual and emotional capacities of the mind. This transition was typical of Puritan natural theology. Barker observed that we were apt to miss this "more sublime part of Man" if we did not seek out models of human excellence, and he accordingly directed his readers "not to take the *measure of the Soul* from such that so debase it, but rather from them in whom it had its best improvements." Looking upon such specimens, commented Thomas Adams, we would surely be constrained to confess that "all the creation hath not more wonder in it, than is in man." Howe likened humanity to "stately ruins" bearing "this doleful inscription—HERE GOD ONCE DWELT." That there existed a creature "that can think, understand, deliberate, argue, &c.," was a fact concerning which there was no doubt. It was also certain that this creature was not eternal or self-made. The great question facing us, therefore, was "*Whose image* the thing produced bears, Or *which* it more resembles; *Stupid, senseless, inactive matter* . . . or the *active, intelligent Being*, whom we affirm the cause of all things?" The phenomenon of a knowing, feeling, intelligent mind stood in such contrast to bare material substance that to affirm that the former arose entirely from the latter, "as the sole and only cause of it," was almost equivalent to saying that something could arise from nothing.[51]

Howe was by this point well acquainted with Descartes' philosophy and its argument (against the medieval-Aristotelian view) that only human beings possessed souls and the power of thought, and that physical mechanism could fully account for every other form of activity in nature. He was also aware of an opinion that would soon be expressed by the philosopher John Locke (1632–1704), namely that while matter could not of itself give birth to mind, it was nevertheless conceivable that the power of thought could be impressed upon it—i.e., that matter was not, as Descartes' rigid

---

50. Howe, *Living Temple* (*Works*, 1:46–53, 156; quotations 51, 50, 49). Cf. Psalm 139:14. Parker, *Tentamina physico-theologica de Deo*. Parker probably derived this analogy from Galen, *On the Usefulness of the Parts of the Body*, 17.1 (vol. 2, pp. 726–27). Hooke, *Micrographia*. Hooke remarked in his preface (p. iv) that the microscope would do for the earth what the telescope had done for the heavens, and that with the aid of this new invention we were now discovering that there existed in the micro-world "almost as great a variety of Creatures, as we were able before to reckon up in the whole *Universe* itself."

51. Barker, *Natural Theology*, 167, 169; Adams, *Meditations Upon the Creed* (*Works*, 3:140); Howe, *Living Temple* (*Works*, 1:225, 64, 80).

ontological distinction between *res cogitans* and *res extensa* had supposed, by definition incapable of thought.⁵² He seemed to recognize, moreover, what could result if the Cartesian view of nature were stripped of this axiom, namely a natural philosophy in which the entire human person could be reduced to a *l'homme-machine* (man-machine), just as Descartes had reduced every animal function to a *bête-machine* (beast-machine) and all non-cognitive human functions to a *l'homme-machine*.

Howe admired Descartes' genius and appreciated his stated motivation for this *bête-machine* theory, namely to reinforce the doctrine of the soul's immortality by sharply distinguishing between animal and human life, but he considered this rationale "a great deal more pious than it is cogent," since there were other ways of avoiding that danger. "Machine" was a most inept designation for animals, for animals possessed the power of sensation, spontaneous motion, and even "the several passions of love, fear, anger, &c., whereof we find so evident indications in brute creatures," none of which were characteristic of machines. No adequate account could be given of these phenomena unless we supposed "a *living principle*, call that by what name you will," soul or otherwise. As for the idea that matter could be made capable of thought, Howe termed it a "misapprehension" but did not consider it terribly objectionable so long as one did not hold that matter could realize such a potential by the mere evolution of its own resources. But however misguided such notions might be, Howe did not consider either Descartes' *bête-machine* or Locke's matter-made-capable-of-thought as a threat to theism. On the contrary, he said, employing a line of reasoning that would reappear again and again in the later history of natural theology and especially in the post-Darwin period, natural philosophers could de-soul the natural world all they wanted: it only added to the staggering marvel of its so-called machinery and made it all the more impossible to account for its origin without God, since "There is the more manifest need of his hand to heighten dull matter, to a qualifiedness for performances so much above its nature."⁵³

---

52. Locke expressed this view in his *Essay Concerning Human Understanding* (IV. iii.6, IV.x.10). It was not published until 1690, however, fifteen years after Howe's *Living Temple*. Howe may been acquainted with Locke's opinion through personal or second-hand acquaintance with Locke, who had written an early draft of the *Essay* in 1671, or he may have had someone else in mind who had made this same point, since he did not specifically mention Locke when discussing it.

53. Howe, *Living Temple* (*Works*, 1:55–80; quotations 58–59, 76–77). Cf. Descartes, *Discourse on Method*, Part 5 (*Philosophical Essays and Correspondence*, 73). Also see

The third cause of atheism Howe identified was the short-sightedness of those who contented themselves with a knowledge of the workings of nature without proceeding further to inquire into their origin. The regular exposure to these phenomena afforded by their scientific learning dulled their sense of wonder, so that "because they can give a very punctual account *that things are so*, they think it now not worth the considering *how they come to be so*." Such persons often remained agnostic because they had never seen a miracle performed, being ignorant all the while of the miracles that were right underneath their scientific nose: "We vainly hunt with a lingering mind after miracles; if we did not more vainly mean by them nothing else but *novelties*, we are compassed about with such; and the greatest miracle is that we see them not."[54]

Howe argued that in the last analysis, the very most that atheists could claim for their "forlorn cause" in the face of all this evidence was a mere logical possibility that "things *might be* as they are" if there were no God. And such slender odds, he maintained, were of no consequence given their own "wild, extravagant suppositions" regarding how the world came to be, which even "if they were admitted *possible*," were so unlikely that they demanded a credulity unlike anything ever dreamed of by the contrary hypothesis. If one adopted such a rule of judgment as a guide in the ordinary affairs of life he would be deemed a madman, for there were "thousands of things not altogether impossible, which yet he would be concluded all together out of his wits" who would believe them. It was not bare logical possibility but the preponderance of evidence that was to determine our assent, and on these grounds the case between theism on the one hand and atheism on the other was easily decided. This appeal to the generally accepted rules of evidence was a common theme in Puritan apologetics.[55]

Descartes' letter to Henry More in this volume, pp. 292–97. For a later Puritan treatment of Cartesian physics, see John Ray, *Wisdom of God Manifested in the Works of the Creation*, Part I, 23–45.

54. Howe, *Living Temple* (*Works*, 1:51, 53). The Newtonian philosopher and apologist Samuel Clarke (1675–1729) would later make the same argument in an unpublished letter replying to the question of why God did not perform miracles more often in order to make his existence more evident: "No Miracle is (in Truth) a stricter Proof of the Being of God, than are the principal Works of Nature, which require the very same Power to effect them, as any Miracle does; & tis nothing but mere Custom and careless inattentiveness, which makes men think continued Works not to be the Effects of the great Power as occasional ones." Quoted in James Dybikowski, "Natural Religion," 3:145.

55. Howe, *Living Temple* (*Works*, 1:124–27, quotation 124). For parallel examples regarding the rules of evidence, see Hopkins, *Exposition on the Ten Commandments*

Howe concluded his argument by remarking that quite apart from its irrationality, atheism had nothing to commend it from the point of view of aesthetics. It stripped the human race of its dignity, robbed us of heavenly consolation against the miseries of life, blighted the joy of philosophy, and left its adherents uncertain at the hour of death as to whether they were on the threshold of non-existence or divine punishment: "Atheism clothes the world in black, and draws a dark and duskish cloud over all things; doth more to damp and stifle all relishes of intellectual pleasure, than it would of sensible to extinguish the sun."[56] The natural theology of Puritans, however, was not without its own dark clouds.

(*Works*, 1:289–90); Barker, *Natural Theology*, 48; Bates, *Considerations of the Existence of God*, 235–36; Bates, *Divinity of the Christian Religion Proved*, 167; Charnock, *Misery of Unbelievers* (*Works*, 4:324); Baxter, *Unreasonableness of Infidelity*, 1:33; 2:34–35, 37–38, 55–56; 4:27, 32; Baxter, *Reasons of the Christian Religion*, 310, 328, 340, 416; Baxter, *More Reasons for the Christian Religion*, 154–55.

56. Howe, *Living Temple* (*Works*, 1:125).

6

Providence, Evil, and Immortality

> "So in all the beauty of [the world], we read our Maker's goodness; in all the deformity of it, our own badness."
>
> —Thomas Adams, 1629

> "If we only regard things as they pass in the sensible World, we shall be in danger of being over-tempted to Atheism."
>
> —William Bates, 1676

Puritans were not unaware of the one seemingly great thing that could be brought forward in favor of atheism, namely the existence and especially prevalence of evil in the world. This was, as we have seen, among the elementary questions of natural theology that Abraham Pierson included in *Some Helps for the Indians*. Indeed, the Puritan doctrine of providence made the problem a far more pressing one for them than for some of their contemporaries and for most modern theologians. Believing that God had "foreordained whatsoever comes to pass" made it easier for them, as I have argued, to reconcile providence with the idea of a physical world largely governed by natural law. But it also meant that whatever transpired in the theatre of nature and in human history had to finally be traced through its secondary causes to the sovereign determination of a God who had decided that it should be so. Like virtually every theologian in the history of Christianity, Puritans rejected the notion that God was the author of evil, but they did not hesitate to affirm that God both permitted and foreordained its original entry into the world and directed its every movement by a "powerful bounding," so that while the "sinfulness" of evil actions proceeded "only from the creature," the actions themselves were exactly what God had decreed.[1]

Puritans did not believe that the power of contrary choice was an essential component of human freedom, so they could not explain the entrance of evil into the world, as some theologians have, by appealing to a divine gift of free will that in the very nature of the case demanded such a risk. The cause of man's fall was indeed "his abuse of free will," said William Ames, but this abuse, he added, could have been prevented had God not withheld the "strengthening and confirming grace by which the act of sinning might have been hindered."[2] God could have rendered human beings incapable of doing evil, yet they still would have been free; and his sovereign grace could likewise transform at any moment every devil and fallen sinner into a sinless saint without in any way compromising their freedom. After all, angels and the saints in heaven were no longer subject to the possibility of defecting to sin, and they were no less free for this benefit. Moreover, God himself was incapable of evil, yet still most free.

The essence of a free act did not therefore lie in one's ability to choose the opposite, but in one's self-conscious desire for the thing chosen. This philosophy of human freedom was articulated by Augustine (354-430 AD) during the Pelagian controversy; subsequently adopted in the Middle Ages by Thomas Aquinas and during the Reformation by Calvin, Luther, Zwingli, Bullinger, Peter Martyr Vermigli, and others; and it would eventually be developed with unprecedented philosophical precision in Jonathan Edwards' (1703-58) *Freedom of the Will* (1754). It allowed rational beings incapable of sin—whether divine, angelic or human—to be worthy of praise for their good actions, and it also meant that fallen human beings and devils who apart from the intervention of divine grace were no longer capable of choosing the good could still be held responsible for their evil actions. Moreover, choices could be predetermined and free (i.e., not coerced) at the same time.[3] The upshot of all this for Puritan natural theology was that

1. *Westminster Confession of Faith*, 5.4. Also see 3.1, and note in 3.3-4 the distinction between the "predestination" of the elect to salvation and the "foreordination" of the reprobate to perdition. Cp. Calvin, *Institutes*, 2.4.2: "Therefore we see no inconsistency in assigning the same deed to God, Satan, and man."

2. Ames, *Marrow of Theology*, 1.11.11 (p. 114).

3. See, e.g., Hopkins, *Discourse upon Providence* (*Works*, 3:383); Ames, *Marrow of*

both the advent and continuance of human wickedness were ultimately traceable to God's free decision.

As for natural evils, no one familiar with Puritan sermons will need to be told how these were handled. The miseries of human life, whether they stemmed from the evil deeds of others or from nature, were manifestations of the divine curse on the world for sin. As Thomas Adams put it:

> When we see any ataxy or deformity in the creatures, let us look back to the apostasy of our parents, and confess in the sorrow of our hearts, that our wretched sins have defiled heaven and earth, and drawn a curse upon the whole fabric of nature. As a man lets a well furnished house to a careless and sluttish tenant, whose uncleanness defiles it. So in all the beauty of it, we read our Maker's goodness; in all the deformity of it, our own badness.[4]

Since everyone was born a sinner and continued to sin every day, man's natural condition was a damnable one, and the worst of his calamities were far less than the eternal punishment merited by his sin. In the context of seventeenth-century Christianity, there was of course nothing unusual about such an assertion, harsh as it may sound to modern ears—theistic and atheistic alike. What distinguished Puritanism in this regard, however, was not only the prominent place it accorded this teaching, so that its ministers routinely preached divine wrath and hell-fire with the goal of awakening parishioners out of their nominal Christianity and bringing them to sincere repentance and true godliness, but also its strong emphasis on the difficulty of this transition from formal religiosity to genuine spiritual experience. Being "born again," to use the language of the New Testament, was no easy affair in Puritanism. There was a wide variation among Puritans regarding the degree to which these themes were pronounced and the extent to which they were balanced by a presentation of divine mercy and goodness. But all Puritan preachers and most of their parishioners were well versed in this sober side of the human encounter with God.[5] While scholars have

---

Theology, 1.26.28 (p. 159). For a sampling of Augustine, see his *On Grace and Free Will*, 20.41–21.43; *City of God*, 5.9–10, and esp. 22.30: "Are we to say that God himself is not free, because he cannot sin?" On the predestinarianism of Augustine and Aquinas and its relationship to Reformation developments, see my "Dante and the Doctrine of Original Sin."

4. Adams, *Meditations Upon the Creed* (*Works*, 3:118–19; also see p. 126).

5. The belief in predestination also played into this picture, but historians have tended to exaggerate its influence and to misunderstand its role in Puritan preaching. For the balance between divine wrath and love in Puritanism, see Cohen, *God's Caress*. The sixty-seven "relations" or "confessions" of would-be communicant members taken

been correct to point out that it is a mistake to characterize Puritanism as a gloomy movement, that mistake is not without any historical foundation. Where there is so much smoke, there often is some fire.

The problem of evil thus looked rather different in Puritan theology than it does in our modern context. Had a Puritan minister been asked why bad things happen to good people, he would likely have replied that the question needed to reverse the order of the adjectives. Increase Mather no doubt summed up the Puritan perspective when he commented that there was "so much sin committed in the earth every day, as that if God should put the government of the world into the hands of a mere creature, though endued with all the Patience of all men and Angels, he could not bear with such Indignities, but would certainly set the world on fire the next hour."[6] Given the universality of human sinfulness, the fact that there was so much suffering in the world was merely what one ought to have expected given the holiness and justice of God. Accordingly, the two great questions the problem of evil posed to Puritanism were why God had allowed evil to enter the world, and why he did not deliver everyone from its grip, seeing it was perfectly within his power to do so. Puritans believed that God's purpose in creating the world was to glorify himself—that is, to manifest to the fullest possible extent the perfections of his nature,[7] so they had to approach these questions by asking how each of these facts ultimately contributed to this end.

The standard answer to the first question was that evil had been permitted in order for God to manifest the full riches of his wisdom and goodness in redemption. The second and obviously more difficult question was only addressed infrequently and never—so far as I have been able to find—in comprehensive fashion. Puritans usually contented themselves with merely vindicating the justice of God, which they attempted to do in

---

down by Thomas Shepard are a valuable source for the religious experience of Puritan laity in New England. Fifty-one of these are in Selement and Woolley (eds.), *Thomas Shepard's Confessions*; the remaining sixteen are in McCarl, "Thomas Shepard's Relations of Religious Experience." Jesus' discourse with Nicodemus (John 3:1–10) is the biblical source of "born again" language. The idea also figures prominently in Paul's writings. See, e.g., Rom 6:4, 1 Cor 5:17, Gal 6:15.

6. Increase Mather, *The Doctrine of Divine Providence*, 19.

7. See, e.g., Perkins, *Golden Chaine* (*Workes*, 1:16); Ames, *Marrow of Theology*, 1.7.12 (p. 95); Preston, *Life Eternall*, 1:144; Adams, *Meditations Upon the Creed* (*Works*, 3:119–20); *Westminster Confession of Faith*, 3.3; *Westminster Shorter Catechism*, Q. 7; Gale, *Court of the Gentiles: Part IV*, bk. 2, chap. 9, § 1, p. 471; Charnock, *Existence and Attributes of God*, 2:228–30.

this particular by employing the answer Augustine had derived from his reading of St. Paul and handed down to medieval theologians: that since God did not owe mercy to fallen sinners, it could be withheld or bestowed at his pleasure. One can, nevertheless, piece together a Puritan reply to this greater question of how, even if selective salvation were consistent with divine justice, it could be reconciled with God's wisdom and goodness, seeing that human free will was no obstacle to universal redemption. Their answer was the same one that Thomas Aquinas had given in passing, namely that the glory of God's goodness was maximized by the display of its different aspects—his mercy in redeeming the penitent, his justice in punishing the wicked: "God wills to manifest his goodness in men, in those whom he predestines in the manner of mercy by sparing them, in those he reprobates in the manner of justice by punishing them."[8]

Baxter concurred with these doctrines but took a more sympathetic approach to the subject. It was his usual style to litter his treatises with every objection he could think of, and to express these in the strongest terms; and in reading them one can easily sense that their author was a man who knew what it was to doubt, even though, as we have seen, he never had any doubts about the existence of God. His own experience of unbelief, he said, had taught him the truth of the maxim, "*Nil tam certum quam quod ex dubio certum est*" (nothing is so certain as what after doubt is made certain);[9] and it was this orientation that made him one of the most thorough apologists in the history of Christianity. He was as much concerned to convince himself as others.

Baxter began his treatment of the problem of evil with a pointed presentation of the miseries of life. We are born in weakness and thereafter subject to innumerable anxieties, conflicts, unsatisfied desires, loneliness, poverty, pains and diseases of the body, fear of death, and at last death itself. We are troubled by enemies, rulers, children, and even our friends. Take a look at the vast panorama of humanity and one finds it "like a Dungeon of ignorance, like an Hospital of mad-men for folly and distractedness, like a

---

8. "Voluit igitur Deus in hominibus quantum ad aliquos, quos praedestinat, suam repraesentare bonitatem per modum misericordiae parcendo, et quantum ad aliquos, quos reprobat, per modum justitiae puniendo." Aquinas, *Summa Theologiae*, Ia. 23, 5, ad 3. For Puritan statements to the same effect, see Perkins, *Golden Chaine* (*Workes*, 1:95, also the diagram accompanying p. 11); Adams, *Meditations Upon the Creed* (*Works*, 3:177); Baxter, *Reasons of the Christian Religion*, 100, 388; Charnock, *Existence and Attributes of God*, 1:533.

9. Baxter, *Autobiography*, 27; *Reasons of the Christian Religion*, 365.

band of Robbers for injury and violence, like Tigers for cruelty, like snarling Dogs for contention, and, in a word, like Hell for wickedness." And as if all this were not enough, "you tell us of a Hell for most at last." Were we to conclude that a God of infinite goodness and power presided over all this? "These thoughts," he conceded, "have seriously troubled some."[10]

As in all such problems, Baxter replied, one had to begin with what was known and proceed from there. To resolve uncertainties by rejecting certainties was a sure recipe for epistemological failure. What was most certain to him, of course, was the existence of the God of classical theism—"infinite, eternal, and unchangeable, in his being, wisdom, power, holiness, justice, goodness, and truth," as the *Westminster Shorter Catechism* succinctly put it. Now since "Truth and Truth is not contradictory," it followed that there had to be a way of reconciling the existence of such a Creator with the manifest evils in the world. And indeed there was when a second certainty was brought into the picture, namely sin: "Nothing is more sure than that *God is most wise and good*; and nothing should be more easily known to us, than that *we are very blind and bad*." Indeed, the greater part of evils in the world were—*homo homini lupus*—what we ourselves inflicted on one another. The rest were what God inflicted on the human race for its sin. Although this punishment was an evil insofar as its recipients were concerned, it was good from the point of view of God's justice.[11]

But Baxter believed there was another consideration that substantially mitigated the problem of evil, namely the likely existence of a plurality of worlds. Our "narrow sight," he commented, was prone to look on a mere "spot or parcel of God's work" and then judge the whole "according to the particular interest of that parcel." Baxter was in fact among the first English writers to argue strongly for a plurality of worlds, though he has been overlooked by scholars who have treated the history of the idea.[12] John Howe and Cotton Mather were two other Puritans who subscribed to it, and Matthew Henry was enthusiastically open to the idea as well; but unlike Baxter they did not employ it in the context of theodicy.[13]

10. Baxter, *Reasons of the Christian Religion*, 97–98.

11. *Westminster Shorter Catechism*, Q. 4; Baxter, *Reasons of the Christian Religion*, 96–99 (quotation 96); Baxter, *Gods Goodness Vindicated*, 43.

12. Crowe, *The Extraterrestrial Life Debate, 1750–1900*; Dick, *Plurality of Worlds*.

13. Baxter, *Reasons of the Christian Religion*, 99; Howe, *Discourse Concerning the Redeemer's Dominion over the Invisible World*, 144–54; Cotton Mather, *Christian Philosopher*, 29; Henry, Commentary on Luke 15:1–10: "O the numberless beings, *for aught we know numberless worlds of beings*, that never were lost nor stepped aside from the laws

Baxter made frequent references to the writings of Pierre Gassendi (1592–1655), an influential French Catholic theologian, philosopher, and astronomer, and he embraced Gassendi's conviction that the vast regions of space were in all probability inhabited by numerous forms of intelligent life. He reminded his readers that according to Scripture, there was at least one other species of intelligent life in the universe besides ourselves, namely the angels; and he argued that considering the fecundity of divine creation on Earth and what the telescope had lately revealed regarding the staggering dimensions of space and our ignorance of even the planets within our solar system, there was good reason to suppose that there were many other such intelligent species:

> Ask any Astronomer, that hath considered the innumerable number of the fixed Stars and Planets, with their distances, and magnitude, and glory, and the uncertainty that we have whether there be not as many more, or an hundred or thousand times as many, unseen to man, as all those which we see . . . . I say, ask any man who knoweth these things, whether all this earth be any more in comparison of the whole creation, than one Prison is to a Kingdom or Empire, or the paring of one nail, or a little mole, or wart, or a hair, in comparison of the whole body. . . . I know it is a thing uncertain and unrevealed to us, whether all these Globes be inhabited or not: but he that considereth, that there is scarce any uninhabitable place on earth, or in the water, or air, but men, or beasts, or birds, or fishes, or flies, or worms and moles do take up almost all, will think it a probability so near a certainty, as not to be much doubted of, that the vaster and more glorious parts of the Creation are not uninhabited; but that they have Inhabitants answerable to their magnitude and glory . . . . I make no question but our number to theirs is not one to a million at the most.

Now for all we knew, mankind and the once angelic demons might be the only fallen creatures among all the intelligent species in such a universe; and if this were so, theodicy would suddenly be cast in a quite different light. Baxter invited his readers to reflect on what their apprehension of the problem of evil would be if they knew that God intended to save the entire human race and damn only the devils. While the Bible would not allow that idea, the scenario was analogous to, indeed surpassed by, what might in fact be the case if the universe were populated with myriads of upright beings. How would we view the problem of evil, for instance, if we knew

---

and ends of their creation!" (emphasis mine).

that only one out of every hundred thousand or hundred million intelligent creatures would be damned, "and that only for *final impenitency* in the contempt of the mercy which would have saved him." One could object, Baxter conceded, that the earth might after all be the only planet on which intelligent life existed, and that even if there were innumerable others, they might contain as many hell-bound souls as our own. To the first of these objections, he repeated the aforementioned reasons for believing that it was far more probable than not that there were in fact other worlds. To the second, he answered that if we considered "how much the superior Orbs do in glory excel this dirty Earth," the prospect of their being equally sinful and miserable was an unlikely hypothesis. In any case, the fact remained that we had insufficient grounds for concluding that there was as much evil in the universe at large as in our little corner of it, much less for rejecting the existence or goodness of God.[14]

After all this, however, there still remained for Puritanism the question of why divine judgments and blessings seemed to be inequitably distributed, and especially why those who had been redeemed by Christ and forgiven their sins came up with the short end of God's providential stick as often as if not more frequently than irreligious souls. Observing that "the works of God sometimes seem to run counter with his word: so that there is a dark and amazing intricacy in the ways of providence," Increase Mather remarked that

> Not only wise but good men have sometimes been put to a nonplus here. The God of Truth, hath in his word said, it shall go well with the righteous, and ill with the wicked, and yet he so orders things by his providence, as that the righteous see nothing but miserable days in this world, and the vilest of men are at the same time in the highest prosperity. *Jer.* 12. 1. The Pen-man of the seventy-third Psalm was sadly puzzled, and had like to have lost himself with amazement at this Thing.[15]

---

14. Baxter, *Reasons of the Christian Religion*, 99–101, 249–50, 388–93 (quotations 388–89, 390, 392). Also see his *Gods Goodness Vindicated*, 29–35, where he repeated the argument and commented, "Though some peevish men have wrangled at what I said of this . . . I am so far from flattering their self conceited wisdom that I will say it over again" (30).

15. Increase Mather, *Doctrine of Divine Providence*, 43. Also see Charnock, *Discourse on Providence* (*Works*, 1:30–31, 38). Compare a remark from Luther's *Bondage of the Will*: "Behold! God governs the external affairs of the world in such a way that, if you regard and follow the judgment of human reason, you are forced to say, either that there is no God, or that God is unjust; as the poet said: 'I am often tempted to think there are

Puritans sought to answer this riddle partly by pointing to the disciplinary and purgative functions of suffering in the lives of the righteous, and partly by connecting it to another key component of natural theology: the belief in an afterlife. Since God was holy and just, there had to be a state beyond death in which the inequities of the present state of things would be rectified. This ancient resolution of the problem of providence, of course, was capable of being reversed. Why not conclude that there was no God at all, or at least no providence, since his supposed government of human affairs seemed almost non-existent sometimes? Indeed, William Bates conceded that "if we only regard things as they pass in the sensible World, we shall be in danger of being over-tempted to Atheism."[16]

The Puritans' first reply to this can easily be anticipated in light of their extreme confidence in the ability of reason to demonstrate the existence of God. Hardly anything in the world was more evident than that there was a God, and it would accordingly be a most injudicious procedure to resolve one uncertainty by rejecting the "most certain, intelligible verity among all the whole world of Certainties," as Baxter called the existence of God.[17] But what of the second possibility, that there was indeed a Deity, but not such a one as had any interest in or at least interaction with human

---

no gods.' See the great prosperity of the wicked, and by contrast the great adversity of the good.... Hereupon some of the greatest minds have fallen into denying the existence of God, and imagining that Chance governs all things at random." *Luther: Selections From His Writings*, (ed. Dillenberger), 201. Calvin similarly comments that "when we consider the matters of this world, it is a very hard thing to persuade [ourselves] that God doth guide them as he thinketh best.... We begin to doubt, and enter into terrible thoughts, saying: What? if God had any care of the world, and things were guided by him, should we not see another manner of government than we do?... God so letteth loose the bridle to the wicked that a man would think their life happy: contrarywise we see the good and godly to be tormented, and to be in pain and anguish, so as a man would think that God had forsaken them, and that he thought no more of them." John Calvin, *Sermons on Job*, serm. 81, on Job 21:16–21, p. 379.

16. Bates, *Considerations of the Existence of God*, 207. Like Increase Mather (*Doctrine of Divine Providence*, 27), Bates went on (p. 209), to recount the tale of the fifth century BC Athenian poet Diagoras, who was "hardened in irreclamable Atheism" after seeing a servant whose theft he had personally witnessed stand unharmed after thrice declaring his innocence before a statue of Zeus and declaring that the god should strike him dead with thunder if he were lying. In the margin Bates referenced an apt verse from Juvenal: "Some attribute every event to the play of fortune. / They hold that the sky revolves without a guiding spirit, / and that nature itself brings round the phases of day and year. / So without compunction they lay their hands on any altar." Juvenal, *The Satires*, 13.86–89 (p. 114).

17. Baxter, *Unreasonableness of Infidelity*, 3:276.

affairs? Puritans responded that such a notion was inconsistent with the infinite perfections of God. Omnipresence without providence, said Charnock, would be turned into "an idle careless presence ... a presence to no purpose, which cannot be imagined of God." The same was true of God's immeasurable knowledge, power, wisdom and goodness, none of which were at all compatible with the idea of a God who took no care for or interest in the world he had made; so that "to deny God this active part of his power, is to render him weak, foolish, cruel, or all."[18] Rejecting providence, said Howe, would "so maim the notion of God, as to make it quite *another thing*." And alas, he lamented, this was an all-too-common shift for those who wished there were no God but were constrained by reason to conclude otherwise. They were willing to acknowledge a Deity so long as it was not one who would meddle in their affairs or to whom they would owe any worship or affection. Worst of all, however, was the way Epicureans "complimented [God] out of this world" under cover of a mock exaltation of his transcendent majesty:

> Yet all this while they court him at a great rate, and all *religion* is taken away under pretence of *great piety*. Worship they believe he cares not for, because he is full and needs nothing. In this world he must not be, for it is a place unworthy of him. He must have had no hand in framing, nor can they think it fit he should have any in the government of it; for it would be a great disturbance to him, and interrupt his pleasures. The same thing as if certain licentious courtiers, impatient of being governed, should address themselves to their prince in such a form of speech, that it is beneath him to receive any homage from them, [as] it would too much debase [his] majesty; that his dominions afford no place fit for his residence, and therefore it would be convenient for him to betake himself into some other country, that hath better air and accommodation for delight; that diadems and sceptres are burdensome things, which therefore if he will quit them, he may wholly give up himself to ease and pleasure.

What real connection could religion have to such a God, who had quite abandoned the world and had no desire for communion with human beings created in his image? God being in his own essence an inscrutable mystery, our chief concern in knowing him was to find out what he was "*in relation to* us." If the answer to that question was essentially nothing or next to nothing, in what way could God be the object of religion? Charnock

---

18. Charnock, *Existence and Attributes of God*, 1:393, 2:88 (also see 1:469).

summed up the Puritan perspective on the issue. Denying providence, he asserted, "destroys all religion."[19]

Scholars familiar with the various brands of ancient Stoicism will be aware that there was a pious form of a-providential, or rather semi-providential theology to which the Puritans could have but did not address themselves, perhaps largely out of ignorance. One thinks especially of the writings of Epictetus (c. AD 35–c. 135), which made a tremendous impression on Herman Witsius.[20] Epictetus' religion reduced providence to an all-embracing divine determinism. He held that God had predestined the entire course of history (with the seeming exception of human choices), but he did not think that God continued to intervene in human affairs, nor did he believe that the absence of this intervention made impossible a life of praise for and communion with the Maker of the universe. God's connection with nature and history was of an eternal rather than historical character, and a life of piety accordingly consisted in praising God's goodness and cheerfully submitting to a divine will that had ordered all things to the common and ultimate good of the universe.[21]

The problem of providence was, as Puritans themselves confessed, the weak link in their natural theology—or as they would have rather put it, the least strong link. I have suggested that one reason for the doubts to which both lay and clerical Puritans were subject was their craving for intense religious experience. While in the throes of unbelief, Thomas Shepard compensated for the absence of the Holy Spirit ("I did not feel it in me") by impressing upon himself a sense of the immanence of God in nature and in the everyday affairs of life: "I also began to see, nay, feel, God in fire, meat, every providence, and that his many providences and creatures are but God's hands and fingers whereby he takes hold of me, etc."[22] My guess is that a second and related cause of religious doubting

---

19. Howe, *Living Temple* (*Works*, 1:143, 134, 141, 144–45); Charnock, *Discourse on Providence* (*Works*, 1:39)

20. See Witsius, *Sacred Dissertations on the Lord's Prayer*, 200–201; Witsius, *Sacred Dissertations on the Apostles' Creed*, iv.9, v.19, viii.99, xiii.17, 18, 21 (vol. 1, pp. 76–77, 114–15, 226, 363–68).

21. See *The Discourses of Epictetus*. Christopher Gill's characterization (pp. xxi, xxii) of Epictetus' Deity as impersonal is undermined by numerous passages in this volume, among them 1.16.15–21 (p. 40), which Witsius hailed as "devout," "pious" and "truly admirable" (*Dissertations on the Apostles' Creed*, viii.99 [1:226–27]).

22. Journal entries for December 10–11, 1641, in *Autobiography and Journal* (ed. McGiffert), 137–38.

among some Puritans was their occasional inability to discover any rhyme or reason in the providential workings of a God whom they believed to be in complete control of every detail in the world. We have seen that this was what tempted Cotton Mather to deism, and remarks like Bates' "if we only regard things as they pass in the sensible World, we shall be in danger of being over-tempted to Atheism," and Increase Mather's "Not only wise but good men have sometimes been put to a non-plus here," may well have reflected the experience of a number of their contemporaries. And indeed, no one acquainted with the doleful laments of Job and the ancient Hebrew poets—as the psalm-singing Puritans certainly were—will need to be told that the question "Where is God?" was hardly a new one in the history of religious experience.

Nevertheless, Puritans were certainly not the only Christians who were serious about religious experience, nor were they the first to believe in an all-determining God. Besides, a perceived absence of divine providence would have presented difficulties to any system that retained a prominent role for ongoing divine intervention in human affairs. This difficulty was naturally heightened by the universal providentialism of Puritans, but it was by no means entirely dependent on that tenet. So the reasons I have proposed to account for their struggles with unbelief can only provide part of the explanation. The remainder has to be sought in the broader and difficult question of what caused the emergence of atheism in the western world during the seventeenth century. One would also want to know whether these doubts were peculiar to or at least more prominent in the religious experience of Puritans, or whether Puritans were simply more willing to acknowledge them than some of their contemporaries were. Both of these inquiries, of course, lie beyond the scope of this study. Had Puritans themselves been asked to account for the phenomenon of atheism, most would have probably replied by pointing to the debilitating effects of original sin on mankind's capacity for communion with God. As the English Puritan and biblical commentator John Trapp (1601–69) put it, only "one in whom common reason is faded and dried up" could be an absolute atheist; "And yet this witless, sapless, senseless creature, this wild-ass colt, is every mother's child of us by nature."[23]

---

23. Trapp, *Mellificium Theologicum*, 6:844. This work was first published as an appendix to Trapp's *Commentary or Exposition upon All the Epistles and the Revelation of John the Divine* (London, 1647).

Matthew Barker was one Puritan who did attempt to delve further into the problem of atheism, and much of his analysis sounds strikingly similar to what several historians and sociologists of religion have proposed as an explanation for the emergence of atheism. Some of his explanations were the standard ones. Pride, guilt, sensuality, and the natural estrangement of the heart from God were the latent seeds of atheism which given the proper environment would inevitably come to full flower. Unbelief was also driven by a simple failure to reflect on reality. People were "so *immersed* in the Affairs of the World" that they could "find no time to sit down and consider" the great questions of human existence or even the wonders of nature. There was also the compounded effect of practical atheism. The more people observed "how little the generality of Mankind do take notice of [God]," the more they were "tempted to think thereby there is no such Being," for "actions carry more *evidence* to the World than words, and so *Atheism* is propagated by Example." And of course there was the problem of providence. The "strange *administration* of things in the World," he observed, often made it difficult even for those who wanted to believe: "Hence Men conclude there is no *Government* of the World; and if so, then no God."[24]

But Barker also noted some new developments. An increased awareness and understanding of natural causes displaced for some the idea of a world continually governed by its Creator, or at the very least provided an explanatory framework sufficient for those disinclined to inquire into the origin and reason of the framework itself. Machiavellianism taught politicians to employ religion merely as an instrument of power. The emergence of religious pluralism did further damage:

> Again, *Atheism* ariseth in the hearts of men from the *diversity* of *Opinions* that have been, and still are, in the World about Religion. . . . As it fared in *Philosophy*, the many differences of Opinions therein, made some at last turn *Scepticks*, and doubt of everything. And so in *Divinity*, according to the known and true *Apothegm*, *Theologia Sceptica tandem exit in Atheismo*; Sceptical Divinity ends in Atheism. And men by seeing the various *Judgments* that are about Religion, begin to question everything, and fix in nothing, till at last they settle in Atheism.

Pluralism also meant that instead of unifying human society, religion now divided it, especially among those who took their faith seriously—"which makes Men take great offence, and think disdainfully of Religion that hath

---

24. Barker, *Natural Theology*, 48, 49, 42–43.

such Effects attending it." Last but not least, opined Barker, was the banishment of superstition and the transition from the rituals and picturesque ceremonies of Roman Catholicism to the bare simplicity of an iconoclastic Protestantism. The general drift of Protestantism, he thought, was to diminish the role of popular religion and nominal Christianity and force people to choose between a serious faith and no faith at all:

> When the Gospel comes, it doth detect and condemn *Superstition*, which in many is the whole of their Religion. And when that is taken away, their Religion, and respect to a *Deity* doth fall with it.... Now when such Superstitious fear is removed by the knowledge of the Gospel, and no other true fear of God planted in the room of it, the Sense of a *Deity* will decay and decline in such a Soul.... Some put all their Religion in a Form, or a *Ceremony*, and when that is taken away, what have they more?... [I]n the *Pictures* and *Images* of the Romish Church... some kind of Reverence and Adoration is maintained in the Hearts of the People.... When all a man's religion is upheld by these Crutches, if you remove them, it falls to the ground.[25]

The phenomenon of religious pluralism, of course, was not about to go away. Just as English Puritans saw their last hopes of an exclusive national establishment vanish with the Restoration of 1660, and after them Anglicans with the 1689 Act of Toleration, so too the Puritan hegemony in New England began to break down in the 1680s. Freedom of religion and the geographical expanse of the new world not only opened the way for any and every kind of sect, but finally enabled religious skeptics to express their views openly and in print rather than confining them to private conversations in pubs and coffee-houses. When Protestant intellectuals who encountered these challenges in the eighteenth century insisted that Christianity was a reasonable religion, that science was so far from being an enemy to belief that it was on the contrary among its greatest allies, that the light of nature formed the ordinary prolegomena to the light of faith, and that on a level playing field of reason alone the evidences for special revelation could defeat deism, and all the more could natural theology overcome atheism—it was nothing new. That mold had long since been cast by their Puritan forbears.

---

25. Barker, *Natural Theology*, 39–60 (quotations pp. 45–46, 58, 58–59).

Appendix 1

The Role of John Locke in the History of Natural Theology and Evidentialism

JOHN LOCKE (1632–1704) is often identified as a pivotal figure in the history of evidentialism and even natural theology in the English-speaking world. The extent of his personal interest in religion has sometimes been questioned, but the publication of his private papers in recent years has put this matter beyond doubt. As one of his modern editors remarks, "An assuredly irreversible conclusion of these studies is the deep and pervasive influence of religion on Locke's thought," to where "his various philosophical enquiries inevitably impinge upon or lead back to theology." Indeed, Locke spent the final years of his life writing a biblical commentary, *Paraphrases and Notes on the Epistles of St. Paul*.[1]

What historians of religion have regarded as remarkable and novel in Locke are his assertions that it was reason's right to judge the credentials of divine revelation, that nothing in such a revelation could be contrary to reason, and that natural religion was the foundation on which special revelation was to be constructed. Historian Roy Porter, for instance, has given the following summation of what he terms Locke's "pathbreaking" proposal:

> Locke argued that the thinking man must be a believer, precisely because Christianity's central doctrines—belief in an omnipotent, omniscient, benevolent Creator, the duty of obeying and

---

1. John Locke, *Writings on Religion*, ed. Victor Nuovo (Oxford: Clarendon, 2001), xvi, lvii. Locke had completed the first five epistles of the English Bible (Romans, First and Second Corinthians, Galatians, Ephesians) when he died in 1704. They were published separately between 1705 and 1707 and collected in volume three of the second and third editions of *The Works of John Locke, Esq.* (1722, 1727).

Appendix 1: The Role of John Locke

worshipping Him, and so forth—were all perfectly consonant with reason and experience. Being a Christian was a rational commitment; but the reasonable Christian was not obliged to accept features of traditional faith at which his reason baulked. No irrational leaps of faith were required.[2]

This characterization of Locke is correct except for the fact that it overlooks, as we will see, Locke's endorsement of the critical theological category "above reason." But it should now be clear that by seventeenth-century standards, whether Puritan or Anglican, these views of the role of reason in religion were anything but "pathbreaking." Indeed, they were entirely conventional. Locke certainly believed that nothing in Scripture could be "contrary" to reason, but so did his contemporaries, the overwhelming majority of whom would likewise have shared his confidence in the rational grounds of theism and Christianity. Indeed, about the only criticism Locke received on this score from the orthodox corner was that he had compromised the argument from universal consent and that his suggestion that matter might through divine power be made capable of thought had negated one of the chief philosophical arguments for the immortality of the soul. Locke in fact conceded this latter criticism and replied that it was to special rather than natural revelation that the honor of firmly securing this doctrine was to be credited.[3] If anything, then, Locke was chastised for *detracting* from natural theology, not for unduly enlarging its bounds.

Nevertheless, there was a significant controversy surrounding the anonymous publication of Locke's *Essay Concerning Human Understanding* (1690) and especially his *Reasonableness of Christianity as Delivered in the Scriptures* (1695), and this seems to be what has led to some of the mistaken views among historians about his influence on the role of reason in religion. What was all the fuss about?

---

2. Porter, *The Enlightenment*, 33. For similar assessments see May, *The Enlightenment in America*, 11; Dybikowski, "Natural Religion," 3:143; Outram, *The Enlightenment*, 39; and an early instance in David Hume (1711–76). "LOCKE seems to have been the first Christian," he has Cleanthes say to Demea, "who ventured openly to assert, that *faith* was nothing but a species of *reason*, that religion was only a branch of philosophy, and that a chain of arguments, similar to that which established any truth in morals, politics, or physics, was always employed in discovering all the principles of theology, natural and revealed." *Dialogues Concerning Natural Religion*, Part I, in Hume, *Principal Writings on Religion*, 40–41.

3. Burnet, *Remarks upon an Essay Concerning Humane Understanding*, 8–13; Locke, *Reply to the . . . Answer to his Second Letter*, 419–21, 429, 437–40, 446–51.

Appendix 1: The Role of John Locke

The answer lies in Locke's doubts about the doctrines of the atonement and especially the Trinity. It was this that brought him into controversy with some of his contemporaries. The first salvo in this battle was fired by the Calvinist Anglican cleric John Edwards (1637–1716), whose *Thoughts on Atheism* (1695), a harangue against the rising tide of Socinianism in England, charged Locke with being a closet Socinian ("he is all over Socinianized") and his *Reasonableness of Christianity* with maintaining that the only doctrine necessary for Christians to believe was that Jesus was the Messiah. Fuel was added to the fire the following year when John Toland (1670–1722) published his *Christianity Not Mysterious*, which explicitly employed Locke's philosophy of ideas to reject the doctrine of the Trinity. Toland's publication prompted a reply from the erudite bishop Edward Stillingfleet (1635–99), *A Discourse in Vindication of the Doctrine of the Trinity* (1697). Stillingfleet does not appear to have been aware that Locke was the author of *The Reasonableness of Christianity*, which had been anonymously published two years previously.[4] Hence, unlike Edwards, he did not accuse Locke of being a Socinian, and most of his treatise was directed against Toland. He did, however, devote a small part of his treatise to criticizing the theory of ideas in Locke's *Essay*.[5]

Locke did not take these criticisms lying down. To Edwards he replied in a forty-page pamphlet that he had nowhere maintained that Christians only had to believe that Jesus was the Messiah; he had simply said that this was the only belief *necessary for salvation*. Edwards was not assuaged, however. Noting a number of similarities between how Locke and the Socinians interpreted certain passages in the New Testament, he immediately attacked Locke again in his *Socinianism Unmask'd* (1696), a work of biting wit and satire to which Locke replied with a 480-page *Second Vindication*.[6] In response to Stillingfleet, Locke penned over a thousand pages exonerating his *Essay* from any necessary connection with Toland's views, defending his philosophy from various criticisms of Stillingfleet,

---

4. Both *An Essay Concerning Human Understanding* and *The Reasonableness of Christianity* were first published anonymously. Locke's authorship of the *Essay* was revealed when he appended his name and wrote an introduction for the second edition (1694), but his *Second Vindications of the Reasonableness of Christianity* (1697) remained anonymous, and it is not clear to me when it became known that Locke had written the work.

5. Edwards, *Thoughts Concerning the Several Causes and Occasions of Atheism*, 104–23 (quotation 113); Stillingfleet, *Vindication of the Doctrine of the Trinity*, 234–62.

6. [Locke], *Vindication of the Reasonableness of Christianity*; Edwards, *Socinianism Unmask'd*; [Locke], *Second Vindication of the Reasonableness of Christianity*.

Appendix 1: The Role of John Locke

and arguing back and forth about misunderstandings and misrepresentations.[7] All of this material makes for instructive if tedious reading, no small part of which is due to Locke's combative style of engagement.[8] He seems to have recognized his shortcoming in this regard and appended a little apology for his manner after reviewing the proofs of his first *Letter to the Right Reverend Edward* (1697). Nevertheless, there was little shift in the tone of the two rejoinders he wrote in response to Stillingfleet's replies; if anything it became more caustic.

Locke's main reply to Edwards concerning his *Reasonableness of Christianity*—"there is not one word of *Socinianism* in it"—was technically correct.[9] There was nothing overtly Socinian in the book, and Locke had never claimed that belief in Jesus as the Messiah was the only doctrine Christians needed to confess. He had also insisted, in good Puritan style, that this belief would avail for nothing without sincere repentance for sin. The impenitent, he said, would not "be received into the eternal bliss of his Kingdom, how much soever they believe in him." His assertion that those who had never heard the gospel could be saved if they responded to the light of nature's call to repentance was mildly controversial but (as discussed above in chapter 4) by no means outside the bounds of seventeenth-century orthodoxy, and Edwards nowhere criticized him for it.[10]

But no intelligent theologian could have failed to recognize several glaring omissions in Locke's anonymously authored book. Its very title implied a distinction between the reasonableness of Christianity *as delivered in the Scriptures* and the reasonableness of Christianity as expressed in certain theological systems; and the contents of the book indicated that it was not simply Calvinist theology that Locke was dissenting from (any number

---

7. Locke, *A Letter to the Right Reverend Edward, Lord Bishop of Worcester*; Locke, *Reply to the . . . Answer to his Letter*; Locke, *Reply to the . . . Answer to his Second Letter*. For the exact chronology of Locke's controversy with Stillingfleet, see J. R. Milton, "Locke, John (1632–1704)," in *DNB*.

8. As J. R. Milton (op. cit.) notes, the debate "revealed in public Locke's defects as a controversialist . . . the reader is offered page after page of close-range pummelling, interspersed with episodes of sarcasm and bad temper." John Edwards similarly observed Locke's "Angry fits and Passionate Ferments, which, tho he strives to palliate, are easily discernible, for he feels himself Wounded, and is not able to disguise it" (*Socinianism Unmask'd*, 3).

9. [Locke], *Vindication of the Reasonableness of Christianity*, 13. Again in the *Second Vindication*, 344: "I challenge him to shew one word of Socinianism in it."

10. [Locke], *Reasonableness of Christianity, as Delivered in the Scriptures*, 194–99, 203 (quotation), 251–54.

Appendix 1: The Role of John Locke

of Anglican divines might have applauded that move) but something much more fundamental. The most obvious clues came from what Locke left out of the treatise. He discussed at great length the office and person of Christ without once mentioning his divinity. And when, after having argued that pagans ignorant of the gospel could be saved, he took up the objection of what need there was in that case for Christ to come into the world, he enumerated all of the standard replies with the exception of the one that would have been most obvious to any orthodox theologian in England at the time, namely that without the death of Christ to atone for human sin there could have been no salvation for anyone. A theologically sensitive reader could not help but infer that Locke was skeptical, if not disbelieving, of the divinity of Christ and that he embraced the Socinian view of redemption, namely that Christ had not come as a priest to atone for sin but simply as a teacher of the human race.[11]

Regarding his debate with Stillingfleet over the connection of his *Essay* to Toland's *Christianity not Mysterious*, it is probably fair to grant Locke's denial that his philosophy lent itself in any particular way to Unitarianism.[12] The controversy would not have grown to the length and size it did had Locke complied with Stillingfleet's request that he openly declare himself a Trinitarian. But he refused to do so and merely repeated over and over again that nothing he had written bore on that question, the same method he was simultaneously pursuing in his separate controversy with Edwards. It is abundantly clear, however, to the careful reader of Locke's replies to Edwards and Stillingfleet, that while he may not have been ready to declare himself a Unitarian, he was at the very least uncertain about the doctrine of the Trinity.[13] And indeed, Locke's "Adversaria Theologica," a private note-

---

11. [Locke], *The Reasonableness of Christianity*, 251–54, 255–90 (cf. 214). Locke was also heterodox on the subject of original sin. See his "Peccatum originale" (*Writings on Religion*, 229–30); and compare the commentary on Rom 5:12–19 (a *locus classicus* for the doctrine of original sin) in his *Paraphrase and Notes on the Epistles of St. Paul* (*Works of John Locke*, 3:281–84).

12. See Biddle, "Locke's Critique of Innate Principles and Toland's Deism." John Valdimir Price similarly notes that the connection scholars have drawn between Locke's *Reasonableness of Christianity* and Toland's *Christianity Not Mysterious* is "very tenuous: while the two books have some premises in common, their conclusions are radically antithetical." "Introduction" to Toland, *Christianity Not Mysterious*, xii., n. 11.

13. The following passage, from p. 224 of Locke's final rejoinder (*Reply to the . . . Answer to his Second Letter*), which Stillingfleet's death prevented him from answering, is the best specimen of Locke's evasive yet revealing method: "My Lord, my Bible is faulty again, for I do not remember, that I ever read in it either of these Propositions, in these

Appendix 1: The Role of John Locke

book from 1694 containing his brief arguments for and against the Trinity, shows him coming down strongly on the side of the anti-Trinitarians.[14]

It was the Socinian features of Locke's theology, then, that proved controversial, not his evidentialism nor his view of the role of reason in religion. As was the case with most early Socinians and Unitarians, his objections to the Trinity were primarily based on Scriptural considerations rather than rationalistic objections to the doctrine. His *Essay* maintained the time-honored distinction between doctrines "contrary to reason" and "above reason,"[15] and Locke made it clear that doctrines falling into the latter category were to be accepted on the authority of divine revelation. As he put it in the postscript of his first letter to Stillingfleet,

> The Holy Scripture is to me, and always will be, the constant Guide of my Assent; and I shall always hearken to it, as containing infallible Truth, relating to Things of the highest Concernment. And I wish I could say, there were no Mysteries in it: I acknowledge there are to me, and I fear always will be. But where I want the Evidence of Things, there yet is Ground enough for me to believe, because God has said it: And I shall presently condemn and quit any Opinion of mine, as soon as I am shown that it is contrary to any Revelation in the Holy Scripture.[16]

---

precise Words, *There are three Persons in one Nature* [the Nicean formulation of the Trinity], or, *There are two Natures and one Person* [the Nicean formulation of the relationship between Christ's human and divine natures]. When your Lordship shall shew me a Bible wherein they are so set down, I shall then think them a good instance of *Propositions offered me out of Scripture*; till then, whoever shall say, that they are Propositions in the Scripture, when there are no such Words so put together, to be found in Holy Writ, seems to me to make a new Scripture in Words and Propositions, that the Holy Ghost dictated not. I do not here question their Truth, nor deny that they may be drawn from the Scripture: But I deny, that these very Propositions are in express Words in my Bible. For that is the only thing I deny here; if your Lordship can shew them me in yours, I beg you to do it." A similar passage occurs is in Locke's *Second Vindication*, 235.

14. John Locke, "Adversaria Theologica," in King, *The Life of John Locke*, 2:186–94.

15. Locke, *Essay Concerning Human Understanding*, IV. 18. 7 (p. 694): "There being many Things wherein we have very imperfect Notions, or none at all; and other Things, of whose past, present, or future Existence, by the natural Use of our Faculties, we can have no Knowledge at all; these, as being beyond the Discovery of our natural Faculties, and above *Reason*, are, when revealed, *the proper matter of Faith*."

16. Locke, *A Letter to the Right Reverend Edward*, 226–27.

Appendix 2

Table of Puritans Represented in this Study

Name	Dates	English/American	Subscribed to 1662 Act of Uniformity?
Adams, Thomas	1583–1652	English	n/a
Agas, Benjamin	bap. 1622, d. 1689	English	no
Allen, James	1632–1710	American	n/a
Ames, William	1576–1633	English	n/a
Ball, John	1585–1640	English	n/a
Ball, Thomas	1590–1659	English	n/a
Barker, Matthew	1619–98	English	no
Bates, William	1625–99	English	no
Baxter, Richard	1615–91	English	no
Bedford, James	?	English	no
Bolton, Robert	1572–1631	English	n/a
Boyle, Robert	1627–91	English	n/a
Capel, Richard	1586–1656	English	n/a
Cartwright, Thomas	1534/5–1603	English	n/a
Case, Thomas	bap. 1598, d. 1682	English	no
Charnock, Stephen	1628–80	English	no
Chauncy, Charles	bap. 1592, d. 1672	English-American (imig. in 1638, to Plymouth)	n/a

APPENDIX 2: TABLE OF PURITANS REPRESENTED IN THIS STUDY

Name	Dates	English/American	Subscribed to 1662 Act of Uniformity?
Cotton, John	1584–1652	English-American (imig. in 1633, to Boston)	n/a
Danforth, Samuel	?	English	no
Davenport, John	1597–1670	English-American (imig. in 1637, to New Haven, Ct.)	n/a
Eliot, John	1604–90	English-American (imig. in 1631, to Boston)	n/a
Fairclough, Samuel	1625–91	English	no
Fitch, James	1622–1702	American (Norwich, Ct.)	n/a
Flavel, John	bap. 1630, d. 1691	English	no
Gale, Theophilus	1628–79	English	no
Goodwin, Thomas	1600–80	English	no
Greenham, Richard	early 1540s–1594	English	n/a
Gurnall, William	bap. 1616, d. 1679	English	yes
Henry, Matthew	1662–1714	English	n/a
Hooker, Thomas	1586?–1647	English-American (imig. 1633, to Cambridge, then Hartford, Ct.)	n/a
Hopkins, Ezekiel	1634–90	English	yes
Howe, John	1630–1705	English	no
Hurst, Henry	1629–90	English	no
Lawrence, Edward	d. 1695	English	no
Lee, Samuel	1625?–1691	English-American (imig. 1686, to Bristol, R.I.)	no
Manton, Thomas	bap. 1620, d. 1677	English	no
Mather, Cotton	1663–1728	American	n/a
Mather, Increase	1639–1723	American	n/a

APPENDIX 2: TABLE OF PURITANS REPRESENTED IN THIS STUDY

Name	Dates	English/American	Subscribed to 1662 Act of Uniformity?
Mitchell, Jonathan	1624–68	American	n/a
Morrice, Roger	1628/9–1702	English	n/a
Norton, John	1606–63	English-American (imig. in 1635, to Boston)	n/a
Owen, John	1616–83	English	no
Pemberton, Matthew	?	English	?
Pemble, William	1591/2–1623	English	n/a
Perkins, William	1558–1602	English	no
Pierson, Abraham	bap. 1611?, d. 1678	English-American (imig. in 1640, to Boston, then Southampton, N.Y.)	n/a
Poole, Matthew	1624?–79	English	no
Preston, John	1587–1628	English	n/a
Ray, John	1627–1705	English	no
Read, Joseph	?	English	no
Richardson, Alexander	d. 1629	English	n/a
Rogers, Richard	1551–1618	English	n/a
Sangar, Gabriel	1608–78	English	no
Scudder, Henry	d. 1652	English	n/a
Shepard, Thomas	1605–49	English-American (imig. in 1633, to Boston)	n/a
Spencer, Thomas	fl. 1628–29	English	n/a
Sylvester, Matthew	1636/7–1708	English	no
Taylor, Thomas	1576–1632	English	n/a
Trapp, John	1601–69	English	yes
Tuckney, Anthony	1599–1670	English	no
Turner, John	?	English	no
Twisse, William	1577/8–1646	English	n/a

Appendix 2: Table of Puritans Represented in this Study

Name	Dates	English/American	Subscribed to 1662 Act of Uniformity?
Vincent, Thomas	1634–78	English	no
Watson, Thomas	d. 1686	English	no
Wilkins, John	1614–72	English	yes
Willard, Samuel	1640–1707	American	n/a
Willet, Andrew	1561/2–1621	English	n/a
Wright, Samuel	?	English	n/a

Bibliography

Primary Sources

Adams, Thomas. *The Main Principles of Christian Religion*. London: no printer given, 1675.

———. *The Works of Thomas Adams*. 3 vols. Edinburgh: James Nichol, 1861–66. Reprint. Eureka, CA: Tanski, 1998.

Al-Ghazali, Abu Hamid Muhammad. *The Incoherence of the Philosophers*. Translated by Michael E. Marmura. Provo, UT: Brigham Young University Press, 2002.

Allen (also Allin), James. *Man's Self-Reflection*. Boston, 1699. Originally published 1680.

———. *Thunder and Earthquake, a Loud and Awful Call to Reformation. Consider'd in a Sermon Preached at Brooklyn [Brookline], November the First, Upon a Special Fast, Occasion'd by the Earthquake, Which happen'd in the Evening after the 29th Day of October 1727. Now Published with Englargements*. 2nd ed. Boston: Printed by Gamaliel Rogers for Joseph Edwards, 1727.

Ames, William. *The Marrow of Theology*. Translated by John D. Eusden. Grand Rapids: Baker, 1997.

———. *The Substance of Christian religion*. London: Printed by T. Mabb, 1659.

———. *Technometry*. Translated by Lee W. Gibbs. Philadelphia: University of Pennsylvania Press, 1979.

Aquinas, Thomas. *Summa Contra Gentiles*. Translated by Anton C. Pegis et al. Garden City, NY: Hanover House, 1955–57. Reprint. Notre Dame, IN: University of Notre Dame Press, 1975.

———. *Summa Theologiae*. Blackfriars edition, translated by Thomas Gilby et al. 60 vols. New York: McGraw-Hill, 1964–73.

Bacon, Francis. *Essays*. Amherst, NY: Prometheus, 1995.

Ball, John. *A Short Catechism. Contayning the Principles of Religion*. London: Printed for Edward Brewster, 1645.

———. *A Short Treatise Contayning all the Principal Grounds of Christian Religion*. London: Printed for E. Brewster and George Sawbridge, 1656. This is Ball's commentary on his *Short Catechism*.

Bibliography

Barker, Matthew. *Natural theology, or, The knowledge of God from the works of creation accommodated and improved, to the service of Christianity*. London: Printed for Nathaniel Ranew, 1674.

Barnard, John. "Earthquakes under the Divine Government." In *Two Discourses Addressed to Young Persons; To which is added, A Sermon Occasioned by the Earthquake, Which was October 29. 1727*. Boston: Printed for S. Gerrish, 1727.

Bates, William. *Considerations of the Existence of God, and of the Immortality of the Soul, with the recompenses of the future state: for the cure of infidelity, and the hectick evil of the times*. London: Printed by J. D. for Brabazon Aylmer, 1676.

———. *The Divinity of the Christian Religion, proved by the evidence of reason, and divine revelation*. London: Printed by J. D. for Brabazon Aylmer, 1677.

———. *The Harmony of the Divine Attributes in the Contrivance and Accomplishment of Man's Redemption*. London: Printed by J. Darby for Nathaniel Ranew and Jonathan Robinson, 1674.

———. *The Works of the Late Reverend and Learned William Bates*. London: Printed for B. Aylmer, 1700.

Bavinck, Herman. *The Last Things: Hope for This World and the Next*. Edited by John Bolt and translated by John Vriend. Grand Rapids: Baker, 1996.

Baxter, Richard. *The Autobiography of Richard Baxter*. Edited by N. H. Keeble. London: J. M. Dent & Sons, 1974.

———. *The Certainty of Christianity Without Popery*. London: Printed for Nevil Simons, 1672.

———. *A Christian Directory*. Morgan, PA: Soli Deo Gloria, 2000. Reprinted from volume one of the four-volume edition of *The Practical Works of Richard Baxter* (London: George Virtue, 1846), with a new introduction by J. I. Packer.

———. *Gods Goodness Vindicated*. London: Printed for N. Simmons, 1671.

———. *Methodus Theologiae Christianae*. London: Typis M. White & T. Snowden, 1681.

———. *More Reasons for the Christian Religion, and No Reason Against it*. London: Printed for Nevil Simmons, 1672.

———. *The Practical Works of the Rev. Richard Baxter*, 23 vols. London: James Duncan, 1830.

———. *The Reasons of the Christian Religion. The First Part, of Godliness: Proving by Natural Evidence the Being of God, the Necessity of Holiness, and a future Life of Retribution; the Sinfulness of the World; the Desert of Hell; and what hope of Recovery Mercies intimate. The Second Part, of Christianity: Proving by Evidence Supernatural and Natural, the certain Truth of the Christian Belief: and answering the Objections of Unbelievers. First meditated for the well-setling of his own Belief; and now published for the benefit of others*. London: Printed by R. White for Fran. Titon, 1667.

———. *Reliquiae Baxterianae: Or, Mr. Richard Baxter's Narrative of The most Memorable Passages of his Life and Times. Faithfully Publish'd from his own Original Manuscript*. London: Printed for T. Parkhurst, J. Robinson, J. Lawrence, and J. Dunton, 1696. Baxter's *Autobiography*, edited by Neil Keeble, is an abridgement of this work.

———. *The Unreasonableness of Infidelity; Manifested in four discourses . . . . Written for the strengthening of the weak, the establishing of the tempted, the staying of the present Course of Apostasie, and the Recovery of those that have not sinned unto death*. London: Printed by R. W. for Thomas Underhill, 1655. The discourses are separately paginated.

BIBLIOGRAPHY

Bayle, Pierre. *Oeuvres Diverses*. 4 vols. Hildesheim: Georg Olms Verlagsbuchhandlung, 1964–68.

Bolton, Robert. *The Carnall Professor*. London: Printed for R. Dawlman, 1634.

Boyle, Robert. *The Early Essays and Ethics of Robert Boyle*. Edited by John T. Harwood. Carbondale, IL: Southern Illinois University Press, 1991.

———. *The Works*. Edited by Thomas Birch. 3rd ed. 6 vols. Hildesheim: Georg Olms Verlagsbuchhandlung, 1965. With the exception of a new introduction by Douglas McKie, this is a reprint of the second edition of *The Works of the Honourable Robert Boyle* (London, 1772).

Burnet, Thomas. *Remarks upon an Essay Concerning Humane Understanding: in a Letter Address'd to the Author*. London: Printed for M. Wooton, 1697.

Burt, John. *Earthquakes, The Effects of God's Wrath*. Newport, RI: Printed by J. Franklin, 1755.

Byles, Mather. *Divine Power and Anger displayed in Earthquakes*. Boston: Printed by S. Kneeland, 1755.

Calvin, John. *Calvin's Commentaries*. 22 vols. Grand Rapids: Baker, 1999.

———. *Institutes of the Christian Religion*. Edited by John T. McNeil. Translated by Ford Lewis Battles. Philadelphia: Westminster, 1960.

———. *Sermons on Job*. Translated by Arthur Golding. London, 1574. Reprint. Edinburgh: Banner of Truth, 1993.

Capel, Richard. *Capel's Remains . . . Left Written with his own Hand*. London: Printed by T. R. for John Bartlet, 1658.

———. *Tentations: Their Nature, Danger, Cure*. 6th ed. London: Printed by Tho. Ratcliffe for John Bartlet, 1659. Originally published 1633.

Cartwright, Thomas. *A Methodicall Short Catechisme: Containing briefly all the principall grounds of Christian Religion*. London: Printed by B. A. for Thomas Man, 1623. Originally published c. 1604.

———. *A Treatise of the Christian Religion, or, The whole body and substance of divinitie*. London: Imprinted by Felix Kyngston for Thomas Man, 1616. Originally published 1611.

Charnock, Stephen. *The Complete Works of Stephen Charnock*. 5 vols. Edinburgh: James Nichol, 1864–65.

———. *Discourses Upon the Existence and Attributes of God*. 2 vols. New York: Robert Carter & Brothers, 1853. Reprint. Grand Rapids: Baker, 1993. Originally published 1682.

Chauncy, Charles (1592–1672). *Gods mercy shewed to his people in giving them a faithful ministry and schooles of learning for the continual supplyes therof delivered in a sermon preached at Cambridg, the day after the commencement*. Cambridge, MA: Printed by Samuel Green, 1655.

Chauncy, Charles (1705–1787). *The Earth delivered from the Curse, to which it is, at present, subjected. A Sermon Occasioned by the late Earthquakes in Spain and Portugal, as well as New-England; and Preached at the Boston-Thursday-Lecture, January 22, 1756*. Boston: Printed by Edes and Gill, 1756.

———. *Earthquakes a Token of the righteous Anger of God*. Boston: Printed by Edes and Gill, 1755.

Cicero, Marcus Tullius. *De Natura Deorum*. Edited by Arthur Stanley Pease, 2 vols. Cambridge, MA: Harvard University Press, 1955.

Bibliography

———. *Cicero: Tusculian Disputations I*. Edited and translated by A. E. Douglas. Chicago: Bolchazy-Carducci, 1985

———. *The Nature of the Gods*. Translated by P. G. Walsh. Oxford: Oxford University Press, 1997.

Clarke, Samuel. *Medulla Theologiae, or The Marrow of Divinity*. London: Printed by Thomas Ratcliff for Thomas Underhill, 1659.

Cogswell, James. *The Danger of disregarding the Works of GOD: A Sermon Delivered at Canterbury, November 23, 1755. Being the next Sabbath after the late surprizing Earthquake*. New Haven: Printed by James Parker, 1755.

Colman, Benjamin. *The Judgments of Providence in the hand of Christ: His Voice to us in the terrible Earthquake. And the Earth devoured by the Curse. In four Sermons*. Boston: Printed for J. Phillips, 1727.

Cooper, William. *The Danger of People's loosing [sic] the good Impressions made by the late awful Earthquake. A Sermon Preach'd a Month after it happen'd*. Boston: Printed by B. Green, 1727.

Cotton, John (1584–1652). *A Briefe Exposition with Practical Observations upon the Whole Book of Ecclesiastes*. London: Printed by T. C. for Ralph Smith, 1654.

———. *The Correspondence of John Cotton*. Edited by Sargent Bush, Jr. Chapel Hill: University of North Carolina Press, 2001.

Cotton, John (1693–1757). *A Holy Fear of God, And His Judgments. Exhorted To: In A Sermon Preach'd at Newton, November 3. 1727. On a Day of Fasting and Prayer, Occasion'd by the Terrible Earthquake That Shook New-England, on the Lords-Day Night before*. Boston: Printed by B. Green, 1727.

Danforth, John. *A Sermon Occasioned by the Late Great Earthquake, And the Terrors that attended it*. Boston: Printed by Gamaliel Rogers, 1728.

Danforth, Samuel. *An Astronomical Description of the late Comet Or Blazing Star, As it appeared in New-England in the 9th, 10th, 11th, and in the beginning of the 12th Moneth, 1664. Together with a brief Theological Application thereof*. Cambridge, MA: Printed by Samuel Green, 1665.

The Day–Breaking, if not the Sun–Rising of the Gospell With the Indians in New-England. London: Printed by Rich. Cotes for Fulk Clifton, 1647. Anonymously authored by "a Minister of Christ in New England," possibly Thomas Shepard or John Wilson.

Descartes, René. *Philosophical Essays and Correspondence*. Edited by Roger Ariew. Indianapolis, IN: Hackett, 2000.

———. *The World and Other Writings*. Edited and translated by Stephen Gaukroger. Cambridge: Cambridge University Press, 1998.

Edwards, John. *Socinianism Unmask'd*. London: Printed for J. Robinson, 1696.

———. *Some Thoughts Concerning the Several Causes and Occasions of Atheism*. London: Printed for J. Robinson, 1695.

Eliot, John. *The Eliot Tracts: With Letters from John Eliot to Thomas Thorowgood and Richard Baxter*. Edited by Michael P. Clark. Westport, CT: Praeger, 2003.

———. *The Logick Primer: Some logical notions to initiate the Indians in the knowledge of the rule of reason and to know how to make use thereof: especially for the instruction of such as are teachers among them*. Cambridge, MA: Printed by M. J., 1672.

Epictetus. *The Discourses of Epictetus*. Edited by Christopher Gill. Translated by Robin Hard. London: J. M. Dent, 1995.

Fitch, James. *The first Principles of the Doctrine of Christ; together with stronger meat for them that are skil'd in the word of righteousness*. Boston: Printed by John Foster, 1679.

Bibliography

Flavel, John. *The Works of John Flavel.* 6 vols. London: W. Baynes & Son, 1820. Reprint. Carlisle, PA: Banner of Truth, 1997.

Fox, John. *GOD by his Power causes the Earth and its Inhabitants to tremble. The Substance of Two Sermons, On I. Sam. IXV. 15. Preached soon after the Earthquake, at Woburn.* Boston: Printed for N. Belknap, 1728.

Foxcroft, John. *The Voice of the Lord, From The Deep Places of the Earth. A Sermon Preach'd on the Thursday-Lecture in Boston in the Audience of the General Court, at the opening of the Sessions, Nov. 23. 1727. Three Weeks after the Earthquake.* Boston: Printed for S. Gerrish, 1727.

Foxcroft, Thomas. *The Earthquake, a Divine Visitation.* Boston: Printed by S. Kneeland, 1756.

Gale, Theophilus. *The Court of the Gentiles: Or, A Discourse touching the Original of Human Literature, both Philologie and Philosophie, from the Scriptures, and Jewish Church, In order to a Demonstration of 1. The Perfection of God's Word, and Church Light. 2. The Imperfection of Nature's Light, and mischief of Vain Philosophie. 3. The right use of Human Learning, and especially sound Philosophie: Part I—Of Philologie.* Oxfordshire, UK: Printed by Hen. Hall for Tho. Gilbert, 1669.

———. *The Court of the Gentiles: Part II—Of Barbaric and Grecanic Philosophie.* 2nd ed. London: Printed by J. Macock for Thomas Gilbert, 1676. First edition published 1670.

———. *The Court of the Gentiles: Part III—The Vanity of Pagan Philosophie.* London: Printed by A. Maxwell and R. Roberts for T. Cockeril, 1677.

———. *The Court of the Gentiles: Part IV—Of Reformed Philosophie.* London: Printed by J. Macock for Thomas Cockeril, 1677.

Galen. *On the Usefulness of the Parts of the Body.* 2 vols. Translated by Margaret Tallmadge May. Ithaca, NY: Cornell University Press, 1969.

Gookin, Nathaniel. *The Day of Trouble near, The Tokens of it, and a Due Preparation for it; In Three Sermons On Ezekiel VII. 7. . . . To which is added, A Sermon on Deuteronomy V. 29. Preach'd the Wednesday after that Awakening Providence; And an Appendix, Giving some Account of the Earthquake, as it was in Hampton.* Boston: Printed for D. Henchman, 1728.

Greenham, Richard. *The Workes of the Reverend and Faithful Servant of Jesus Christ, M. Richard Greenham. . . . The Fift[h] and Last Edition.* London: Printed for William Welby, 1612. Originally published 1599.

Gurnall, William. *The Christian in Complete Armour.* 2 vols. in 1. Glasgow: Blackie & Son, 1864. Reprint. Edinburgh: Banner of Truth, 1995. Originally published in three volumes, 1662–65.

Grotius, Hugo. *De jure belli ac pacis.* Edited by P. C. Molhuysen. Lugduni Batavorum: Apud A. W. Sijthoff, 1919.

———. *The Law of War and Peace.* Translated by Francis W. Kelsey. Indianapolis: Bobbs-Merrill, 1962.

Henry, Matthew. *The Complete Works of Matthew Henry: Treatises, Sermons, and Tracts.* 2 vols. London: A. Fullarton, 1855. Reprint. Grand Rapids: Baker, 1997.

———. *Matthew Henry's Commentary on the Whole Bible.* 6 vols. Peabody, MA: Hendrickson, 1991. Originally published 1707–21.

Hooke, Robert. *Micrographia: Or, Some Physiological Descriptions of Minute Bodies Made By Magnifying Glasses.* London: Printed by Jo. Martyn and Ja. Allestry, 1665.

Bibliography

Hooker, Thomas. *An Exposition of the Principles of Religion*. London: Printed for R. Dawlman, 1645.

———. *The Immortality of Mans Soule, Proved both by Scripture and Reason*. London: Printed by Peter Cole, 1645.

———. *The Soules Vocation or Effectual Calling to Christ*. London: Printed by John Haviland, 1638.

Hopkins. Ezekiel. *The Works of Ezekiel Hopkins*. Edited by Charles W. Quick. 3 vols. Philadelphia: Leighton, 1874. Reprint. Morgan, PA: Soli Deo Gloria, 1997.

Howe, John. *A Discourse Concerning the Redeemer's Dominion over the Invisible World*. London: Printed for Tho. Parkhurst, 1699.

———. *Sermons on Several Occasions*. 2 vols. London: Printed by H. Woodfall, 1744.

———. *The Works of the Rev. John Howe*. 3 vols. London: William Tegg, 1848.

Hume, David. *Principal Writings on Religion*. Edited by. J. C. A. Gaskin. New York: Oxford University Press, 1993.

Hunter, Michael, ed. *Robert Boyle by Himself and his Friends*. London: Pickering, 1994.

The Judgment of Non-conformists of the Interest of Reason in Matters of Religion. London: no printer given, 1676. The signatories were Richard Baxter (the likely author), Thomas Manton, William Bates, Thomas Case, Gabriel Sangar, Matthew Pemberton, Matthew Sylvester, Henry Hurst, Roger Morrice. Edward Lawrence, Benjamin Agas, James Bedford, Samuel Fairclough, John Turner and Joseph Read.

Juvenal. *The Satires*. Translated by Niall Rudd. Oxford: Clarendon, 1991.

Kant, Immanuel. *Immanuel Kant's Critique of Pure Reason*. Translated by Norman Kemp Smith. New York: St. Martin's, 1965.

Keeble, N. H., and Geoffrey F. Nuttall, eds. *Calendar of the Correspondence of Richard Baxter*, 2 vols. Oxford: Clarendon, 1991.

Leclercq, J., H. M. Rochais, and C. H. Talbot, eds. *Sancti Bernardi Opera*. 8 vols. Rome: Editiones Cistercienses, 1957–77.

Lee, Samuel. *The Joy of Faith, or A treatise opening the true nature of faith*. Boston: Printed by Samuel Green, 1687.

Locke, John. *An Essay Concerning Human Understanding*. Edited by Peter H. Nidditch. New York: Oxford University Press, 1979.

———. *A Letter to the Right Reverend Edward, Lord Bishop of Worcester*. London: Printed for A. and J. Churchill, 1697.

———. *Mr. Locke's Reply to the Right Reverend the Lord Bishop of Worcester's Answer to his Letter*. London: Printed by H. Clark, 1697.

———. *Mr. Locke's Reply to the Right Reverend the Lord Bishop of Worcester's Answer to his Second Letter*. London: Printed by H. C., 1699.

———. *The Reasonableness of Christianity: As Delivered in the Scriptures*. Edited by John C. Higgins-Biddle. New York: Oxford University Press, 1999

———. *The Works of John Locke*. 3 vols. London: Printed for Awnsham Churchill, 1722.

———. *Writings on Religion*. Edited by Victor Nuovo. Oxford: Clarendon, 2001.

[Locke, John]. *The Reasonableness of Christianity, as Delivered in the Scriptures*. London: Printed for Awnsham and John Churchill, 1695.

———. *A Second Vindication of the Reasonableness of Christianity*. London: Printed for A. and J. Churchill, 1697.

———. *A Vindication of the Reasonableness of Christianity, &c. From Mr. Edwards's Reflections*. London: Printed for Awnsham and John Churchill, 1695.

Bibliography

Luther, Martin. *Martin Luther: Selections from his Writings*. Edited by John Dillenberger. New York: Doubleday, 1962.

Manierre, William R., II. *The Diary of Cotton Mather, D.D., F.R.S. for the Year 1712*. Charlottesville, VA: University of Virginia Press, 1964.

Manton, Thomas. *By Faith: Sermons on Hebrews 11*. Carlisle, PA: Banner of Truth, 2000.

Mather, Cotton. *The Christian Philosopher*. Edited by Winton U. Solberg. Urbana, IL: University of Illinois Press, 1994. Originally published 1721.

———. *Diary of Cotton Mather*, 2 vols. Massachusetts Historical Society Collections, seventh series, vols. VII–VIII. Boston: Massachusetts Historical Society, 1911–12.

———. *An Epistle to the Indians*. Boston: Printed by Bartholomew Green, 1700.

———. *A Man of Reason: A Brief Essay to demonstrate, That all Men should hearken to Reason; and, What a World of Evil would be prevented in the World, if Men would once become so Reasonable*. Boston: Printed for John Edwards, 1718.

———. *Reason Satisfied: And Faith Established*. Boston: Printed by J. Allen for N. Boone, 1712.

———. *Reasonable Religion: Or, the Truth of the Christian Religion Demonstrated. . . . With Incontestable Proofs, that those who would Act Reasonably, must Live Religiously*. Boston: Printed by T. Green for Benjamin Eliot, 1700.

———. *The Terror of the Lord. Some Account of the Earthquake That shook New England, In the Night, Between the 29 and 30 of October, 1727. With a Speech, Made unto the Inhabitants of Boston, Who assembled the Next Morning, for the proper Exercises of Religion, On so Uncommon and so Tremendous an Occasion*. 3rd ed. Boston: Printed for S. Kneeland, 1727.

Mather, Increase. *Diary by Increase Mather, March, 1675–December, 1676. Together with Extracts From Another Diary by Him, 1674–1687*. Edited by Samuel A. Green. Cambridge, MA: John Wilson and Son, 1900.

———. *A Discourse Concerning Earthquakes. Occasioned by the Earthquakes which were in New-England, in the Province of Massachusetts-Bay, June 16. and in Conecticot-Colony, June 22. 1705; Also, Two Sermons*. Boston: Printed by Timothy Green for Benjamin Eliot, 1706.

———. *A Discourse Concerning the Existence and Omniscience of God. Plainly Proving, 1. That there is a God. 2. That the God of Heaven knows all Things. Being the Substance of several Sermons*. Boston: Printed by J. Allen for Daniel Henchman, 1716.

———. *A Discourse Proving that the Christian Religion is the only True Religion: Wherein, the necessity of Divine Revelation is Evinced, in several Sermons*. Boston: Printed for & Sold by the Booksellers, 1702.

———. *The Doctrine of Divine Providence Opened and Applied: Also Sundry Sermons on Several other Subjects*. Boston: Printed by Richard Pierce for Joseph Brunning, 1684.

———. *Heavens Alarm to the Word, or a sermon wherein is shewed, that fearful sights and signs in heaven are the presages of great calamities at hand*. Boston: Printed by John Foster, 1681.

———. *Kometographia, or, A discourse concerning comets wherein the nature of blazing stars is enquired into: with an historical account of all comets which have appeared from the beginning of the world unto this present year*. Boston: Printed by S. G. for S. S., 1683.

———. *Some Important Truths About Conversion, Delivered in sundry Sermons*. London: Printed for Richard Chiswell, 1674.

Bibliography

Mayhew, Jonathan. *A Discourse On Rev. XV. 3d, 4th. Occasioned by the Earthquakes in November 1755*. Boston: Printed by Edes & Gill, 1755.

———. *The expected Dissolution of all things, a Motive to universal Holiness*. Boston: Printed by Edes & Gill, 1755.

———. *Practical Discourses Delivered on Occasion of the Earthquakes in November, 1755*. Boston: Printed by Richard Draper and Edes and Gill, 1760.

McCarl, Mary Rhinelander. "Thomas Shepard's Relations of Religious Experience, 1648–1659." *William and Mary Quarterly*, 3rd Ser., 48/3 (1991) 432–66.

Mix, Stephen. *Extraordinary Displays of the Divine Majesty & Power, are to Try Men, and Impress the Fear of God on their Hearts, that they Sin Not. Being the Substance of Two Sermons Occasioned by a Terrible Earthquake in New-England, and other parts of Northern America; the Night immediately following the Sabbath-Day, October 29, 1727. Publickly Delivered in Wethersfield, on November the 5th. and 12th. the Sabbaths next Succeeding the said Earthquake. Something Enlarged*. London: Printed by T. Green, 1728.

Morrill, Nathanael. *The Lord's Voice in the Earthquake . . . Preach'd in the Parish of Rye, in New-Castle, in New-Hampshire, in New-England, Novemb. 16. 1727. Being a Day of Publick Fasting thro'out the Province*. Boston: Printed for Richard Jenness and Joseph Lock, 1728.

Nieuwentyt, Bernard. *The Religious Philosopher: Or, the Right Use of Contemplating the Works of the Creator*. Translated by John Chamberlayne. 3 vols. London: Printed by T. Wood for J. Senex, 1718–19. First published in 1714 as *Het regt gebruik der werelt beschouwingen* (The Right Use of the Contemplation of the World).

Norton, John. *A Brief Catechisme*. Cambridge, MA: Printed by S. G. and M. J., 1660.

———. *A Brief and Excellent Treatise Containing the Doctrine of Godliness, or living unto God. Wherein the body of divinity is substantially proposed, and methodically digested, by way of question and answer*. London: Printed by John Field, 1648.

———. *The Orthodox Evangelist. Or a Treatise Wherein many Great Evangelical Truths . . . are briefly Discussed*. London: Printed by John Macock, 1654.

Noyes, James. *A Short Catechism*. Cambridge, MA: Printed by Samuel Green, 1661.

O[verton], R[ichard]. *Mans Mortalitie*. Amsterdam: Printed by John Canne, 1644. This was the first edition of *Man Wholly Mortal*, and bears the same subtitle.

———. *Man Wholly Mortal. Or, a Treatise Wherein It is proved, both Theologically and Philosophically, That as whole man sinned, so whole man died; contrary to that common distinction of Soul and Body: And that the present going of the Soul into heaven or hell, is a meer Fiction: And that at the Resurrection is the beginning of our immortality; and then actual Condemnation and Salvation; and not before. With Doubts and Objections answered and resolved, both by Scripture and Reason; discovering the multitude of Blasphemies and Absurdities that arise from the Fancie of the Soul. . . . The second Edition, by the Author corrected and enlarged* London: no printer given, 1655.

Owen, John. *The Works of John Owen*. Edited by William H. Goold. 24 vols. London: Johnstone and Hunter, 1850–55.

Paine, Thomas. *The Doctrine of Earthquakes. Two Sermons Preached at a particular Fast in Weymouth, Nov. 3. 1727. The Friday after the Earthquake. Wherin [sic] this terrible Work appears not to proceed from natural Second Causes, in any orderly Way of their Producing: But from the Mighty Power of GOD immediately interposed; and is to the World, A Token of GOD's Anger, &c. and Presage of Terrible Changes. With Examples*

Bibliography

of many Earthquakes in History,—illustrating this doctrine. Boston: Printed for D. Henchman, 1728.

Parker, Samuel. *Tentamina physico-theologica de Deo*. London: Typis A. M., 1665.

Pascal, Blaise. *Pensées*. Translated by A. J. Krailsheimer. New York: Penguin, 1966.

Payson. Edward. *Pious Heart-Elations: Being The Substance of a Sermon In Publick On November 29th. in Consideration of present Awful Providences amongst us; and on the Sabbath following in the Forenoon. December 3d. 1727*. Boston: Printed by B. Green, 1728.

Pemble, William. *Vindiciae gratiae. A Plea for Grace. More especially the grace of faith*. London: Printed by R. Young for I. Bartlett, 1627.

Perkins, William. *The Arte of Prophecying*. Translated by Thomas Tuke. London: Felix Kyngston, 1607. First published in 1592 as *Prophetica, sive, De sacra et unica ratione concionandi tractatus*.

———. *A Christian and Plaine Treatise of the manner and order of Predestination*. Translated by Francis Cacot and Thomas Tuke. London: Printed for William Welby, 1606. First published in 1598 as *De praedestinationis modo et ordine*.

———. *The Workes of that Famous and Worthy Minister of Christ in the Universitie of Cambridge, Mr. William Perkins*. 3 vols. London: Printed by John Legatt, 1631. Quotations from volume one of Perkins' *Workes* are taken from the 1635 edition.

Pierson [also Peirson], Abraham. *Some Helps for the Indians; Shewing them how to Improve their Natural Reason, to know the true God, and the Christian Religion. 1. By leading them to see the Divine Authority of the Scriptures. 2. By the Scriptures, the Divine truths necessary to Eternal salvation*. Cambridge, MA: Printed for Samuel Green, 1658.

Plato. *The Laws*. Translated by Trevor J. Saunders. London: Penguin, 1975.

Poole, Matthew. *A Commentary on the Holy Bible*. 3 vols. Edinburgh: Banner of Truth, 1962. First published as *Annotations on the Holy Bible* (2 vols., 1683–85).

———. *A Seasonable Apology for Religion, being the subject of two sermons lately delivered in an auditory in London*. London: Printed by J. M. for Tho. Parkhurst, 1673.

Prentice, Thomas. *Observations Moral and Religious, on the late terrible Night of the Earthquake*. Boston: Printed by S. Kneeland, 1756.

Preston, John. *Life Eternall, or A treatise of the knowledge of the divine essence and attributes. Delivered in XVIII sermons*. 4th ed. London: Printed by E. P., 1634. Originally published in 1631.

———. *Sermons Preached Before his Majestie; and upon other speciall occasions*. London: Printed for Leonard Greene, 1630.

Prince, Thomas. *Earthquakes the Works of God and Tokens of his just Displeasure*. Boston: Printed for D. Henchman, 1727.

———. *An Improvement of the Doctrine of Earthquakes, Being the Works of GOD, and Tokens of his just Displeasure. Containing an Historical Summary of the most remarkable Earthquakes in New-England, from the first Settlement of the English here, as also in other Parts of the World since 1666*. Boston: Printed by D. Fowle, 1755.

Ray, John. *Three Physico-Theological Discourses . . . With Practical Inferences*. 2nd. ed., rev. London: Printed for Samuel Smith, 1693. The first edition of 1692 bore the title, *Miscellaneous Discourses concerning the Dissolution and Changes of the World*.

———. *The Wisdom of God Manifested in the Works of the Creation*. London: Printed for Samuel Smith, 1691.

Bibliography

———. *The Wisdom of God Manifested in the Works of the Creation, In Two Parts. . . . The Second Edition, very much enlarged.* London: Printed for Samuel Smith, 1692.

Richardson, Alexander. *The Logicians School-Master: Or, A Comment Upon Ramus Logicke.* London: Printed for John Bellamie, 1629.

Roberts, Alexander, and James Donaldson, eds. *Ante-Nicene Fathers.* 10 vols. 1885. Reprint. Peabody, MA: Hendrickson, 1999.

Rogers, John (1684-1755). *The Nature and Necessity of Repentance, with the Means and Motives to it. A Discourse Occasion'd by the Earthquake. Preached at Boxford, in part on the Publick Fast, Dec. 21. 1727.* Boston: Printed for S. Gerrish, 1728.

Rogers, John (1712-89). *Three Sermons On different Subjects and Occasions. The First, On the Pleasure which affects the Hearts of virtuous Men, at the View of publick Happiness. . . . The Second, On the Vanity of Prayer and Fasting; when they are not joined with Reformation of Manners. The Last, On the Terribleness, and the moral Cause of Earthquakes.* Boston: Printed by Edes & Gill, 1756.

Rogers, Richard. *Seven Treatises Containing such Directions as is Gathered out of the Holie Scriptures.* London: Printed by Felix Kyngston for Thomas Man, 1610. Originally published in 1603.

Salter, Samuel, ed. *Eight Letters of Dr. Anthony Tuckney, and Dr. Benjamin Whichcote. . . . Written in September and October, MDCLI.* London: Printed for J. Payne, 1753. Bound together with Benjamin Whichcote's *Moral and Religious Aphorisms* but separately paginated with its own title page.

Schaff, Philip, ed. *Nicene and Post-Nicene Fathers.* First Series. 14 vols. 1886-89. Reprint. Peabody, MA: Hendrickson, 1999.

Schaff, Philip, and Henry Wace, eds. *Nicene and Post-Nicene Fathers.* Second Series. 14 vols. 1890-1900. Reprint. Peabody, MA: Hendrickson, 1999.

Scudder, Henry. *The Christian's Daily Walk, in Holy Security and Peace.* Harrisonburg, VA: Sprinkle, 1984. Originally published in 1627.

Selement, George, and Bruce C. Woolley, eds. *Thomas Shepard's Confessions.* Boston: Colonial Society of Massachusetts *Collections* (XVIII), 1981.

Sewall, Joseph. *The Duty of a People to Stand in Aw[e] of GOD, and not Sin, When under His terrible Judgments. A Sermon Preach'd at the South Meeting House in Boston, the Evening after the Earthquake.* 2nd ed. Boston: Printed for D. Henchman, 1727.

———. *Repentance the sure Way to Escape Destruction. Two Sermons on Jer. 18. 7, 8.* Boston: Printed for D. Henchman, 1727.

Shepard, Thomas. *A Short Catechism Familiarly Teaching the Knowledg[e] of God, and of our Selves, familiarly teaching the knowledg of God and of our selves.* Cambridge, MA: Printed by Samuel Green, 1654.

———. *The Works of Thomas Shepard.* 3 vols. Boston: Doctrinal Tract and Book Society, 1853. Reprint. New York: AMS Press, 1967.

Silverman, Kenneth, ed. *Selected Letters of Cotton Mather.* Baton Rouge: Louisiana State University Press, 1971.

Smith, Josiah. *The Greatest Sufferers Not always the Greatest Sinners. A Sermon Delivered in Charlestown, in the Province of South-Carolina, February 4th. 1727,8. Occasioned by the Terrible Earthquake in New-England.* Boston: no printer given, 1730.

Spencer, Thomas. *The Art of Logick, Delivered in the Precepts of Aristotle and Ramus.* London: Printed by John Dawson, 1628.

Stillingfleet, Edward. *A Discourse in Vindication of the Doctrine of the Trinity.* London: Printed by J. H., 1697.

Bibliography

Suarez, Francisco. *On Creation, Conservation, and Concurrence: Metaphysical Disputations 20, 21, and 22.* Translated by Alfred J. Freddoso. South Bend, IN: St. Augustine's, 2002.

———. *The Metaphysical Demonstration of the Existence of God: Metaphysical Disputations 28-29.* Translated by John P. Doyle. South Bend, IN: St. Augustine's, 2004.

Taylor, Thomas. *The Principles of Christian Practice.* London: Printed by R. Y., 1635.

Thayer, H. S., ed. *Newton's Philosophy of Nature: Selections From His Writings.* New York: Hafner, 1953.

Toland, John. *Christianity Not Mysterious.* London: Routledge/Thoemmes, 1995.

Trapp, John. *Commentary on the Old and New Testaments.* 6 vols. London: Richard Dickinson, 1865-68. Reprint. Eureka, CA: Tanski, 1997. Volume six of this set contains Trapp's *Mellificium Theologicum: The Marrow of Many Good Authors,* first published as an appendix to Trapp's *Commentary or Exposition upon All the Epistles and the Revelation of John the Divine* (1647).

———. *Theologia Theologiae.* London: Printed by K. B. for George Badger, 1641.

Twisse, William. *A Discovery of D. Jacksons Vanitie.* London, 1631.

Vaughan, Alden T., ed. *The Puritan Tradition in America, 1620-1730.* Rev. ed. Hanover, NH: University Press of New England, 1997. Originally published in 1972.

Vincent, Thomas. *The Shorter Catechism of the Westminster Assembly Explained and Proved from Scripture.* Carlisle, PA: Banner of Truth, 1998. Originally published in 1673.

Voltaire. *Oeuvres Complètes de Voltaire.* Edited by Louis Moland. 52 vols. Paris: Garnier, 1877-85. Reprint. Nendeln: Kraus, 1967.

Watson, Thomas. *A Body of Divinity: Contained in Sermons on the Westminster Assembly's Shorter Catechism.* London: Banner of Truth, 1965. Originally published in 1692.

Webb, John. *Some Plain and Necessary Directions to obtain Eternal Salvation.* Boston: Printed for Benjamin Gray, 1729.

Westminster Confession of Faith. 1646 ed. Glasgow: Free Presbyterian, 1990. Also contains the *Westminster Shorter Catechism* and the *Westminster Larger Catechism.*

Whichcote, Benjamin. *Moral and Religious Aphorisms.* Edited by Samuel Salter. London: Printed for J. Payne, 1753.

Wigglesworth, Samuel. *Religious Fear of God's Tokens. Explained and Urged; In a Sermon Preached at Ipswich, November 1. 1727. Being a Day of Humiliation on account of the terrible Earthquake, October 29. 1727.* Boston: Printed for D. Henchman and T. Hancock, 1728.

Wilkins, John. *A Discourse concerning the Beauty of Providence, in all the rugged passages of it.* London: Printed for Sa. Gellibrand, 1649.

———. *Sermons Preached Upon several Occasions Before the King at White-Hall.* London: Printed by H. Cruttenden for Robert Sollers, 1677.

———. *Sermons Preached upon Several Occasions . . . never before Published.* London: Printed for Tho. Basset, 1682.

———. *Of the Principles and Duties of Natural Religion: Two Books.* London: Printed by A. Maxwell, 1675.

Willard, Samuel. *A Compleat Body of Divinity, in Two Hundred and Fifty Expository Lectures on the Assembly's Shorter Catechism.* Boston: Printed by B. Green and S. Kneeland for B. Eliot and D. Henchman, 1726. These were monthly lectures delivered by Willard between 1688 and 1707.

Bibliography

Willet, Andrew. *Hexapla: That is, a six-fold commentarie upon the most divine epistle of the holy apostle S. Paul to the Romanes.* Cambridge: Leonard Greene, 1620. Originally published in 1611.

Williams, Eliphalet. *The Duty of a People, under dark Providences, or symptoms of approaching Evils, to Prepare to Meet their God. A Discourse Delivered at East-Hartford, November 23, 1755. The next Sabbath after the late Terrible Earthquake.* New London, CT: Printed by Timothy and John Green, 1756.

Williams, William. *Divine Warnings to be Received with Faith & Fear.* Boston: Printed for Samuel Gerrish, 1728.

Winthrop, John. *A Lecture on Earthquakes; Read in the Chapel of Harvard-College in Cambridge, N.E. November 26th 1755.* Boston: Printed by Edes & Gill, 1755.

Witsius, Herman. *The Economy of the Covenants Between God and Man: Comprehending a Complete Body of Divinity.* Translated by William Crookshank. 2 vols. London: R. Baynes, 1822. Reprint. Escondido, CA: den Dulk Christian Foundation, 1990. First Latin edition published in 1677.

———. *Sacred Dissertations on the Apostles' Creed.* Translated by Donald Fraser. 2 vols. Glasgow: Khull, Blackie & Co., 1823. Reprint. Escondido, CA: The den Dulk Christian Foundation, 1993. First Latin edition published in 1681.

———. *Sacred Dissertations on the Lord's Prayer.* Translated by William Pringle. Edinburgh: T. Clark, 1839. Reprint. Escondido, CA: The den Dulk Christian Foundation, 1994. First Latin edition published in 1689.

Xenophon. *Memorabilia.* Boston: Ginn, 1903. Reprint. Salem, NH: Ayer, 1985.

Secondary Sources

Abraham, Gary A. "Misunderstanding the Merton Thesis: A Boundary Dispute between History and Sociology." *Isis* 74/3 (1983) 368–87.

Ahlstrom, Sydney E. *A Religious History of the American People.* New Haven: Yale University Press, 1972.

Aldridge, Owen A. "Natural Religion and Deism in America before Ethan Allen and Thomas Paine." *William and Mary Quarterly*, 3rd Ser., Vol. 54/4 (1997) 835–48.

Aylmer, G. E. "Unbelief in Seventeenth-Century England." In *Puritans and Revolutionaries: Essays in Seventeenth-Century History presented to Christopher Hill*, edited by Donald Pennington and Keith Thomas, 22–46. Oxford: Clarendon, 1978.

Ball, Bryan W. *The Seventh-day Men: Sabbatarians and Sabbatarianism in England and Wales, 1600–1800.* Oxford: Oxford University Press, 1994.

Berman, David. *A History of Atheism in Britain: From Hobbes to Russell.* London: Croom Helm, 1989.

Biddle, John C. "Locke's Critique of Innate Principles and Toland's Deism." *Journal of the History of Ideas* 37/3 (1976) 411–22.

Bozeman, Theodore Dwight. *To Live Ancient Lives: The Primitivist Dimension in Puritanism.* Chapel Hill, NC: University of North Carolina Press, 1988.

Bremer, Francis J., ed. *Puritanism: Transatlantic Perspectives on a Seventeenth-Century Faith.* Boston: Massachusetts Historical Society, 1993.

Brooke, John Hedley. "Science and the Fortunes of Natural Theology: Some Historical Perspectives." *Zygon* 24 (1989) 3–22.

Bibliography

———. *Science and Religion: Some Historical Perspectives.* Cambridge: Cambridge University Press, 1991.

Bristol, Roger P. *Index to Supplement to Charles Evans' American Bibliography.* Charlottesville, VA: University of Virginia Press, 1971.

———. *Supplement to Charles Evans' American Bibliography.* Charlottesville, VA: University of Virginia Press, 1970.

Brooks, Benjamin. *The Lives of the Puritans.* 3 vols. London: James Black, 1813. Reprint. Pittsburgh, PA: Soli Deo Gloria, 1994.

Brown, John. *Puritan Preaching in England: A Study of Past and Present.* London: Hodder and Stoughton, 1900.

Buckley, Michael J. *At the Origins of Modern Atheism.* New Haven: Yale University Press, 1987.

Bush, Douglas. *English Literature in the Earlier Seventeenth Century: 1600–1660.* New York: Oxford University Press, 1946.

Bush, Sargent Jr. *The Writings of Thomas Hooker: Spiritual Adventure in Two Worlds.* Madison, WI: University of Wisconsin Press, 1980.

Butterfield, Herbert. *The Origins of Modern Science: 1300–1800.* London: Bell and Sons, 1950.

Champion, J. A. I. *The Pillars of Priestcraft Shaken: The Church of England and Its Enemies, 1660–1730.* Cambridge: Cambridge University Press, 1992.

Cogley, Richard W. *John Eliot's Mission to the Indians before King Philip's War.* Cambridge, MA: Harvard University Press, 1999.

Cohen, Charles Lloyd. *God's Caress: The Psychology of Puritan Religious Experience.* Oxford: Oxford University Press, 1986.

———. "The Post-Puritan Paradigm of Early American Religious History." *William and Mary Quarterly*, 3rd Ser., Vol. 54/4 (1997) 695–722.

Cohen, I. Bernhard, ed. *Puritanism and the Rise of Modern Science: The Merton Thesis.* New Brunswick, NJ: Rutgers University Press, 1990.

———., and George E. Smith, eds. *The Cambridge Companion to Newton.* Cambridge: Cambridge University Press, 2002.

Collinson, Patrick. *The Elizabethan Puritan Movement.* Berkeley: University of California Press, 1967.

———. *Godly People: Essays on English Protestantism and Puritanism.* London: The Hambledon, 1983.

———. *The Religion of Protestants: The Church in English Society, 1559–1625.* Oxford: Clarendon, 1983.

Coolidge, John S. *The Pauline Renaissance in England: Puritanism and the Bible.* Oxford: Clarendon, 1970.

Cox, Robert. *The Literature of the Sabbath Question.* 2 vols. London: Simpkin, Marshall, & Co., 1865.

Craig, William Lane. *The Kalam Cosmological Argument.* London: Macmillan, 1979.

Crocker, Robert, ed. *Religion, Reason, and Nature in Early Modern Europe.* Dordrecht: Kluwer Academic, 2001.

Crowe, Michael J. *The Extraterrestrial Life Debate, 1750–1900: The Idea of a Plurality of Worlds from Kant to Lowell.* Cambridge: Cambridge University Press, 1986.

Dahm, Jon J. "Science and Apologetics in the Early Boyle Lectures." *Church History* 39/2 (1970) 172–86.

Bibliography

Daly, Robert. *God's Altar: The World and the Flesh in Puritan Poetry.* Berkeley: University of California Press, 1978.

Dear, Peter. "Miracles. Experiments, and the Ordinary Course of Nature." *Isis* 81/4 (1990) 663–83.

Deason, Gary B. "The Protestant Reformation and the Rise of Modern Science." *Scottish Journal of Theology* 38/2 (1985) 221–40.

Dennison, James T., Jr. *The Market Day of the Soul: The Puritan Doctrine of the Sabbath in England, 1532-1700.* Lanham, MD: University Press of America, 1983.

Dick, Steven J. *Plurality of Worlds: The Origins of the Extraterrestrial Life Debate from Democritus to Kant.* Cambridge: Cambridge University Press, 1982.

Dillenberger, John. *Protestantism and Natural Science.* New York: Doubleday, 1960. Reprint. Westport, CT: Greenwood, 1977.

Dybikowski, James. "Natural Religion." In *Encyclopedia of the Enlightenment*, edited by Alan Charles Kors, 3:142–50. 4 vols. Oxford: Oxford University Press, 2003.

Eddy, M. D. "The Rhetoric and Science of William Paley's *Natural Theology*." *Literature & Theology* 18/1 (2004) 1–22.

Emerton, Norma. "The Argument from Design in Early Modern Natural Theology." *Science and Christian Belief* 1/2 (1989) 129–47.

Evans, Charles. *American Bibliography: A Chronological Dictionary of All Books, Pamphlets, and Periodical Publications Printed in the United States of America from the Genesis of Printing in 1639 Down to and Including the Year 1820.* 14 vols. New York: Smith, 1941–59.

Ferngren, Gary B, ed. *The History of Science and Religion in the Western Tradition: An Encyclopedia.* New York: Garland, 2000.

Fiering, Norman. *Moral Philosophy at Seventeenth-Century Harvard: A Discipline in Transition.* Chapel Hill, NC: University of North Carolina Press, 1981.

Fleming, Donald. "The Judgment upon Copernicus in Puritan New England." In *Mélanges Alexandre Koyré, publiés à l'occasion de son soixante-dixième anniversaire*, 2:160–75. 2 vols. Paris: Hermann, 1964.

Ford, Brian J. "Shining through the Centuries: John Ray's Life and Legacy." *Notes and Records of the Royal Society of London* 54 (2000) 5–22.

Foster, Stephen. *The Long Argument: English Puritanism and the Shaping of New England Culture, 1570-1700.* Chapel Hill, NC: University of North Carolina Press, 1991.

Foster, Frank Hugh. *A Genetic History of the New England Theology.* New York: Russell & Russell, 1963. Originally published 1907.

Gabbey, Alan. "'A Disease Incurable': Scepticism and the Cambridge Platonists." In *Scepticism and Irreligion in the Seventeenth and Eighteenth Centuries*, edited by Richard H. Popkin and Arjo Vanderjagt, 71–91. Leiden: Brill, 1993.

Gerson, L. P. *God and Greek Philosophy: Studies in the Early History of Natural Theology.* London: Routledge, 1990.

Gillett. E. H. (Ezra Hall). *God in Human Thought, or, Natural Theology Traced in Literature, Ancient and Modern, to the Time of Bishop Butler: with a Closing Chapter on the Moral System, and an English Bibliography from Spenser to Butler.* 2 vols. New York: Scribner, Armstrong & Co., 1874.

Greaves, Richard L. "Puritanism and Science: The Anatomy of a Controversy." *Journal of the History of Ideas* 30/3 (1969) 345–68.

Gribben, Crawford. *The Puritan Millennium: Literature & Theology, 1550-1682.* Dublin: Four Courts, 2000.

Bibliography

Haggenmacher, Peter. *Grotius et la doctrine de la guerre juste*. Paris: Presses Universitaires de France, 1983.

Hall, David D. "On Common Ground: The Coherence of American Puritan Studies." *William and Mary Quarterly*, 3rd Ser., Vol. 44/2 (1987) 193–229.

———, ed. *Puritanism in Seventeenth-Century Massachusetts*. New York: Holt Rinehart and Winston, 1968.

———. *Worlds of Wonder, Days of Judgment: Popular Religious Belief in Early New England*. New York: Knopf, 1989.

Hall, Michael G. *The Last American Puritan: The Life of Increase Mather, 1639-1723*. Middletown, CT: Wesleyan University Press, 1988.

Hall, A. Rupert. *The Revolution in Science, 1500-1750*. New York: Longman, 1983.

Harrison, Peter. "Miracles. Early Modern Science, and Rational Religion." *Church History* 75/3 (2006): 493–511.

Hasper, Pieter Sjoerd. "Aristotle on Infinity." Paper presented at the University of Cambridge conference, "History & Philosophy of Infinity," September 20–23, 2013. http://www.philosophie.uni-muenchen.de/lehreinheiten/philosophie_3/personen/hasper/verg_sem/lv_sose_2011/unendlichkeit/hasper_aris_infin.pdf

Heyd, Michael, "Protestant Attitudes towards Science in the 17th and early 18th Centuries." In *Les Églises Face Aux Sciences: du Moyen Age au XXe siècle*, edited by Olivier Fatio, 71–89. Geneva: Librairie Droz S. A., 1991.

Hill, Christopher. *Economic Problems of the Church: From Archbishop Whitgift to the Long Parliament*. Oxford: Clarendon, 1956.

———. "Puritanism, Capitalism and the Scientific Revolution." *Past and Present* 29 (1964) 88–97.

———. "Science, Religion and Society in the Sixteenth and Seventeenth Centuries." *Past and Present* 31 (1965) 110–12.

Hindson. Edward, ed. *Introduction to Puritan Theology*. Grand Rapids: Baker, 1976.

Holifield. E. Brooks. *Theology in America: Christian Thought from the Age of the Puritans to the Civil War*. New Haven: Yale University Press, 2003.

Hooykaas, Reijer. *Religion and the Rise of Modern Science*. Grand Rapids: Eerdmans, 1972.

Hornblower, Simon, and Antony Spawforth, eds. *The Oxford Classical Dictionary*. 3rd ed. New York: Oxford University Press, 1996.

Howe, Daniel Walker. "The Impact of Puritanism on American Culture." In *Encyclopedia of the American Religious Experience*, edited by Charles H. Lippy and Peter W. Williams, 2:1057–74. 3 vols. New York: Scribner's Sons, 1988.

Hunter, Michael. *Robert Boyle (1627-1691): Scrupulosity and Science*. Woodbridge, UK: Boydell, 2000.

Hunter, Michael, ed. *Robert Boyle Reconsidered*. Cambridge: Cambridge University Press, 1994.

Jaeger, Werner. *The Theology of the Early Greek Philosophers*. Oxford: Clarendon, 1947. Reprint. Westport, CT: Greenwood, 1980.

Katz, David S. *Sabbath and Sectarianism in Seventeenth Century England*. Leiden: Brill, 1988.

Kearney, H. F. "Merton Revisited." *Science Studies* 3/1 (1973) 72–78.

———. "Puritanism, Capitalism and the Scientific Revolution." *Past and Present* 29 (1964) 81–101.

Keeble, N. H. *Richard Baxter: Puritan Man of Letters*. Oxford: Clarendon, 1982.

Bibliography

Kelter, Irving A. "The Refusal to Accommodate: Jesuit Exegetes and the Copernican System." *Sixteenth Century Journal* 26/2 (1995) 273–83.

Keynes, Geoffrey. *John Ray, 1627–1705: A Bibliography, 1660–1970*. Amsterdam: Gérard Th. Van Heusden, 1976.

King, Peter. *The Life of John Locke, with Extracts from his Correspondence, Journals, and Common-Place Books*. 2 vols. London: Henry Colburn and Richard Bentley, 1830. Reprint. Bristol, UK: Thoemmes, 1991.

Kittredge, George L. "Cotton Mather's Election into the Royal Society." *Publications of the Colonial Society of Massachusetts* 14 (1913) 81–114.

———. "Further Notes on Cotton Mather and the Royal Society." *Publications of the Colonial Society of Massachusetts* 14 (1913) 281–92.

Klaaren. Eugene. *Religious Origins of Modern Science: Belief in Creation in Seventeenth-Century Thought*. Grand Rapids: Eerdmans, 1977.

Kocher, Paul H. *Science and Religion in Elizabethan England*. San Marino, CA: The Huntington Library, 1953.

Koesler, Helmut. "ΝΟΜΟΣ ΦΥΣΕΩΣ: The Concept of Natural Law in Greek Thought." In *Religions in Antiquity: Essays in Memory of Erwin Ramsdell Goodenough*, edited by Jacob Neusner, 521–41. Leiden: Brill, 1968.

Koons, Robert C. "A New Kalam Argument: The Revenge of the Grim Reaper." *Nous* 48/2 (2012) 256–67.

Kors, Alan Charles, ed. *Encyclopedia of the Enlightenment*. 4 vols. Oxford: Oxford University Press, 2003.

Ladell, A. R. *Richard Baxter: Puritan and Mystic*. New York: MacMillan, 1925.

Lake, Peter. *Anglicans and Puritans? Presbyterianism and English Conformist Thought from Whitgift to Hooker*. London: Allen & Unwin, 1988.

———. "Defining Puritanism—again?" In *Puritanism: Transatlantic Perspectives on a Seventeenth-Century Faith*, edited by Francis J. Bremer, 3–29. Boston: Massachusetts Historical Society, 1993.

LeMahieu, D. L. *The Mind of William Paley: A Philosopher and His Age*. Lincoln, NE: University of Nebraska Press, 1976.

Lindberg, David C., and Ronald L. Numbers, eds. *God and Nature: Historical Essays on the Encounter between Christianity and Science*. Berkeley: University of California Press, 1986.

———. *When Science & Christianity Meet*. Chicago: University of Chicago Press, 2003.

Lindberg, David C., and Robert S. Westman, eds. *Reappraisals of the Scientific Revolution*. Cambridge: Cambridge University Press, 1990.

Livingstone David N., D. G. Hart, and Mark A. Noll, eds. *Evangelicals and Science in Historical Perspective*. New York: Oxford University Press, 1999.

Lowrie, Ernest Benson. *The Shape of the Puritan Mind: The Thought of Samuel Willard*. New Haven: Yale University Press, 1974.

Maddison, R. E. W. *The Life of the Honourable Robert Boyle*. London: Taylor & Francis, 1969.

Marshall, Wallace W. "Dante and the Doctrine of Original Sin." *Dante: Rivista Internazionale di studi su Dante Alighieri (*International Journal of Dante Studies*),* Anno III (2006) 21–40.

Mason, S. F. "Bishop John Wilkins, F.R.S. (1614–72): Analogies of Thought-Style in the Protestant Reformation and Early Modern Science." *Notes and Records of the Royal Society of London* 46/1 (1992) 1–21.

BIBLIOGRAPHY

———. "Science and Religion in 17th Century England." *Past and Present* 3 (1953) 28–44.
Matthew, H. C. G., and Brian Harrison, eds. *Oxford Dictionary of National Biography*. 60 vols. Oxford: Oxford University Press, 2004.
May, Gerhard. *Creatio ex Nihilo: The Doctrine of "Creation out of Nothing" in Early Christian Thought*. Translated by A. S. Worrall. Edinburgh: T. & T. Clark, 1994.
May, Henry F. *The Enlightenment in America*. New York: Oxford University Press, 1976.
Mayr, Otto. *Authority, Liberty, & Automatic Machinery in Early Modern Europe*. Baltimore: Johns Hopkins University Press, 1986.
McGiffert, Michael, ed. *God's Plot: The Paradoxes of Puritan Piety, Being the Autobiography and Journal of Thomas Shepard*. Amherst, MA: University of Massachusetts Press, 1972. This older edition of *God's Plot* contains the entirety of Shepard's journal, which is cut by some 50 percent in the 1994 edition in order to make room for thirty-three of the confessions of Shepard's parishioners.
———. *God's Plot: Puritan Spirituality in Thomas Shepard's Cambridge*. Rev. and expanded ed. Amherst, MA: University of Massachusetts Press, 1994.
McKim, Donald K. *Ramism in William Perkins' Theology*. New York: Lang, 1987.
McLachlan, H. John. *Socinianism in Seventeenth-Century England*. New York: Oxford University Press, 1951.
Mencken, H. L. *A Mencken Chrestomathy*. New York: Knopf, 1949.
Meyer, D. H. "The Uniqueness of the American Enlightenment." *American Quarterly* 28/2 (1976) 165–86.
Middlekauf, Robert. *The Mathers: Three Generations of Puritan Intellectuals, 1596–1728*. Berkeley: University of California Press, 1999. Originally published in 1971.
Miller, Perry. *The New England Mind: From Colony to Province*. Cambridge: Harvard University Press, 1954.
———. *The New England Mind: The Seventeenth Century*. New York: MacMillan, 1939.
Morgan, John. *Godly Learning: Puritan Attitudes towards Reason, Learning, and Education, 1560–1640*. Cambridge: Cambridge University Press, 1986.
———. "The Puritan Thesis Revisited." In *Evangelicals and Science in Historical Perspective*, edited by David N. Livingstone, D. G. Hart, and Mark A. Noll, 43–74. New York: Oxford University Press, 1999.
———. "Puritanism and Science: A Reinterpretation." *The Historical Journal* 22/3 (1979) 535–60.
Morison, Samuel E. *The Founding of Harvard College*. Cambridge: Harvard University Press, 1935.
———. *Harvard College in the Seventeenth Century*. 2 vols. Cambridge: Harvard University Press, 1936.
———. *The Intellectual Life of Colonial New England*. 2nd ed. New York: New York University Press, 1956.
Muller, Richard. *Post-Reformation Reformed Dogmatics: The Rise and Development of Reformed Orthodoxy, ca. 1520 to ca. 1725*. 2nd. ed. 4 vols. Grand Rapids: Baker, 2003.
Murray, Iain. *The Puritan Hope: Revival and the Interpretation of Prophecy*. London: Banner of Truth, 1971.
Noll, Mark. *America's God: From Jonathan Edwards to Abraham Lincoln*. Oxford: Oxford University Press, 2002.
———. *The Old Religion in a New World: The History of North American Christianity*. Grand Rapids: Eerdmans, 2002.

Bibliography

———. "The Rise and Long Life of the Protestant Enlightenment in America." In *Knowledge and Belief in America: Enlightenment Traditions and Modern Religious Thought*, edited by William M. Shea and Peter A. Huff, 88–124. Cambridge: Cambridge University Press, 1995.

Norton, Arthur O. "Harvard Text-Books and Reference Books of the Seventeenth Century." Colonial Society of Massachusetts, *Transactions*, XXVIII (1935) 361–438.

Nuttall, Geoffrey F. *Richard Baxter*. London: Thomas Nelson and Sons, 1965.

Orme, William. *The Life and Times of Richard Baxter: With a Critical Examination of his Writings*. 2 vols. London: Duncan, 1830.

Osler Margaret J. *Divine Will and the Mechanical Philosophy: Gassendi and Descartes on Contingency and Necessity in the Created World*. Cambridge University Press, 1994.

Outram, Dorinda. *The Enlightenment*. Cambridge: Cambridge University Press, 1995.

Parker, Kenneth. *The English Sabbath: A Study of Doctrine and Discipline from the Reformation to the Civil War*. Cambridge: Cambridge University Press, 1988.

Platt, John. "The Denial of the Innate Idea of God in Dutch Remonstrant Theology: From Episcopius to Van Limborch." In *Protestant Scholasticism: Essays in Reassessment*, edited by Carl R. Trueman and R. Scott Clark, 213–26. Carlisle, UK: Paternoster, 1999.

———. *Reformed Thought and Scholasticism: The Arguments for the Existence of God in Dutch Theology, 1575–1650*. Leiden: Brill, 1982.

Popkin, Richard H., and Arjo Vanderjagt, eds. *Scepticism and Irreligion in the Seventeenth and Eighteenth Centuries*. Leiden: Brill, 1993.

Porter, Roy. *The Enlightenment*. 2nd. ed. New York: Palgrave, 2001.

Rabb, Theodore K. "Religion and the Rise of Modern Science." *Past and Present* 31 (1965) 111–26.

Raven, Charles E. *John Ray, Naturalist: His Life and Works*. Cambridge: Cambridge University Press, 1950.

Ringer, Fritz. "The Intellectual Field, Intellectual History, and the Sociology of Knowledge." *Theory and Society* 19/3 (1990) 269–94.

Rivers, Isabel. *Reason, Grace, and Sentiment: A Study of the Language of Religion and Ethics in England, 1660–1780*. 2 vols. Cambridge: Cambridge University Press, 1991, 2000.

Rowe, William L. *The Cosmological Argument*. Princeton: Princeton University Press, 1975.

Ruse, Michael. "Robert Boyle and the Machine Metaphor." *Zygon* 37/3 (2002) 581–96.

Ryken, Leland. *Wordly Saints: The Puritans as They Really Were*. Grand Rapids: Zondervan, 1986.

Selement, George. "Perry Miller: A Note on His Sources in The New England Mind: The Seventeenth Century." *William and Mary Quarterly*, 3rd Ser., 31/3 (1974) 453–64.

Shapiro, Barbara J. *John Wilkins, 1614–1672: An Intellectual Biography*. Berkeley: University of California Press, 1969.

Solberg, Winton U. "Science and Religion in Early America: Cotton Mather's Christian Philosopher." *Church History* 56 (1987) 73–92.

Sprunger, Keith L. *The Learned Doctor William Ames: Dutch Backgrounds of English and American Puritanism*. Urbana, IL: University of Illinois Press, 1972.

Staloff, Darren. *The Making of an American Thinking Class: Intellectuals and Intelligentsia in Puritan Massachusetts*. New York: Oxford University Press, 1998.

Stout, Harry. *The New England Soul: Preaching and Religious Culture in Colonial New England*. New York: Oxford University Press, 1986.

BIBLIOGRAPHY

Thomson, Keith. *Before Darwin: Reconciling God and Nature.* New Haven: Yale University Press, 2005.

Tulloch, John. *Rational Theology and Christian Philosophy in England in the Seventeenth Century.* 2 vols. Edinburgh: Blackwood, 1872.

Turner, James. *Without God, Without Creed: The Origins of Unbelief in America.* Baltimore: Johns Hopkins University Press, 1985.

Van Biema, David. "Mother Teresa's Crisis of Faith." *Time*, 23 Aug 2007.

Van De Wetering, Maxine. "Moralizing in Puritan Natural Science: Mysteriousness in Earthquake Sermons." *Journal of the History of Ideas* 43/3 (1982) 417–38.

Vartanian, Aram. *Diderot and Descartes: A Study of Scientific Naturalism in the Enlightenment.* Princeton, NJ: Princeton University Press, 1953.

Vaughn, Alden T. *The Puritan Tradition in America, 1620–1730.* 2nd ed. Hanover, NH: University Press of New England, 1997. Originally published in 1972.

Walker, D. A. "Puritanism and Natural Theology After the Restoration of 1660." Ph.D. diss., Council for National Academic Awards, 1989.

Walker, James. *The Theology and Theologians of Scotland.* 2nd ed., rev. Edinburgh: T. & T. Clark, 1888.

Walsham, Alexandra. *Providence in Early Modern England.* New York: Oxford University Press, 1999.

Walters, Kerry S., ed. *The American Deists: Voices of Reason and Dissent in the Early Republic.* Lawrence, KS: University Press of Kansas, 1992.

Weber, Max. *The Protestant Ethic and the Spirit of Capitalism.* Translated by Talcott Parsons. New York: Scribner's Sons, 1930.

Webster, Charles, ed. *The Intellectual Revolution of the Seventeenth Century.* London and Boston: Routledge and Kegan Paul, 1974.

Webster, Tom. *Godly Clergy in Early Stuart England: The Caroline Puritan Movement, c. 1620–1643.* Cambridge: Cambridge University Press, 1997.

Winship, Michael P. "Prodigies, Puritanism, and the Perils of Natural Philosophy: The Example of Cotton Mather." *William and Mary Quarterly*, 3rd Ser. 51/1 (1994) 92–105.

———. *Seers of God: Puritan Providentialism in the Restoration and Early Enlightenment.* Baltimore: Johns Hopkins University Press, 1996.

———. "Were There Any Puritans in New England?" *New England Quarterly* 74/1 (2001) 118–38.

Woodall, "The Relationship between Science and Scripture in the Thought of Robert Boyle." *Perspectives on Science and Christian Faith* 49/1 (1997) 32–39.

Wright, Conrad. *The Beginnings of Unitarianism in America.* Boston: Starr King, 1955.

———. "Rational Religion in Eighteenth-Century America." In *The Liberal Christians: Essays on American Unitarian History*, 1–21. Boston: Beacon, 1970.

Index of Persons

Abelard, Peter, 84
Abraham, Gary, 71n27
Adams, Thomas, 37n13, 65n10, 71, 83n5, 116, 120, 122, 123n7, 124n8
Agas, Benjamin, 63n5
Al-Ghazali, Abu Hamid Muhammad, 100–101
Aldridge, Owen, 5
Allen, James, 83n5
Alsted, Johann Heinrich, 1, 53
Ames, William, 5, 53–54, 71, 100–101, 106, 111n41, 121, 123n7
Aquinas, Thomas, 12, 77, 99, 121, 122n3, 124
Aristotle, 22, 68, 81, 94, 95n8, 99–100, 102
Arnobius, 21n6
Augustine, 100, 121, 122n3, 124
Aylmer, G.E., 48n39

Bacon, Francis, 70, 75
Ball, Bryan, 22
Ball, John, 36, 45n32, 94n5, 100n16, 101n19
Ball, Thomas, 27
Barker, Matthew, 1, 10–11, 18, 19n3, 22, 25, 37, 39, 50, 75, 81–82, 87, 89, 94n5, 96n10, 100n16, 101n19, 110–11, 114n49, 116, 132–33
Barlow, John, 71
Bates, William, 12, 18, 21n6, 37, 40, 50–52, 58n73, 60–61, 62n6, 70–72, 75n40, 77–79, 87, 89n17, 94n5, 97, 100n16, 101–2, 111, 119n55, 120, 128, 131
Bavinck, Herman, 86
Baxter, Richard, 7, 11, 20–21, 30–31, 34–36, 37n13, 38, 41, 43n29, 45n32, 45n34, 46, 48–52, 54, 56–58, 62, 73, 75, 77, 80, 87–91, 96, 98, 100n16, 101n19, 102, 114n49, 119n55, 124–28
Bayle, Pierre, 98
Bedford, James, 63n6
Berman, David, 48n39
Bernard of Clairvaux, 84
Biddle, John, 139n12
Bolton, Robert, 65, 67
Boyle, Robert, 4, 21, 24–25, 29–30, 42–43, 61n4-5, 70n26, 76–77, 82, 95, 111–12
Bozeman, Theodore, 66
Brooke, John Hedley, 71n27
Bruce, Robert, 56
Bullinger, Heinrich, 83, 86, 121
Burnet, Thomas, 136n3
Bush, Sargent Jr., 78

Calvin, John, 7, 9–10, 13, 40n20, 81, 88n15, 95n5, 121, 128n15
Capel, Richard, 7–9, 25, 33–36, 44, 47, 57, 64–65, 67–68
Cartwright, Thomas, 37n13, 83–84
Case, Thomas, 62n6

Index of Persons

Charnock, Stephen, 8, 11, 19–21, 24n14, 26, 37, 40, 43n29, 50, 55, 58, 60, 72–73, 75, 77–78, 79n47, 81n1, 82n2, 89n17, 94n5, 95, 97–98, 100–101, 111, 115n49, 119n55, 123n7, 124n8, 127n15, 129–30
Chauncy, Charles, 68, 71
Cicero, Marcus Tullius, 74, 75n38, 81, 94, 95n5, 102, 112
Clarke, Samuel (1675–1729), 4–5, 118n54
Clarke, Samuel (1599–1682), 33n2
Cohen, Charles, 3n2, 122n5
Cohen, I. Bernhard, 71n27
Collinson, Patrick, 3, 18, 22n12, 67
Cotton, John, 26–27
Cox, Robert, 22n11
Craig, William Lane, 101
Crocker, Robert, 12n20
Cromwell, Oliver, 112

Daly, Robert, 2
Danforth, Samuel, 105n25
Davenport, John, 35
Democritus, 102
Descartes, René, 107–108, 116–17, 118n53
Diogenes Laertius, 102
Dybikowski, James, 136n2

Eddy, M.D., 112–13n46
Edwards, John, 137–39
Edwards, Jonathan, 121
Eliot, John, 10, 38–39, 42–43, 69
Epictetus, 130
Epicurus, 102

Fairclough, Samuel, 63n6
Fiering, Norman, 5, 53n58
Flavel, John, 50, 60
Fleming, Donald, 4

Gabbey, Alan, 12n20, 48n39
Gale, Theophilus, 17, 59n1, 70n26, 75, 77, 82n2, 86–87, 94n5, 98, 100n16, 101n19, 123n7

Galen of Pergamum, 66n11, 114, 115n49, 116n50
Gassendi, Pierre, 126
Gerson, L. P., 94
Goodwin, Thomas, 27, 43n28
Greaves, Richard, 76
Greenham, Richard, 48, 64–67
Grotius, Hugo, 97–98
Gurnall, William, 3, 34, 44–45

Haggenmacher, Peter, 98n13
Hall, David, 3n2, 105
Hall, Michael, 105
Henry, John, 103n21
Henry, Matthew, 3, 11, 40, 43n29, 60–61, 67, 89n17, 91–92, 125
Henry, Philip, 3
Herbert, Edward of Cherbury, 50, 90
Hill, Christopher, 2
Holifield, E. Brooks, 78
Hooke, Robert, 115
Hooker, Thomas, 23, 53, 60, 65n10, 71, 95, 100n16, 109
Hopkins, Ezekiel, 3, 11, 18, 25–26, 37, 44n31, 49–50, 70, 75, 94n5, 97–98, 100n16, 114n49, 118n55, 121n3
Howe, Daniel, 9
Howe, John, 35, 37–40, 41n22, 47, 52, 54, 58n75, 93, 94n5, 97n11, 99–100, 101n19, 112–19, 125, 129
Hume, David, 102, 112, 136n2
Hurst, Henry, 62n6
Hutton, Sarah, 12n20

Jaeger, Werner, 96n9
Juvenal, 128

Kant, Immanuel, 99–100
Kearney, H. F., 6n6
Kittredge, George, 74n37
Koesler, Helmut, 95-96n8
Koons, Robert, 101n17

Lake, Peter, 3
Lawrence, Edward, 63n6

Index of Persons

Lee, Samuel, 37n13, 40–41, 54n64, 59, 65–66, 75–76, 115n49
Leucippus, 102
Lindberg, David, 15n25
Locke, John, 5, 15, 50, 116–17, 135–40
Lowrie, Ernest, 5, 51
Lucretius, 102
Luther, Martin, 9, 66n12, 121, 127–28n15

Maimonides, Moses, 99
Manton, Thomas, 19n3, 28, 37, 39, 60, 62n6, 69–70, 83, 101n19
Mather, Cotton, 5, 7, 9–11, 29–30, 51–53, 55n66, 63–67, 74–77, 93, 95n5, 101n19, 103–4, 106, 111–12, 115n49, 125, 131
Mather, Increase, 7, 9–10, 19, 26, 29–30, 37, 40, 51–53, 59, 69, 91, 95n5, 98, 100n16, 101n19, 104–107, 115n49, 123, 127, 128n16, 131
Mather, Lydia, 75, 76n42
May, Gerhard, 94n2
May, Henry, 136n2
Mayr, Otto, 113n46
Mencken, H. L., 2
Meyer, D. H., 5
Middlekauf, Robert, 104–5
Miller, Perry, 4, 59, 64
Mitchell, Jonathan, 7, 29–30, 41
Morgan, John, 64, 65n10, 71n27
Morison, Samuel, 68
Morrice, Roger, 62n6
Muller, Richard, 13
Murray, Iain, 76n41

Newton, Isaac, 5, 77
Nieuwentyt, Bernard, 112–13
Noll, Mark, 5–6
Norton, John, 75n38
Numbers, Ronald, 15n25
Nuovo, Victor, 135

Osler, Margaret, 103n21
Outram, Dorinda, 136n2
Overton, Richard, 23
Owen, John, 19n3, 20, 22, 36–37, 45n32, 46–47, 52, 58, 80, 83–84, 88, 89n16

Paley, William, 73–74, 112, 115
Parker, Samuel, 115–16
Pascal, Blaise, 8–9, 20, 21n6, 54
Paul of Venice, 100
Pease, Arthur, 94n4
Pemberton, Matthew, 62n6
Pemble, William, 17, 21n7, 25n17, 43n28, 45n33, 46n35, 48, 57
Perkins, William, 8, 17–19, 25, 36, 39, 44n31, 64, 66–67, 68n19, 89n17, 94n5, 99, 101n19, 109–10, 123n7, 124n8
Pierson, Abraham, 41–42, 101n19, 110, 120
Plato, 18, 65, 66n11, 68, 81, 84, 87, 94n4, 95, 99, 102
Platt, John, 13n22
Poole, Matthew, 43n29, 50, 70, 75n40, 114
Porter, Roy, 15, 135–36
Preston, John, 8, 26–27, 32, 37, 39, 44n31, 56–57, 65n10, 75, 94n5, 99, 101, 110, 112, 123n7
Prince, Thomas, 104

Raven, Charles, 74
Ray, John, 53, 73–75, 118n53, 123n7
Raymond of Sebunde, 1
Read, Joseph, 63n6
Renwick, James, 55–56
Richardson, Alexander, 71
Ringer, Fritz, 6
Rivers, Isabel, 12n20
Robie, Thomas, 106n27
Rogers, Richard, 64, 67
Rowe, William, 99n15
Ryken, Leland, 2

Sangar, Gabriel, 62n6
Sarasohn, Lisa, 103n21
Scudder, Henry, 32, 35–36, 101n19
Seneca, Lucius Annaeus, 68, 81, 87
Shapiro, Barbara, 87n12
Shepard, Thomas, 7, 17, 22n12, 27–30, 37, 39n17, 43, 55, 75, 101n19, 123n5, 130
Socrates, 81, 87, 95
Solberg, Winton, 5, 53n57

Index of Persons

Southey, Robert, 71
Spencer, Thomas, 59
Spinoza, Baruch, 99
Stillingfleet, Edward, 137–40
Suarez, Francisco, 53–54
Sylvester, Matthew, 62n6

Taylor, Thomas, 65n10
Tertullian, 97
Thomson, Keith, 73
Toland, John, 137, 139
Trapp, John, 3, 43n29, 45n32, 46, 82n2, 131
Tuckney, Anthony, 12, 45n32, 61
Tulloch, John, 12n20
Turner, James, 6
Turner, John, 63n6
Twisse, William, 32–34, 46, 52–53, 100

Vartanian, Aram, 108
Vaughn, Alden, 74n37
Vermigli, Peter Martyr, 121
Vincent, Thomas, 19, 36, 44n31, 45n32, 94n5, 100n16, 101n19

Voltaire, 108

Walker, D. A., 55
Walker, James, 56n69
Walters, Kerry, 5
Watson, Thomas, 19, 26, 37, 73n34, 95n5
Webster, Tom, 71n29
Whichcote, Benjamin, 12, 45n32, 61n4
Wilkins, John, 4, 11, 87, 107n29
Willard, Samuel, 36, 45n32, 55n66, 61, 74, 75n38, 83n5, 98, 100n16, 101n19, 115n49
Willet, Andrew, 11, 84–85, 87, 101n19
Winship, Michael, 3
Witsius, Herman, 43, 89n17, 130
Wright, Conrad, 5
Wright, Samuel, 65n10

Xenophon, 74, 81, 87

Zanchi, Jerome, 83
Zwingli, Ulrich, 83, 86, 121

Subject Index

Animals, 72, 108, 110–11, 113, 117
Arguments for Christianity
    Existence/immortality of the soul, 6, 23, 109, 117, 128, 136
    Experience of God, 32–33
    Incarnation, the, 66
    Inspiration of the Bible, 36, 42, 44–47, 52, 56–57
    From miracles, 7, 34–35, 44, 62, 118
    From prophecy, 7, 44–45
    Loving God, 22
    Loving neighbor as oneself, 21–22
    Witness of the Spirit, 5, 7, 14, 30n30, 34, 41, 44, 46, 64, 68
Arguments for the Existence of God
    Cosmological Argument, 99–101
    Design Argument, 101–2, 109–18
    Divine attributes, 21, 47, 80, 88–89
    From human nature and mind, 116–17
    Moral Argument, 97–98
    Universal consent, 1, 94–97
    Wager argument, 20–21
Atheism
    Absolute atheism, 24, 27, 30, 51, 131
    Aesthetics of, 119
    Causes of, 20, 41, 114–15, 118, 131–33
    Practical atheism, 8, 24–28
    Rise of, 10, 49–50, 108
    Temptations to (see Doubts)

Calvinism, 2, 6, 9, 22n9, 85–86, 88, 106–7, 121, 137–38
Catechisms/catechesis, 7, 10, 14, 18–19, 21, 22n9, 36, 37n11, 41–42, 44n31, 45n32, 49, 66–67, 83, 94n5, 100n16, 101n19, 106, 123n7, 125
Certainty regarding God's existence, 18–20, 112, 125, 128
Circularity in reasoning, 44, 47
Comets, 104–106
Conversion/regeneration, 11, 14, 39, 41, 46, 60, 78, 82–92, 122, 123n5, 138

Deism, 5, 10–11, 29–30, 50–51
Doubts, 7–9, 20, 28–31, 33–39, 48–49, 54–56, 124

Earthquake sermons, 103–104
Education, 2, 57–59, 68–70, 73n34, 79, 96, 114, 119
Enlightenment, the, 4, 14–15
Eschatology, 72–73, 76
Evidence, rules of weighing, 118
Evidentialism, 1–2, 4–6, 10–12, 14, 44–46, 49, 62, 66, 78, 135–40
Evil, problem of, 120–27
Extraterrestrial life, 125–27

Faith, 5, 7, 10–11, 29–32, 34, 37, 39–41, 44, 45n33, 46, 49–52, 54, 56–57, 60–61, 64–65, 68–69, 75, 78, 83, 88, 90–91, 96, 133, 140n15

Subject Index

Fall, the, 4, 59, 92, 120–22, 131
Foundationalism, 8, 10, 13–14, 39–44
Free will, 121–22

Holy Spirit, 5, 7, 14, 34, 41–42, 44, 46, 62, 64, 68, 78, 82–83, 84n7, 85, 88, 90, 92, 130

Imago Dei, 13, 82, 88, 116, 119, 129
Immanence of God, 130
Incomprehensibility of God (see Mystery)
Indians, missions to, 10, 38–39, 41–43, 69, 110, 120
Islam, 58, 90

Jews, 76–77n42

Logical possibility, 118

Mechanical philosophy, rise and impact of, 102–109
Miracles, 7, 34–35, 44–45, 62, 114, 118
Mystery
    In God (incomprehensibility), 11–12, 22, 33, 41, 65, 74–75, 77–78, 129
    In Nature, 75–77
    In Religion, 11–12, 61, 65, 78, 137, 140

Natural law (ethical), 1, 22
Natural laws (scientific), 102–10, 132

Original sin (see the Fall)

Philosophers, 17, 23, 43n28, 70, 81–82, 86–87, 94, 96, 101n17, 108
Philosophy, study of, 68, 70, 119
Polytheism, 41, 87, 97
Predestination (see Sovereignty of God)

Progress, hope for, 76
Providence, 9–10, 21, 127–32
Puritanism, definition of, 2–3
Purpose of creation, 21, 24, 71–72, 123

Reason, role and capabilities of, 2, 4–6, 11–13, 15, 17, 20, 24, 34–35, 59–68, 70, 78–79, 140
Repentance (see conversion)
Roman Catholicism, 45, 48, 58, 62, 67, 84, 86, 133

Sabbatarian controversy, 21–22
Science and Puritanism, 4, 14–15, 70–74, 76–77, 102–117, 126–27, 132
Sects (enthusiasts), 2, 23, 46, 62, 67
Smallpox inoculation controversy, 74
Sociological conditioning of religious beliefs, 23, 27, 56–58, 62, 67, 96–97, 122, 132–33
Socinianism, 12–13, 34, 62, 84, 137–40
Soul (see Arguments for Christianity)
Sovereignty of God, 76, 106–7, 120–21, 123–24
Superstition, 48n40, 96, 103, 133

Unevangelized, possibility of salvation for, 11, 80, 82–92, 138–39

Watch analogy, 112–113
Westminster Assembly, Confession and Catechisms, 10, 12, 14n24, 19, 21–22, 27, 32, 36, 58, 61, 81n1, 83, 88n15, 92n27, 106, 107n29, 121n1, 123n7, 125
Wonder, sense of, 22, 53, 70, 111, 114, 132
Worship, 1–2, 21–22, 24, 81, 87n11, 89, 92, 95, 129, 136

Scripture Index

Genesis
1:1 — 82n2

1 Kings
18:17–40 — 56

Job
21:16–21 — 128n15

Psalms
14:1 — 19
49:20 — 43n29
73:12–14 — 127
138:8 — 92n28
139:14 — 115

Proverbs
20:27 — 41

Jeremiah
10:2 — 106n27

Matthew
22:35–40 — 21n8

Mark
8:31–33 — 90n19

Luke
15:1–10 — 125
24:21 — 90n19

John
3:1–10 — 123n5
12:47 — 92n27

Acts
10:35 — 92n28
17:22 — 40n20
17:28 — 68n19

Romans
5:12–19 — 139n11
6:4 — 123n5
11:15 — 77n42
11:36 — 54

1 Corinthians
1:20–25 — 81, 82n2
5:17 — 123n5
15:33 — 68n19

Galatians
6:15 — 123n5

Titus
1:12 — 68n19

Hebrews
11:6 — 90

1 Peter
3:15 — 51

Revelation
4:11 — 54

www.ingramcontent.com/pod-product-compliance
Lightning Source LLC
Chambersburg PA
CBHW071458150426
43191CB00008B/1380